n its coverage, uplifting in its message, engaging in its
, and powerful in its significance, *Streets of Gold* is a New
phony in words and numbers. Immigrants today, as in the
a better life for themselves. But upward mobility comes
erations, and the success of the immigrant child does not
expense of the one with US-born parents. There is greater
nd harmony in this version of the American Dream than
y and dissonance."

—Claudia Goldin, Henry Lee Professor of Economics,
Harvard University, and author of *Career & Family:
Women's Century-Long Journey toward Equity*

ts *of Gold*, Ran Abramitzky and Leah Boustan have written
aging book on the enduring but underappreciated success
erican immigration. Interweaving anecdotes drawn from
es, including their own personal stories, with conclusions
systematic big data analyses using tools from modern
search, they paint a vivid and wide-ranging picture of the
mmigration over time and the effects on American soci-
e us to meet not only spectacular success stories like Tino
quickly moved from being born in Mexico to graduat-
arvard and becoming a justice on the California supreme
o the more common story of Louis Bilchick, whose family
y but steadily up the economic ladder. Along the way, they
and fiction and bust many of the myths that pervade and
urrent discussion on immigration policy. As an immigrant
citizen, I highly recommend this inspiring book for any-
d in the debates on immigration."

—Guido Imbens, The Applied Econometrics Professor,
Stanford University, and Nobel laureate, economics

ted data, empathetic personal histories, joyous writing,
tions, and a compelling counter-zeitgeist narrative make
ld an essential read for all Americans confused by the
or surrounding immigration. Abramitzky and Boustan
the travails of first-generation immigrants, the startling

Praise
Streets o

"This wonderful and highly readable
the record straight about the hot-but
must-read for anyone who cares abou
benefit from coming to the US, but
versity, skills, and energy that they
evidence suggests that native worker

—DARON ACEMOGLU, Instit
and coauthor of *Why Na*

"In this fascinating book, Abramitz
ploy the tools of data science to con
immigration in America. Combinin
thoughtful narratives, they weave a
lions of immigrant families achieved
century and a half. The result is a set
will help reshape the narrative abou
the United States."

—RAJ CHE
of Pub

"While Americans are intensely pol
history can help change minds. And
and millions of them, about the am
of American immigration. It is a spl
data to illuminate our past and wha

—ANGUS DEATON, Nobe
of *Deaths of*

"Complex
compositio
World Sym
past, make
through ge
come at the
continuity
discontinui

"With *Stree*
a highly eng
story of An
many sourc
drawn from
economic re
changes in
ety. They tak
Cuellar, wh
ing from H
court, but al
moved slowl
separate fac
confuse the
and Americ
one intereste

"Unprecede
practical sol
Streets of G
partisan ran
demonstrate

economic success of the second generation, the rapid pace of cultural 'Americanization,' the lack of wage threat to American-born workers, and the similarity of these patterns for the two waves of immigration bringing Europeans (in the late nineteenth century) and Latin Americans (in the late twentieth century) into our country. Despite all the rancor, we who are of immigrant heritage are reminded how remarkable a country is America."

—DAVID LAITIN, Watkins Professor of
Political Science, Stanford University

"The optimism that runs through *Streets of Gold*—immigrants are and have always been a 'grand bargain' for America—is based on the rock-solid evidence of Ran Abramitzky and Leah Boustan's rigorous deep dive into millions of census records and Ancestry.com filings. The stories they tell then become a powerful means of communicating the truth about the unique phenomenon of the American immigrant experience."

—DOUG MASSEY, Henry G. Bryant Professor of
Sociology and Public Affairs, Princeton University

"A book as timely as it is magisterial. Two of the most respected and accomplished scholars of economic history demonstrate that much of what you thought you knew about the historical experience of immigrants coming to the United States in the past turns out to be wrong. Armed with reams of new data, elegantly written, and meticulously researched, *Streets of Gold* revisits many of the most pertinent and perplexing social and economic issues in the history of immigration with often-surprising results."

—JOEL MOKYR, Northwestern University

"*Streets of Gold* is the conversation you always wanted to have about where Americans come from. Abramitzky and Boustan have discovered new ways of answering that question in this fascinating and hard-to-put-down history of American immigration, based on new sources of data, and conveyed by powerful storytelling."

—ALVIN E, ROTH, Nobel laureate, economics,
and author of *Who Gets What and Why*

"*Streets of Gold* is a pathbreaking book. Mining a treasure trove of big data over more than a century, Ran Abramitzky and Leah Boustan manage to show the surprising continuity between past and present patterns of immigrant integration in the United States. Their data show that most immigrants, even across widely different backgrounds, achieve success over two to three generations, much as in the past. This book is a must-read for those interested in the role of immigration in American society."

—ANDREW SELEE, president, Migration Policy Institute

"An absolute treasure, the perfect book on immigration—substantive and data-driven, but leaving room for the stories of immigrants, good and bad. This is a timely book, but it will be read for many years."

—ZACK WEINERSMITH,
New York Times–bestselling author of *Soonish*

STREETS
OF GOLD

STREETS
OF GOLD

America's Untold Story of Immigrant Success

RAN ABRAMITZKY
LEAH BOUSTAN

PUBLICAFFAIRS
New York

PublicAffairs
Hachette Book Group
1290 Avenue of the Americas, New York, NY 10104
www.publicaffairsbooks.com
@Public_Affairs

Printed in the United States of America
First Edition: May 2022

Published by PublicAffairs, an imprint of Perseus Books, LLC, a subsidiary of Hachette Book Group, Inc. The PublicAffairs name and logo is a trademark of the Hachette Book Group.

The Hachette Speakers Bureau provides a wide range of authors for speaking events. To find out more, go to www.hachettespeakersbureau.com or call (866) 376-6591.

The publisher is not responsible for websites (or their content) that are not owned by the publisher.

Library of Congress Cataloging-in-Publication Data
Names: Abramitzky, Ran, author. | Boustan, Leah Platt, author.
Title: Streets of gold : America's untold story of immigrant success / Ran Abramitzky, Leah Boustan.
Description: First edition. | New York : PublicAffairs, 2022. | Includes bibliographical references and index.
Identifiers: LCCN 2021050335 | ISBN 9781541797833 (hardcover) | ISBN 9781541797826 (ebook)
Subjects: LCSH: Immigrants—United States—Economic conditions. | Children of immigrants—United States—Economic conditions. | United States—Emigration and immigration—Economic aspects. | United States—Emigration and immigration—Government policy.
Classification: LCC HD8081.A5 A27 2022 | DDC 331.6/20973—dc23/eng/20211021
LC record available at https://lccn.loc.gov/2021050335

ISBNs: 9781541797833 (hardcover), 9781541797826 (ebook)

LSC-C

Printing 1, 2022

To Noya and Ra'anan, with love

Contents

STREETS
OF GOLD

1

"I CAME WITH FIFTY CENTS AND THAT'S IT!"

OVERTURNING AMERICA'S IMMIGRATION MYTHS

> *I came to America because I heard the streets were paved with gold. When I got here, I found out three things: First, the streets weren't paved with gold; second, they weren't paved at all; and third, I was expected to pave them.*
>
> —Unknown Italian immigrant, painted on the wall of the Ellis Island Museum

FOR OVER TWO CENTURIES, IMMIGRATION HAS BEEN A DEfining element of America's culture, society, and economy. Yet, our national conversations about immigration are driven largely by myths. These myths can be either positive or negative: for every uplifting tale of an immigrant striking it rich, there is an ominous story of an immigrant undermining American culture from within. For many Americans, ideas about immigration are based on these tales and the feelings they arouse, not on facts and data. It's no wonder immigration is one of those divisive issues that everyone thinks they understand. Ultimately, immigration myths color how voters think about immigration and affect immigration policy.

Our aim in this book is to rebuild the story of immigration to America from the ground up, uncovering the patterns that emerge from data on millions of immigrants' lives. Our journey to get the facts right has taken us to many unexplored data sources that span nearly a century and a half of American history, starting around 1880 with the Age of Mass Migration from Europe and running through the present.

Think of us like curious grandchildren searching branches of their family tree online, but a million times over. We started by digging through websites like Ancestry.com that allow the public to search for their relatives. From there, we developed methods to automate these searches so we could follow millions of immigrants and their children in the records as they moved up the economic ladder and integrated into American society. We also read through thousands of immigrant interviews and congressional speeches, and used the latest linguistic tools and machine-learning techniques to systematically analyze these texts. All told, we were able to compile what is the first set of truly big data about immigration.

The immigrants that we follow journey from crowded New York City tenements to leafy suburbs, and from small family farms to growing cities. Our data includes everyone from bankers to errand boys—a bit like following the life stories of everyone in the phone book, rather than only the CEOs or the criminals who make it to the front page of the newspaper. We supplement our research on the past with data on immigrants in America today, using everything from birth certificates to tax records to oral histories. Compiling information on as many immigrants as possible allows us to move beyond myths and nostalgia to tell the true story of immigration that has been hiding in plain sight all along.

The data gives us clues about why immigrants chose to come to the United States, and tells us when they left school, how well they spoke English, the occupations they held over their work lives, their earnings, whom they married, the names they chose for their children, and their children's outcomes as they became adults. With our new data, we can reassess some of the common myths about immigration, contributing a new understanding of the immigrant experience in American history to today's national debate.

Is it really true that past immigrants moved quickly from rags to riches? Are today's immigrants less successful than immigrants in the past, and do today's immigrants integrate more slowly into society than past immigrants? Do immigrants harm US-born workers through added competition for jobs? These are some of the major questions we answer in this book.

OUR FIFTEEN MINUTES OF FAME

Our hope has always been that our findings about the true nature of immigrant success would interest people from all walks of life. So we were thrilled when, one day in 2019, a small part of our research escaped the ivory tower and found its way to late-night TV on Showtime's *Desus & Mero* show. The segment started with Desus, one of the hosts, saying, "Yo, recent study found that children of immigrants do better than children of those born in the US."[1] Somehow he was able to distill our five-year research project about the children of immigrants down to a single sentence.

Our study was overturning two commonly held myths about immigrant prosperity. First, many believe that immigrants who come to the United States today from poor backgrounds will never catch up to the US born. The data reveals a different pattern: children of immigrants from nearly every country in the world, including from poorer countries like Mexico, Guatemala, and Laos, are more upwardly mobile than the children of US-born residents who were raised in families with a similar income level. The second misconception is that immigrants in the past, who came almost exclusively from Europe, were more successful than today's immigrants, who come from around the globe. Our data reveals that, despite major changes in immigration policy over time, immigrants today move up the economic ladder at the same pace as European immigrants did in the past.

With our work as inspiration, Desus and his cohost, The Kid Mero, hit the streets of Queens ("our Ellis Island," they added) to ask passersby what it was like to grow up with immigrant parents. Desus and The Kid Mero are a favorite of younger, Twitter-savvy viewers. The comedy duo act like two friends who just enjoy each other's company, always ready with a laugh to appreciate a good turn of phrase. They share a "Bronx uniform": short, defined beards, baseball caps with a flat brim, The Kid Mero's hoodie and Desus's double T-shirt.

Desus and The Kid Mero now have a career that should make any parent proud—maybe even an immigrant parent—but as students back in the Bronx, they never expected to make it to television. When they first made it big, an interviewer asked them, "What were you guys? Were you comedians? Were you aspiring?" "No," said Desus, "just two guys at school—just funny. Just hang in the hallways and go to class. Actual New York City high school students. . . . We saw each other in summer school. We'd do the little head nod."[2]

That day, Desus and The Kid Mero invited along fellow comedian Hasan Minhaj to the Queens street corner. The comedians are themselves children of immigrants; in fact, their families are very likely captured in our modern datasets. Hasan Minhaj was raised by highly educated immigrant parents in Davis, California. His mother and father, a chemist and a medical doctor, are immigrants from Uttar Pradesh in India. Desus (né Daniel Baker) and The Kid Mero (né Joel Martinez) are children of working-class immigrants from the

Caribbean. Desus jokes that his parents arrived in the country with "a goat and one Bitcoin."[3]

Above the din of the rattling of the elevated train and a constant stream of traffic, the trio interviewed adult children of immigrants who happened to pass by. Everyone talked about the sacrifices that their parents made to get to the United States and about the stories and legends they heard growing up in an immigrant family. Life turned out well for these children of immigrants, even if their successes did not quite live up to their parents' often unrealistic dreams.

Immigrant parents' high expectations of their kids was, in fact, the main topic of conversation in these street interviews. The Kid Mero asked a son of immigrants from the Dominican Republic: "What is the strongest guilt you have received from your parents?" The man answered with an exaggerated eye roll: "Oh man, my Pops reminded me of the struggle of getting from DR [the Dominican Republic] to here, so nothing was good enough."

Another son of immigrants, who described himself as a "brown guy named Usama in Texas"—perfect shorthand for how hard it can be as a child of immigrants trying to fit in—told the story of getting into medical school and deciding to not go. "My mom threw nineteen pots at me. The good ones, too. The glass ones." Hasan recalls how he, too, didn't live up to his own parents' expectations: "The rebellion for me was I was a poli-sci major instead of premed. . . . I really broke out."

Only one person, a South Asian man in a North Face jacket, seemed to be a success in his parents' eyes. Desus: "Are your parents proud of you?" Man: "I would say yes." Hasan: "You said yes with such confidence." The Kid Mero: "You must be a lawyer that's also a doctor." "Ah, you know," the man said, "I never made it to both of those degrees. I became an engineer, though."[4]

Our research underscores what Desus and The Kid Mero heard out on the streets of Queens that cold day. Children of immigrants from all over the globe are making it here in America. Even when their parents struggle and have to work two jobs to get by, the children of immigrants rise.

We make these broad statements not because of a few man-on-the-street interviews, but on the basis of systematic analysis of many immigrant records. For more than a decade, we have built large data-sets, overturning many of the defining myths in America's immigration history. What we share with you is the final product of our research, along with the stories behind the data and a flavor of how the findings come together.

THE "STREETS OF GOLD" MYTH

When Democrat Jon Ossoff of Georgia was sworn into office in January 2021, becoming one of the youngest senators in US history, he carried in his breast pocket a copy of two ship manifests: one for his paternal great-grandfather, Israel Osshowsky, who arrived in the United States in 1911, and one for his great-grandmother, Annie, who joined her husband in the United States in 1913.[5] Later that day, Ossoff mentioned this sentimental gesture on social media, marveling that "a century later, their great grandson was elected to the U.S. Senate." This is the promise of America, Ossoff implied, that the sons and daughters of immigrants from all around the world can rise to the halls of power.

As economic historians who study the past with the hope of illuminating the present, we took special note of the manner that Ossoff chose to honor his ancestors: not with a sepia-toned photograph or a family heirloom but with passenger records, listing his great-grandparents by name at the very moment they set foot on American shores.

After his swearing in, we couldn't help but look up Ossoff's great-grandfather in the historical census records on Ancestry.com, a source that we have turned to many times over the years. We found that by 1920, Israel Osshowsky had already changed his last name to Ossoff and was living with his wife, Annie, and their five young children in Peabody, Massachusetts, where he worked as a laborer in a leather factory.

By leaving Lithuania for Peabody, Israel Ossoff had likely already doubled his fortunes. A century ago, poverty was higher in many European countries than in the United States, so immigrants had a lot to gain by crossing the Atlantic. Escaping their financial plight was what 44 percent of immigrants who arrived during this period reported as the reason they came to America, while 34 percent were following family members and 20 percent were fleeing persecution, according to details gathered by the Ellis Island Foundation.[6]

Looking at historical census data gives an even better fix on the financial value of moving versus staying home. In one of our research projects, we followed pairs of brothers born in Norway, one of whom left for the United States by 1900 while the other remained behind. (We focused on Norway because the Norwegian census data happens to be highly complete.) Brothers who immigrated to the United States earned nearly twice as much as their siblings back home.[7]

The best estimates suggest that much the same is true today: immigrants can more than double their earnings by moving to the United States.[8] So the impetus to immigrate is as strong as ever. Its only the countries that are different: you don't see many immigrants from Norway to the United States these days because Norway has become one of the richest nations in the world, with a higher median income per person than the United States. Today, most immigrants hail from countries that, relative to the United States, are far poorer than European home countries were a century ago. Consider the fact that nine of the ten countries sending the largest numbers of immigrants to the United States these days are ranked between the 90th and 150th countries in the world in terms of GDP per capita (out of 195)—countries like El Salvador, India, and Vietnam. Korea is the only large immigration partner that cracks the top fifty.[9]

Our research shows that crossing the Atlantic in the past—or the Rio Grande today—is the biggest step on immigrants' ladder of upward economic mobility. In this way, America really does have golden streets that allow newcomers to quickly make more than they could have earned at home.

But we also find that moving up the economic ladder in America—and catching up to the US born—takes time. Nearly a decade after arrival, Israel Ossoff was still working as a laborer, a job that today would probably earn the minimum wage. Census records indicate that ten years later, he reported being in the "express business," with a truck that hauled leather goods from the factory in Peabody. It was only by 1940, close to thirty years after his first arrival, that Israel converted this small business into ownership of a local gas station.[10]

HOW IMMIGRANTS PAVED THEIR WAY TO AMERICAN PROSPERITY

Although Jon Ossoff himself is an outlier for ending up on Capitol Hill, his family is a good illustration of our work tracing the rising fortunes of immigrant families through historical data. The Ossoffs represent only one entry in our larger ledger, a dataset that follows millions of immigrant families through historical census records from their arrival onward. The very power of such large datasets is that we do not need to rely on the recollections of a small number of immigrants who left diaries or memoirs, and we do not need to wonder whether a particular story is typical or an exception.

Indeed, when we turn to the big data, we find that many of Americans' widely held beliefs about immigrant success do not stand up to scrutiny. One of our nation's triumphal myths is that immigrants arriving at Ellis Island a century ago with only a few dollars in their pocket could quickly achieve prosperity through their own hard work and ingenuity. Indeed, many older academic studies—conducted using the sparse information that was available at the time—supported the view that immigrants in the past were able to catch up to the US born remarkably quickly, matching and surpassing their earnings within a few years.[11] By comparison with this rapid ascent, today's immigrants seem to be lagging behind.

But our data tell a different story. In the coming pages, we will provide evidence that will revise myths about immigration in three major ways. First, the nostalgic view of immigrants in the past moving quickly from rags to riches does not fit the facts. Second, newcomers today are just as quick to move up the economic ladder as in the past, and immigrants now are integrating into American culture just as surely as immigrants did back then. And finally, immigrant success does not come at the expense of US-born workers.

The lives that immigrants lead after arriving in the United States have never been as easy as the common nostalgic view. Many of the historical immigrants that we follow through the data were slow to climb up the economic ladder. Often, the move from low-paid jobs to higher-paid positions took a whole lifetime, and many immigrants never caught up to US-born workers in their occupations or earnings. As the unnamed immigrant whose words we use to open the chapter observed, not only were the streets not paved with gold, but immigrants were expected to pave their own way.

In the pace of their economic progress, immigrants of the past were very similar to immigrants today. Immigrants in the past did not rise from poverty to comfort as quickly as we believe, nor are today's immigrants climbing the economic ladder any more slowly than past immigrants. We will see that the story of Israel Ossoff's slow progress can very well be told of immigrant families today.

The true ascent for immigrant families happens in the next generation. The children of immigrants, like in Jon Ossoff's family, or Desus's and The Kid Mero's, achieve incredible economic success—a pattern that has held in the United States for more than a century. We find in the data that the children of immigrants from nearly every country, especially children of poor immigrants, are more upwardly mobile than the children of US-born residents. The children of immigrants from El Salvador are as likely to be economically successful nowadays as were the children of immigrants from Great Britain 150 years ago.

One such success story is Gisel Ruiz, who grew up in California's Central Valley, the daughter of Mexican farm laborers. Her cousin, Alfredo Corchado, grew up alongside Gisel and wrote about their childhood in his memoir, *Homelands*.[12] After school, Gisel worked "hoeing cotton, working atop tomato machines for her father Pilar and mother Martha." Despite their own lack of formal education, her parents encouraged her to go to college. "There was no other way," they told her, to get ahead in America. She graduated from nearby Santa Clara University with a degree in marketing and went on to ascend to the upper ranks of the American business elite, as a top executive at Walmart. Gisel is just one of many children of immigrants who moved up, a few of whom we profile in the book. Although her rise was faster than most, we see variants of Gisel's story repeated in the data time and again.

All in all, we find a common immigrant story of strong economic mobility in both the past and the present. This shared immigrant experience is all the more remarkable given the dramatic changes in immigration policy over time. A century ago, immigrants from Europe and Canada did not require a visa or passport for entry, nor did they need to prove that they had a family member or a job waiting for them (although immigrants from Asia faced many more restrictions). Today, immigrant entry is highly restricted, and many immigrants arrive without documents. But the bottom line remains the same: the American Dream is just as real for immigrants from Asia and Latin America now as it was for immigrants from Italy and Russia one hundred years ago.

Our findings are decidedly more optimistic than other studies that have warned that the children of immigrants from poor countries might be on a path to a permanent underclass.[13] Being raised in America is a great equalizer for immigrant children from many ethnic backgrounds, and parents' country of origin need not be destiny. But one important factor makes us less optimistic: race. As a group, children of Black parents have lower upward mobility than children of white parents, and we find a similar pattern in our data when comparing children of immigrants from Caribbean countries with children of immigrants from Europe or from Asia.[14] But here, too, we find some room for optimism. As we'll show in Chapter 5, many children of immigrants from majority-Black countries (particularly daughters) do remarkably well.

Our data also busts another widely held myth: that today's immigrants are slower to embrace American culture and society than were European immigrants in the past. The data shows that current immigrants do not assimilate into US society any more slowly than past immigrants. Both in the past and today, immigrants make tremendous efforts to join American society. We document the process of cultural assimilation in large datasets using a variety of measures: Do immigrants become fluent in English? Do they leave immigrant enclaves and move to more integrated neighborhoods? Do immigrants or their children marry spouses from other countries of origin or who were born in the United States? We even learn about efforts that immigrants make to fit in by choosing more American-sounding names for their children as they spend more time in the United States and learn more about American culture.

What we find across all these measures is that the pace of cultural assimilation is very similar in the past and present. Not only that, the immigrant groups most accused of unwillingness to assimilate—Southern and Eastern Europeans in the past, Mexicans today—actually tended to assimilate the fastest. And, contrary to common concerns that refugees will remain isolated, we find that refugees assimilate even faster than other immigrants.

The story that emerges when we let the data speak is a happy one, a tale of economic prosperity and cultural integration. In one generation's time, we find that it becomes hard to tell apart the children of immigrants from the children of the US born. Both groups are simply American.

IMMIGRATION DOES NOT HARM THE US BORN

Yet, simply knowing that immigrants themselves eventually thrive is not the end of the story. What if newcomers squeeze out existing residents for jobs or housing or access to public services? In that case, it would be hard to justify the number of immigrants currently entering the country—let alone an increase in immigration.

Indeed, many politicians defend immigration restrictions as a means of supporting the American worker. If we block new immigration, the idea goes, there will be more jobs for the US born. Yet, when we look to the evidence—either for the past or the present—we do not find that immigrants steal the last slice from a fixed pie. Rather, immigrants help the economy grow, contributing to science, innovation, and culture.

To be sure, immigration creates some winners and losers in the labor market—but only in the short term. US-born workers who do the same types of jobs that immigrants tend to face more competition for jobs. But today, immigrants often fill roles that have few available US-born workers: either very highly educated positions in tech and science, or work that requires very little education, such as picking crops by hand, washing dishes, landscaping, and taking care of the elderly. In fact, the workers who can lose out the most in the short term from new immigrant arrivals are not US-born workers but immigrants who themselves came to the United States a few years before.

These days, research into episodes of immigration restriction or new immigrant entry strongly rejects the zero-sum idea that immigrant workers steal American jobs. Immigration policy is not as easy as saying "close the border and jobs will come." Instead, as a nation we should focus on the ways in which immigrants promote a growing economy, with jobs available for all, rather than imagine that there is a fixed set of jobs to divide between immigrants and the US born. The important role of immigration in contributing to population growth is all the more critical now that we are in the midst of what census watchers call "demographic stagnation."[15] To continue building the labor force, immigration is essential for filling key jobs in health care, tech, construction, and manufacturing.[16]

As a country, we are in dire need of shared facts about immigration. Too often, rational discussion of immigration is overwhelmed by anecdotes that can slant the narrative in one direction or another. It is easy to get influenced by daily headlines of a "crisis" at the southern border, which can stoke fears that the country is being overrun by newcomers. As a result, voters overestimate the number of immigrants living in the country and underestimate immigrants' economic contributions, assuming that more immigrants are dependent on welfare than really do use government benefits.[17] Our large datasets comparing immigrants in the past and present bring new evidence to the national discussion on immigration policy.

We realize that different people can reach different conclusions from the same facts. Even to those who are convinced that immigration is good for America, more immigration isn't always better. It would be facile to say that US policy should maximize the number of immigrants. Thus, we do not seek to give simplistic policy solutions.

Our main message is more basic: as a society, we need to design our immigration policy at the level of generations; the immigrants of today are the Americans of tomorrow. Taking a short-term perspective—as candidates focusing on the next election cycle often do—underestimates the potential contributions that immigrants and their children will make to the economy in the future.

It can feel, at times, like bringing facts to the table is futile. There is a vocal and emboldened minority who oppose immigration under the mantle of America First. But the data conveys a clear message: immigration is good for America, and immigrants and their children ultimately become Americans, both then and now.

FAMILY STORIES, NATIONAL MYTHS

Our motivation for writing this book is rooted in our belief in the power of data to discover the truth about immigration and to undermine the simplistic—and ultimately false—notions that for far too long have influenced the way many Americans perceive immigration and immigrants. We hope that learning the real story of immigration to America over the past two centuries will help politicians and voters build immigration policy on a stronger foundation for the next hundred years.

We also have a more personal goal, one we hope resonates with people who see their own face or the faces of their grandparents in the stories we tell. In trying to set the record straight about immigration, we wanted to understand our own family narratives and where we ourselves—as an immigrant and the descendant of immigrants—fit into the American story.

Leah has heard her own family's immigration history many times. With the years of retellings, the stories have a way of becoming tall tales. As one of the passersby interviewed on *Desus & Mero* joked about his father, an immigrant from the Dominican Republic, "My

Pops . . . first told me . . . , 'I came here with fifty dollars"; two years [later, it was,] 'I came with fifty cents and that's it!'"

By combing through immigrants' data on Ancestry.com for our research, Leah learned that—just like our national narratives—a few of her family stories turned out to be myths. For example, Leah had always heard that the clan's generic-sounding last name, Platt, had been changed at Ellis Island from the far more ethnic Platnichky. As it turns out, historical records show that Leah's great-grandparents kept the name Platnichky for many years after immigrating to the United States and changed the name themselves as part of their process of assimilating into American culture. In fact, the very idea of name changes occurring on Ellis Island is more legend than historical reality.[18]

Other family tales turned out to be true. Leah's grandmother Roslyn always insisted that her second-grade teacher encouraged her to change her name from the ethnic-sounding Rose to the stylish name Roslyn, more befitting of a movie star. Although Leah never believed her (what second grader comes home and informs her own parents that her name has changed?), the census data backs up her story that, indeed, her name changed at some point in elementary school.

We also learned in compiling the records that Leah's family's story of economic progress follows the general pattern that we find in the millions of records we share throughout the book. After arriving in America, Leah's great-grandparents worked for the rest of their lives behind the till of their small family store. To help the family make ends meet, some of Hyman and Annie's eight children sold newspapers on the street corner, like characters in the musical *Newsies*, bringing home a penny for every copy sold.

Economic prosperity came in the next generation, and even then, this prosperity was uneven. Leah's grandfather Matthew enrolled in medical school, hoping to provide for his family. By the age of twenty-one, he was an MD, conducting physicals for John Hancock Life

Insurance for $2 a pop (worth $37 today). He was the most financially successful of his eight siblings, eventually opening up his own suburban medical practice. Matthew's occupation was recorded in the 1940 census as a "physician."

Usually, the details uncovered from this detective work are commonplace, but sometimes even family secrets can emerge. The president of Princeton University, Christopher Eisgruber, was raised Catholic but discovered while helping his son find family members in old passenger records for a school project that his own mother was born Jewish. There on the document was the telltale word "Hebrew."

Many family memories are accurate and can be found written down in the data in black-and-white. But some of the family stories are embellished, often transmuting the "fifty dollars" that immigrants had in their pocket upon arrival into "fifty cents." The same is true for the stories Americans tell about immigration more broadly. The nostalgic view of European immigrants arriving penniless but rising quickly is overstated, and this lopsided comparison makes immigrants today look worse. In fact, it has always taken time for immigrants to find their footing, and it is often the children of immigrants who really thrive.

2

FACT-CHECKING THE PAST

CONVERTING MILLIONS OF IMMIGRANT STORIES INTO DATA

In God we trust. All others must bring data.
—Often attributed to W. Edwards Deming,
although true origin is uncertain[1]

OUR ATTEMPT TO REVEAL THE TRUE STORY OF AMERICAN immigration was nearly thwarted before it could even begin. One morning in the fall of 2011, Ran arrived at his office at Stanford to a message light blinking on his phone. What he heard left him in panic: a "cease and desist" call from a lawyer for Ancestry.com, the popular genealogy site.

As part of our research on immigration, we had been using our office computers to gather data from Ancestry.com—enough data to raise the company's suspicions. Most users of the site look up a few relatives to fill out their family tree from census records. We were trying to scale up this search to find as many immigrants as we could, possibly even numbering in the millions.

We had hit on this plan to use Ancestry to reconstruct the story of American immigration one newcomer at a time a few years before, on the day we first met. On that day in 2008, we were both attending an economic history conference as eager young assistant professors. The conference was held on a perfect May day at the Huntington Botanical Gardens in tony San Marino, California.[2]

It was an odd venue for an academic conference, but the organizers had chosen the site deliberately, figuring that the serenity of the setting would inspire creative ideas and interesting collaborations. And for us, the conference did just that. When, after a morning session on interest bans in medieval Islam, the organizers urged attendees to take a long lunch break and wander through the gardens' paths beneath the cloudless blue sky, we were glad to take our conversation outside.

We were crossing a curved wooden bridge spanning a pond brimming with koi below and chatting, among other things, about the power of large datasets, when Ran had an idea. If we want to figure out who came to the United States during the Age of Mass Migration, why don't we use the popular genealogy service Ancestry. com? Imagine the discoveries we could make if we multiply by the thousands what curious grandchildren do individually! If you can find where your four grandparents lived during their childhood, why can't we find four hundred? Or four thousand? Or four hundred thousand? If we could create a large enough dataset, maybe we could uncover some useful facts to contribute to the acrimonious debate about immigration.

Since the site's monthly subscription fee was relatively modest (currently $29.99) we decided to give it a try. We paid for a few accounts and started searching, first by hand and then eventually in a more automated fashion. Our goal was to find as many immigrants as possible soon after they arrived on our nation's shores, and then to follow their fortunes over the decades as they found work, got mar-

ried, and potentially moved from place to place. This chapter explains
how we did it, and how these many lives help us to tell a new version
of the American story.

FROM FAMILY HISTORY TO AMERICAN HISTORY

Family genealogy is a national pastime. Ancestry.com boasts more
than three million paying subscribers and an annual revenue of over
a billion dollars.[3] The popular television show *Finding Your Roots*,
which sketches out the family trees of celebrities and politicians, has
been running on PBS for nearly a decade, with celebrities from Senator Cory Booker to Martha Stewart serving as guests. The book and
miniseries *Roots* may have kicked off the craze in the late 1970s, tracing the semi-fictionalized history of one African American family
through slavery and back to Africa.

Now a big business, Ancestry.com got its start by marketing its
research tools to members of the Church of Jesus Christ of Latter-day
Saints (informally known as the Mormon Church), whose members
are eager to track down all of the members of their family tree. Family
genealogy is the community's solution to a theological question that
arises in a relatively young church: What happens to ancestors who
died before church history began? The church's answer is that these
long-dead relatives can be baptized by proxy. One of Leah's friends, a
man raised in a Mormon family, recalls participating as a teenager in a
community event, volunteering to jump into the baptismal font once
for each name on a list of ancestors for members of his ward.

By 2008, the popularity of the Ancestry site was exploding. A
year later, the company would go public on the NASDAQ stock
exchange. Searching branches on a family tree used to require
paging through parish registers or making trips to dusty archives.
But through Ancestry, an array of digitized historical records became available at the stroke of a computer key: not just the names

of great-uncles and long-lost cousins, but detailed records for these family members, including marriage and death certificates, military conscription lists, and census forms.

So our breakthrough at the Huntington koi pond was to use the records cataloged on Ancestry.com to test various aspects of conventional wisdom about mass immigration from Europe. Before we got started, other economic historians—most notably Joseph Ferrie at Northwestern University—had already created datasets following individuals from one census to another. But Ferrie's method was painstaking: conducted by hand using microfilm, not all that different from what historians and family genealogists had long been doing.[4]

Ancestry.com was much better suited for our purposes. Using its digitized records enabled us to track more deeply and widely the lives of ordinary immigrants from long ago. This one insight has been the basis of much of our subsequent research, including the findings we describe in the rest of this book.

But even before we could get started, the "cease and desist" call that we received from Ancestry's lawyer in 2011 seemed to be jeopardizing the future of our research plans. In fact, during a tense conversation in which Ancestry's lawyer said that we had been violating the site's terms of service, Ran actually worried for a brief moment that he might be sued or possibly even prosecuted.

A year or so prior to the threatening phone message, soon after the conference at the Huntington, we had begun conducting initial experiments on the Ancestry site. These early forays were innocuous enough: we started out by typing in a few names to the Ancestry search bar to see how far we could get. But we quickly ran up against the immensity of the numbers. Thirty million immigrants arrived on American shores in the late nineteenth and early twentieth centuries. In 1900, the United States had seventy-six million residents overall. How could we possibly search for everyone?

Our solution was to write a computer program that automatically searched the Ancestry site for one person at a time. We let this script run for a month, and by the end we had data for around two hundred thousand immigrants and their families. But all these searches also created a mystery for the Ancestry corporate office. What could explain the sudden interest in their product? Why had search numbers increased by thousands over the last month? What they discovered when they dug into the numbers is that many of these searches came from just a few accounts, and those accounts all belonged to us.

Ancestry.com worried that some computer bot was downloading their data to package and resell: the company was concerned that someone was, in effect, stealing their data. That's why Ran got that frightening call from the lawyer. Would our research project be shut down? Would we face charges? By the end of the conversation, once we could explain that we were academics doing research to learn more about immigration, Ancestry.com became very supportive and allowed us to finish the project. These days, the relationship between Ancestry.com and researchers is stronger than ever: the company partners with researchers through the Minnesota Population Center to provide data for academic projects.

Whenever possible, we compare the patterns that we observe in the historical census files to more recent data sources that allow researchers to track households over time—Social Security earnings records, IRS tax records, or birth certificate files.

Statistics don't speak for themselves, of course. In addition to looking for the patterns that emerge from millions of records, we also gathered stories of individual immigrants from hundreds of retrospective interviews compiled by the Ellis Island Oral History Project, and drew on the work of various qualitative researchers who have studied immigrant communities. We also conducted our own survey asking respondents to write about their family immigration history. We ran our survey at a conference for California high school teachers and also circulated it on Twitter. Respondents confided to us about European grandparents who snuck into the country after the border was closed and about Chinese-born parents with science degrees who entered without papers and cleaned houses to build a new life in America. We tell these stories throughout the book.

In the previous chapter, we explained the problem with drawing conclusions from isolated stories, especially stories filtered through the generations. So it may seem odd that we talk about stories of individual immigrants. But we are not contradicting ourselves: when considered in tandem with data, stories can round out our understanding of the past. What's more, when we tell stories in this book, our goal is not to draw conclusions from the stories themselves, but merely to illustrate patterns revealed by our large datasets.

These stories and the survey responses we received provide detailed reflections about life in the home country before immigration, reasons for coming to the United States, the journey to America, and immigrants' lives in the United States since arrival. The stories connect real people to some of the numbers in our datasets, and are a reminder that our quantitative records came about as the result of a complex and often wrenching human process.

We intentionally focus here on the stories of everyday people rather than dramatic tales of extraordinary individuals; ordinary stories reveal the more common experience of the many millions of immigrants who came to America over the last two centuries. Individually, each record reflects a life quietly lived—perhaps as a beloved teacher or a hopeful parent or a kindly neighbor—achieving no fame as a result of their strivings. Together, these stories paint a portrait of the immigrant experience that largely overturns conventional wisdom.

FOLLOWING IMMIGRANTS THROUGH
THE DATA OVER TIME

Annie Moore was the very first immigrant to pass through the new Ellis Island immigration station when it opened for use on New Year's Day 1892. She stepped off the boat from County Cork, Ireland, to great fanfare. Traveling with her two younger brothers, Annie was soon reunited with her parents who had finally saved up enough, after four years in America, to send for their children to join them.

As the story goes, Annie then lived out a true American tale, traveling west and marrying the dashing and enterprising Patrick O'Connell, who made his fortune in real estate. Annie allegedly died in Fort Worth, Texas, after being struck by a streetcar.

Since then, Annie's journey across the Atlantic has become the stuff of legend. It is commemorated with statues at Ellis Island and the Cobh Heritage Centre in Ireland, and is even the subject of a sentimental Irish ballad, "Isle of Hope, Isle of Tears."[5]

But it turns out that this story is not true. Yes, the first immigrant to alight at Ellis Island was named Annie Moore. Yes, she hailed from County Cork, Ireland. But the Annie Moore who settled in Texas, whose family returned to Ellis Island for the ribbon-cutting ceremony on their great-grandmother's statue, is not the right Annie Moore! The real Annie Moore lived out her days in New York City, mother to eight surviving children, and was buried in an unmarked grave in Queens upon her death at the age of fifty.[6] Her children and grandchildren eventually moved into the professions, but she herself "led the kind of small, difficult life common to so many immigrants at the time."[7]

So how did the story of the first woman at Ellis Island become so mythologized, and how was the real story uncovered? According to Megan Smolenyak, the genealogist who discovered the story, the first Moore family grew to believe "an elderly relative's fanciful tale—an innocent exaggeration that morphed into indisputable family lore."

Smolenyak looked through old census records and found out that the
Texas Annie couldn't possibly be the first woman at Ellis Island—
according to the data, she was born in Illinois and was not an immigrant at all.[8]

Like Smolenyak and other genealogists, we, too, have been using
the historical census to reconstruct the truth of immigrants' lives.
From these records, we can document in minute detail how immigrants lived upon first arrival in the United States, and how their
lives changed after spending more time in the country.

The census provides a snapshot of the (free) population residing
in the United States, including immigrants, every ten years going
back to 1790.[9] Until 1960, census manuscripts were prepared using
paper and ink, and these manuscripts were eventually transferred to
rolls of microfilm. Until recently, a family genealogist or a historian
who wanted to look up a particular immigrant would have to scroll
through the rolls, one by one, in a library basement and then copy
down the information found there: What city or rural town did the
person live in? Who else lived in the house with her, and who were
the next-door neighbors? What did he do for a living and when did
he report coming to the United States?

These days, historical census records have been painstakingly
transcribed and made available in digital format. In 1900, for example, seventy-six million people lived in the United States, and the
census kept records for all (or most) of them. Using search tools provided by companies like Ancestry.com, this newly digitized census
data can now be readily accessed from any computer connected to
the internet.

To get a sense of how it is possible to follow an individual across
census manuscripts, let's take a look at one immigrant, James Alexander, soon after he arrived in the United States and track his progress over time. Even though our final dataset relies on software to

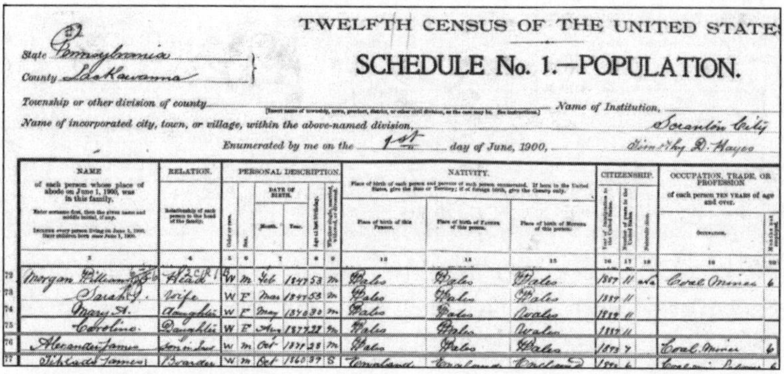

FIGURE 1. A page from the 1900 census manuscript, showing twenty-eight-year-old James Alexander from Wales living in his father-in-law's house. James reports working as a coal miner. CREDIT: US Census Bureau

study large numbers of immigrants, looking at a single immigrant in the original records helps to illustrate the complexity of identifying the same person over time, as well as the richness of the detail that emerges through the process.

We reproduced the census manuscript for James Alexander and discover that he was twenty-eight years old in 1900. James was born in Wales, moved to the United States in 1893, and seven years later was living in his father-in-law's house with his wife, Caroline (shown in Figure 1). The young Welshman worked as a coal miner, as did most of the other men on his block surveyed on the same census manuscript page. James and his neighbors lived in the heart of Pennsylvania's coal country, in Lackawanna County. The other men and women on his block, with last names like Mason and Evans, also hailed from Wales—or in some cases, from England or Ireland. The street was very uniform: all immigrants, all from the same countries of origin, all working in the coal mines.

We can then follow up on James Alexander in the next census, a decade later, and ask: Did he move to a new region or a new neighborhood? Did he switch to a new occupation? When we find James

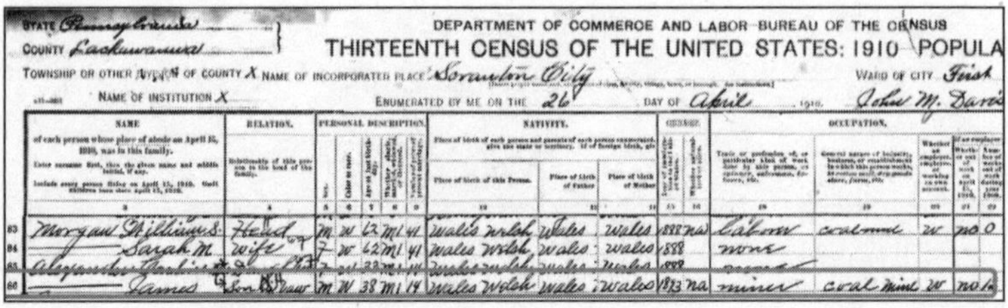

FIGURE 2. A page from the 1910 census manuscript, showing thirty-eight-year-old James Alexander from Wales. James is still working as a coal miner. CREDIT: US Census Bureau

Alexander again in the 1910 census (shown in Figure 2), we verify that he was born in Wales and is now thirty-eight years old, which gives us some confidence that he is the same immigrant we identified before. James is still living with his wife and her parents. He is still working as a coal miner, and he has no children recorded on the census form. Although James's life seems much the same, the neighborhood around him has changed. Half of his neighbors report being born in the portion of Poland then part of the Russian Empire, and a few of the men on his block now report occupations outside of the coal industry—in grocery, dry goods, and tailoring.

Our third snapshot of James's life comes from the 1920 census (shown in Figure 3), when he was forty-eight years old. James is still married to Caroline. Like many women at the time, Caroline did not report an occupation so likely did not work outside the home. The couple lives with Caroline's mother, Sarah, but her father, William, appears to have died before the 1920 census was taken. Also enumerated on the census page is James and Caroline's son, also named William, who is recorded as seventeen years old in 1920 and working as a clerk in an office. The younger William was not listed in the 1910 census even though, presumably, the boy would have been seven years old at that time and living at home with his parents. William's sudden appearance illustrates one of the problems with census data. Sometimes the census takers missed people altogether, especially if the people lived in crowded

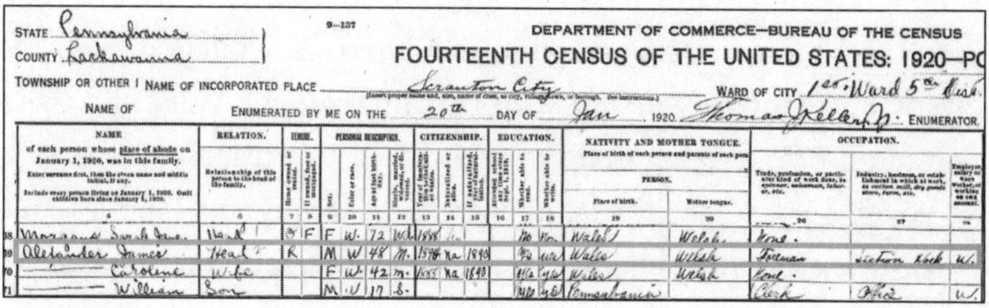
STATE Pennsylvania
COUNTY Lackawanna
9—137
DEPARTMENT OF COMMERCE—BUREAU OF THE CENSUS
FOURTEENTH CENSUS OF THE UNITED STATES: 1920—PC
TOWNSHIP OR OTHER | NAME OF INCORPORATED PLACE Scranton City WARD OF CITY 1st Ward 5th Dist.
NAME OF ENUMERATED BY ME ON THE 20th DAY OF Jan, 1920. Thomas J Keller Jr. ENUMERATOR.

	NAME	RELATION	Home		Sex	Color or race	Age	Single, married, widowed, or divorced	Year of immigration	Naturalized or alien	If naturalized, year	Attended school	Able to read	Able to write	Place of birth	Mother tongue	Trade, profession	Industry, business	Employer, salary or wage worker
68	Morgans Sarah Jane	Head	O	F	F	W	72	Wd	1888				no	no	Wales	Welsh	None		
69	Alexander James	Head	R		M	W	48	M	1896	Na	1898		yes	yes	Wales	Welsh	Foreman	Section Stock	W
70	— Caroline	Wife			F	W	42	M	1888	Na	1898	no	yes	yes	Wales	Welsh	None		
71	— William	Son			M	W	17	S				no	yes	yes	Pennsylvania		Clerk	Office	W

FIGURE 3. A page from the 1920 census manuscript, showing forty-eight-year-old James Alexander from Wales. James now reports his occupation as a foreman (supervisor). CREDIT: US Census Bureau

apartments or down long rural lanes. Because of language barriers, such errors may have been more common in immigrant neighborhoods.

The Alexander family experienced two forms of economic advancement by 1920. Although James still works in the coal industry, he is no longer a miner and now lists his occupation as "foreman." So during his lifetime, he moved up from being a coal miner to supervising other workers at the coal mine. This promotion happened more than twenty years after he first arrived in the United States. What's more, James's seventeen-year-old son, William, works in a white-collar job as a clerk, a position that likely came with a higher paycheck (or at least more opportunity for upward advancement) relative to working as a coal miner and also took place in a safer and cleaner workplace. William was part of the first group of children to benefit from free public high schools, which offered courses in business writing, stenography, and other subjects needed for the modern office.[10] Like many other immigrant families, the immigrants in the Alexander family did not move into white-collar work—but their children did.

Once we assemble records for a large number of immigrants like James Alexander, we can study how immigrants made their way in their new home: Were immigrants really more likely to start out with lower-paying jobs than the US born, but to then quickly catch up?

Whom did immigrants tend to marry? How many children did they have? Did they try to hasten their children's assimilation into US society by giving them American-sounding names? What did their children do for a living and how much did they earn? In this way, we create genealogies for large batches of immigrant families and study their economic mobility and cultural integration in the United States.

If you look up family members like James Alexander on a genealogy website, you can find their life traced out through census records. By opening each census manuscript in turn, you can start to piece together how your relatives' lives evolved. But using this method to trace census records across generations for large numbers of people, instead of for just one family, is prohibitively slow and labor-intensive. To scale up our searches, we automated them: we developed computer algorithms that allow us to search for "links" between individuals whom we first see in an early census (1900, in this example), identifying possible matches for the same individual in subsequent census years.[11]

Old census manuscripts do not record unique personal identification numbers such as Social Security numbers. Instead, what we do have are identifying details like first and last name, which the US government makes available to the public seventy-two years after the original survey was taken.[12] To find possible matches for an individual, we use personal information that includes first and last name, year of birth (or age), and state or country of birth.

The historical data has some downsides. One is that we cannot systematically follow women from childhood to adulthood because our linking approach depends on matching by last name, and women often take their husband's name when they marry. So, up through 1940, we limit our attention to fathers and sons. In other data sources from the modern era (such as birth certificates or tax records for children born in the 1980s and 1990s), we expand our study to consider daughters, as well.

Another difficulty is that even detailed personal information does not always uniquely identify a person. There is only one Ran Abramitzky in America, but many people named James Smith; therefore, it is harder to find a unique match for a James Smith, even if we know his age and place of birth.[13]

Beyond the issue of common names, other problems can arise in the census data. For starters, census takers sometimes made mistakes when they went door-to-door to chronicle the population. Somehow, William Alexander, James's US-born son, did not show up on the 1910 census. Some immigrants, like Leah's great-grandparents, the Platnichkys, change their name after spending time in the United States, making them hard to follow over time. And some links simply can't be made because an immigrant returns to Europe or died between one census period and the next.[14]

Moreover, the records sometimes contain errors introduced when old handwritten census forms are typed in to create a digitized copy.[15] And many respondents, especially in the past, also forgot their birth year and thus reported an inaccurate age on the census form. One clue that tips us off to age misreporting is that far too many people in the past reported themselves as being exactly one hundred years old, which might just be shorthand for "very old."[16]

The good news is that new linking methods can address some of these problems. Certainly, there is nothing we can do to find records that are not there—children who are missed by the census taker, immigrants who return to Europe or who die between census waves, or anyone who changes their name. But we *can* fine-tune our linking method to address names that are typed in incorrectly or ages that are misreported. For names that might be typed in incorrectly, we use algorithms that compare strings of letters for degrees of similarity rather than for an exact match. So rather than declaring Miles and Mike a non-match, we can score the two names on how close they truly are and select matches that are close enough for comfort. For misreported ages, we can try matching people with age bands, rather than requiring exact age matches. After all, the census might be taken at different times of the year, so some individuals may be nine years older (rather than a full ten years older) if their birthday has not yet arrived.

More broadly, we think that any good linking method should do its best to avoid creating false matches, matching individuals to the wrong person (false positives)—yet it should also catch as many of the true matches as possible. Think about the trade-off this way: we could try to be incredibly conservative and only declare two records a match if all of their attributes are the same (spouse's name, children's names, and so on) and if there is no one else in the United States with remotely similar characteristics. But this approach would be so conservative that we would throw away all but the most certain cases. Over the last decade, we (alongside other researchers) have developed several record-linking methods that aim to avoid false matches while recovering as many true matches as possible. We have tested all of the results that we present in this book to make sure that the findings are similar across various linking methods.[17]

Beyond linking challenges, it's important to think about who is included and who is excluded from any dataset, including ours. Immigrants are by definition those who were able to move to America. So families that try to make it to America but are turned away aren't included in our immigrant samples. This set of people is much smaller than the set of immigrants in the past, but it's not insignificant. Back then, fewer than 2 percent of prospective immigrants were either barred from entry or deported. Today, the number of those turned away or deported is higher.[18] Another group of immigrants come to America but eventually choose to return to their home countries (we discuss this group later in the book). Immigrants who make it to America may be different from people who want to but can't immigrate; as a result, we can say more about what happened to immigrants than about would-be immigrants. We can only speculate about what would have happened if a different set of immigrants had entered the country.

3

A BRIEF HISTORY OF
IMMIGRATION TO AMERICA

I N 2020, FORTY-FIVE MILLION PEOPLE IN THE UNITED STATES
were born in another country—about one in seven residents, or
14 percent of the population. Many Americans believe that immigrants make up a larger share of the country than ever before.[1] But they're wrong: immigrants accounted for the same share of the population—14 percent—a century ago, and did so for at least fifty years.

Although the immigrant proportion of the country has remained the same, in many ways, the context of immigration now is very different from back then. Immigrants then used to hail overwhelmingly from Europe, whereas now they come from all over the world, with around seven out of ten immigrants coming from countries in Latin America and Asia. What's more, there were very few restrictions for entry in the past (as long as you were of European origin), so most immigrants lived in the United States legally. Now the demand for immigration outstrips the limited supply of visas for entry, so one in four immigrants enters the country without papers.

In the past, many children from poor families—the "poor, huddled masses" of Europe—immigrated to the United States. Today, immigrants seeking a higher degree or arriving with technical skills are more likely to be admitted through special visa categories. What's perhaps more surprising is that even immigrants who do not work here in high-paid occupations tend to be more educated or wealthier than the average person who remains in their home countries.

These enormous changes in immigration over time make many of our book's key findings—that immigrants today are just as quick as in the past to integrate into the US economy and society—all the more remarkable and unexpected. Before we turn to the big data to reassess myths about immigrants' economic mobility and cultural assimilation, this chapter gives a brief history of immigration to America over the past two centuries.

THE TWO PEAKS OF MASS MIGRATION

Ran opens his undergraduate class at Stanford on the economics of immigration with a data exercise that has all of the excitement of a magic trick. As students file into the wood-paneled seminar room on the first day of class, Ran asks everyone to report on the years of their family's (or their own) arrival in the United States, collecting a small dataset of arrival years from the students in his class. Each time, he wonders: Will the class stories reproduce the historical pattern of immigration to the United States yet again? Lo and behold, what emerges on the board—like a magician revealing his card—is precisely what we have come to call the Immigration U, the two peaks of mass migration to the United States.

To start the experiment, Ran draws a long timeline of American history in chalk. The beginning of the line is marked as "before 1790," reflecting families that settled in the colonies before the Revolution. The end of the line is marked as 2019 or 2020, the year of the class in question. Before stepping away from the board, Ran places his own dot on the timeline in 1999, the year he arrived as an international student to start his PhD at Northwestern.

Ran tells the class his own immigration story: how he dreamed about studying economics in the United States, how grateful he was to finally be admitted, how his wife received a work visa that allowed her to work while he was studying, how much he missed his family in Israel, and how much he struggled with English at the outset. Adjusting to a new country wasn't always easy. He recalls to the students how he nearly found himself homeless when he arrived in America because he had reserved his dorm apartment for the date "09/08," which means August 9 in Israel and September 8 in America. Like many other immigrants, Ran benefited from friends and family ties. He tells the students how his second cousin Melvin and his wife, Sherry, whose family had immigrated to the United States decades earlier, became like his second parents, and how his classmates became like siblings.

Ran then asks the students to come up to the board and place their own dots on the timeline, one dot marking the arrival of each side of their family in the country. One year, the first student to accept the challenge was Dante, who shares a name with the famous Italian poet. One branch of Dante's family first arrived in the United States in the late nineteenth century, and he remembers his own grandmother telling stories of growing up in San Francisco's Little Italy. Next up was Katelyn, whose parents immigrated without papers from Ireland in the 1980s and built up a successful construction business, and then Pam, whose family won the green card lottery

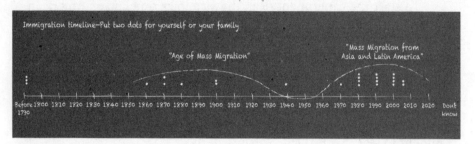

FIGURE 4. The Immigration U as a timeline from Leah and Ran's classes at Princeton and Stanford. Each student was asked to put a dot on the board for when their family first moved to the United States. CREDIT: Illustration by Patti Isaacs. Based on photograph from Leah Boustan's class.

and was able to move to the United States from Cameroon in the 2000s, when she was a little girl. A few more descendants of European immigrants placed their family dots in the late nineteenth or early twentieth centuries, followed by more recent immigrants from Peru, Sierra Leone, and Mexico.

What emerged on the board that year was the unmistakable two-peaked pattern. Most of Ran's students descended from families who had moved during either the first peak of immigration to the United States (before 1920) or the second peak (after 1965). Only one student had family who arrived between the two large eras of mass migration: Carlos, whose grandmother immigrated from Mexico in 1962 "with nothing but a backpack full of clothes." During this period in the middle part of the twentieth century, the United States substantially restricted new immigrant entry.

In most years we have done this in-class survey, only a few students report family who arrived in the country before 1850. We have taught just a handful of descendants of the earliest British immigrants to the country or descendants of men and women who were brought to American shores involuntarily as enslaved persons. These students place their dots on the "before 1790" mark.

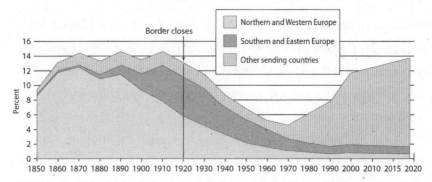

FIGURE 5. Percentage of the US population born abroad, 1850–2019. The first peak of the Immigration U is made up primarily of immigrants from Europe. In the second peak of the Immigration U, immigrants hail from other sending countries (50 percent from Latin America and 25 percent from Asia). CREDIT: Illustration by Patti Isaacs. Underlying data from US Census Bureau.

We demonstrate one such classroom timeline in Figure 4. As usual, a flurry of dots representing the years of arrival of students' families are placed between 1880 and 1920 (the first peak), and then another dense set of dots appear at the end of the line (the second peak), culminating with the international students who immigrated in 2019 or 2020 to earn their college degree.

The students wonder: Maybe the two peaks of immigration only pertain to our class? Or only appear among students who attend elite universities, who come from a particular set of backgrounds?

But no. This U shape would emerge from any reasonably representative group of American residents. We don't need to attempt this magic trick in other groups because the census data graphed in Figure 5 shows us the full picture. The census has asked every resident in the United States to report their place of birth since 1850, and from this question we can figure out what percentage of the population is born abroad: sure enough, we see two peaks of mass immigration, one from 1880 to 1920, and one starting in 1980 and still ongoing today. The two peaks are separated by an immigration valley in between.

EUROPE THEN, THE WHOLE WORLD TODAY

How did these two peaks of mass immigration to the United States emerge? In the decades after the nation's founding, very few immigrants came to the United States. The transatlantic journey on the sailing ships of the era was too dangerous and costly for most people to undertake at the time.

The country's original settlers were relatively small in number and came from two major locations: free immigrants and indentured servants from the United Kingdom, and enslaved persons from Africa.[2] The importation of new slaves was banned in 1808, and so very few men and women arrived in bondage as involuntary immigrants from that year onward. Free immigration also remained low through the 1840s.

Back then, sailing from Europe to America meant a month of discomfort and misery, with a very real chance of death on the way. For every one hundred people who set sail for New York or Boston, one would die along the way.[3] In Vilhelm Moberg's novel *The Emigrants*, about a Swedish family migrating to Minnesota, the journey is nothing but torment. "In the ship's hold . . . ," Moberg writes, "closely packed human beings [are] strangled by the sickness that is caused by a ship's swaying motions at sea—emitting all the sounds that witness the disease." The close quarters spread disease. The death toll reported in the novel is consistent with the mortality rate of one per hundred passengers. Each death is somberly announced as it happens, the body is wrapped in canvas, and three spoonfuls of earth from Sweden is placed in the shroud before the body is lowered into the sea. As the sailors said ominously on the very first day at sail, "There's more room in the hold the farther out we get."[4]

Of course, *The Emigrants* is a fictionalized version of the transatlantic journey before the widespread use of steamship technology. Real accounts also attest to the challenges. One of the most famous travelers to America during this period was Alexis de Tocqueville, a French diplomat from an old aristocratic family who sailed for America with his friend Gustave de Beaumont in 1831. The two men traveled in the nicest possible accommodations, leaving from Le Havre for New York. One historian reconstructed their travels from letters and diary entries, and notes that if the two men "had imagined that the Atlantic crossing would be comfortable . . . they were immediately disillusioned." The journey took thirty-eight days. De Tocqueville reported being "sick and depressed," surrounded by other passengers whose faces were "pale, yellow and green, enough to make all the colours of the rainbow."[5]

By the middle of the nineteenth century, America was entering a new era of mass migration. Annual immigration increased nearly ten-fold from the 1820s to the 1850s and onward. It's no surprise, then, that the timeline of student ancestry on Ran's board starts filling up with dots after 1850.

One major factor in the rise of immigration was the shift from sailing ships to steamships. If we had to pick one date to mark the start of the first peak of mass migration, it would be April 23, 1838, the day that the SS *Great Western* chugged into New York Harbor, the first steamship of its kind. The boat arrived only fifteen days after it departed from Bristol in the United Kingdom, completing the trip more than two weeks faster than the typical transatlantic journey by sail. This new technology lowered the cost—in terms of time, money, and risk—of crossing the Atlantic.

At first, most of the newcomers in this new age of steam travel hailed from the same countries that had sent immigrants to the United States before: the UK, Ireland, Germany, and later Scandinavian countries. As the cost of transatlantic travel continued to fall with further innovation in shipping technology, immigration expanded to poorer countries like Italy, Poland, and the Russian Empire on the European periphery. By 1900, 80 percent of new arrivals to the United States hailed from Southern and Eastern Europe.[6] We have taught many students whose ancestry can be traced back to these years, and Leah's own great-grandparents came to the United States at this time.

European immigrants faced few barriers to entry in the late nineteenth century, but the borders were not open to all who wanted to come. The anti-immigration movement scored early victories with targeted bans against specific immigrant groups, including the 1882 Chinese Exclusion Act. Those immigrants from Asia, Africa, and the Middle East who did make it to America were often denied the opportunity to apply for citizenship because of naturalization acts that restricted citizenship to "free white persons." These rules made it clear that only a certain kind of immigrant—white and of European ancestry—was welcome in the country. When we conduct the timeline exercise in class, we rarely see a student with Asian ancestry place a dot before the 1960s, presumably because the number of Asian immigrants in these years was small.[7]

Asian immigration to the United States represents a path not taken for the country. As such, it is a favorite topic for writers of "alternate history," the genre of historical fiction similar to science fiction in imagining what the world would have been like if a key turning point—like the US Civil War or World War II—had turned out differently.[8] Alternate histories about Asian immigration raise a fascinating question: What if America had continued welcoming immigration from China and Japan in the 1880s, rather than waiting until the liberalization of immigration policy in 1965?

One possibility is that California and the rest of the West Coast would have attracted a large Asian community that, by now, would have had roots in the country that are at least a century deep. Another possibility is that Asian immigration would have remained small even without restrictive legislation because few immigrants from poor countries like China or India would have been able to afford the trip.[9] Of course, since history runs its course only once, it's impossible to answer any historical "what if" question with certainty. The country chose its fork in the road, and the door swung shut to Asian immigration for nearly a century.

The era of immigration from Europe, too, came to a sudden close with the imposition of restrictive immigration quotas in the 1920s. As soon as immigrants from Southern and Eastern Europe began arriving in large numbers near the end of the nineteenth century, anti-immigration politicians began to cite all of their characteristics—young, unmarried, transient, lower skilled, and Catholic or Jewish—as reasons to restrict entry. Josiah Strong, a Protestant clergyman and leader of the Social Gospel movement, listed Catholicism and immigration as two of the seven "perils" facing the nation in his 1885 volume, *Our Country: Its Possible Future and Its Present Crisis*. Catholicism, he believed, was incompatible with American citizenship. "There is an irreconcilable difference," Strong warned, "between papal principles and the fundamental principles of our free institutions." For Catholics, he worried, "the commands of the Pope, instead of the constitution and laws of the land, demand the highest allegiance."[10]

The phrasing and the vehemence of the anti-immigrant rhetoric of that era remind us of anti-Muslim sentiment voiced during Trump's 2016 presidential campaign. "I think Islam hates us," Trump said in March 2016. "We're having problems with the Muslims, and we're having problems with Muslims coming into the country." The problem, as he saw it, stemmed from a fundamental incompatibility—the "irreconcilable difference," as Strong would say—between Islam and Western values. "Frankly, there's no assimilation," Trump announced. Muslim immigrants "want sharia law. They don't want the laws that we have." Whether because of supposed papal principles in the past or sharia law today, politicians often claim that certain types of immigrants can never become truly American.[11]

Influenced by these anti-immigration voices, Congress convened a committee chaired by Senator William Dillingham of Vermont to study the effect of immigration on the economy. A few years later, in 1911, the Dillingham Commission published a more than forty-volume report, proposing a sweeping set of new restrictions on immigration, including limits to the number of immigrant arrivals, strict entry quotas by country of origin, and a ban on immigrants who could not read or write.

During the 1920s, most of the proposed immigration restrictions came to pass. The new entry quotas barred nine out of ten immigrants who would have been able to enter the United States freely only a decade before. What's more, these restrictions were not uniform, but instead were imposed unevenly by countries of origin—with many slots set aside for more long-standing immigrant groups from countries like the UK, and very few slots for the countries in Southern and Eastern Europe. The goal of this policy was not only to reduce immigration, but also to tilt immigration even more heavily toward Western Europe. The policy succeeded in doing exactly that for two generations.[12] We discuss the politics of this period in more detail in Chapter 7.

As a result of these immigration restrictions, there were very low numbers of entrants from the 1920s through 1965. In our own classes, we usually have at most one or two students who can trace their family's arrival to this period of border closure. In the survey about family immigration history that we ran through Twitter and the teachers' conference, there was only one story (out of around three hundred) of immigration from this era, a family lucky enough to gain entry from a displaced persons camp immediately after World War II. A small number of refugees were also accepted from Communist countries in these years. Another source of immigration were the temporary workers from Mexico who participated in the Bracero Program, a guest worker program that authorized the entry of five million temporary workers from 1942 to 1965, but many of those immigrants eventually returned to Mexico.

The immigration quotas of the 1920s shaped midcentury America as surely as the deprivations of the Great Depression of the 1930s, the sacrifices of World War II in the 1940s, and the economic growth of the 1950s. The classic image of the 1950s suburbs—with soldiers home from the war and mothers tending to three or four baby-boom-era kids behind white picket fences—is a story shared by the children or grandchildren of European immigrants, but new immigrants themselves were rare during these years.

The immigration quotas of the 1920s may well have remained the law of the land for a century if not for the shifting geopolitics at the end of World War II and the looming Cold War. If the quotas had remained in place, many of our own students and even Ran himself may not be Americans today.

But with the national solidarity forged during World War II, the terms of the immigration debate shifted. Fears that immigrants could never become truly American were harder to sell to an American public that had recently fought in Europe and the Pacific alongside immigrants and the children of immigrants. The idea of defining peoplehood on the basis of race or national origin also had disturbing echoes of the Nazi ideology that the country had just sacrificed so much to defeat.[13]

Throughout the 1950s, pro-immigration voices sought to redefine the terms of the immigration debate, emphasizing an American identity emerging out of common purpose, rather than blood and soil. Although President Johnson is better remembered today for his landmark civil rights legislation, it was also on his watch that Congress passed the Immigration and Nationality Act of 1965, sweeping away the country-of-origin quotas and nearly doubling the total slots for entry.

The 1965 law set the stage for the immigrant communities living in the country today. Within fifteen years, the United States began to welcome immigrants from around the world, particularly from Asia and Latin America. In 1960, nearly nine out of ten Americans were listed as white on the census, many of whom were descended from immigrants during the first peak of mass migration. Today, only six in ten Americans are listed as white—and immigration from around the world is a major reason.[14] Many of the students in Ran's class who place dots for themselves or their family on the second peak of the timeline are from Latin America, Asia, or Africa.

But politicians in the 1960s didn't expect such a change in country of origin. Senator Ted Kennedy once promised that the 1965 bill "would not inundate America with immigrants from . . . the most populated and economically deprived nations of Africa and Asia."[15] Like most politicians of his day, Kennedy couldn't predict the long-term effect of a core tenet of the 1965 system: family reunification, which allocated a large proportion of visas (nearly two-thirds) to immigrants whose relatives were already living in the United States. During the Johnson era, unlike today, family reunification was a favorite policy of conservatives, who believed that family-based immigration would continue to prioritize the existing European communities to the exclusion of countries in Asia and Latin America who had not (yet) sent immigrants in large numbers. At the time, few politicians from either party could imagine the rising number of immigrants from Mexico, China, and India, which today constitute some of the largest countries of origin.

THE RISE OF UNDOCUMENTED IMMIGRATION

Another unintended consequence of Johnson's sweeping immigration reform was the new attention paid to the category of undocumented immigration. The 1965 bill imposed entry quotas on Mexican and Canadian immigrants for the first time, setting the stage for more than fifty years of policy focus on illegal border crossings, primarily at the southern border. In the same year, Congress phased out the Bracero guest worker program, imagining that eliminating guest workers would preserve agricultural jobs for US-born workers. Yet, with the program shuttered, many of the same Mexican immigrants who had arrived a few years before on Bracero contracts crossed the border, except they were now reclassified as "illegal" immigrants and thus had reason to stay in the United States rather than hazard more border crossings.[16]

If there is one type of immigrant family that is underrepresented in our classes at Stanford and Princeton, it is the children of the undocumented. It's possible that our informal tallies may undercount the true number of such students, particularly if students worry about disclosing their parents' or their own documentation status. But our sense is that the perceived and actual barriers to entering university can be so high that we likely have actually had few students who come from undocumented families.

A common sentiment today, especially on the right, is that legal immigration is fine—maybe even welcomed—but that illegal immigration is a problem. "My grandparents followed all of the rules and immigrated legally," people will say, adding that "immigrants these days are trying to jump the line." But trying to compare the immigration system then and now is like comparing open access of a public park with exclusive entry to a nightclub with a bouncer at the door. Many of the European immigrants who arrived in the past would be excluded under the current rules, when visa slots are limited to a fraction of immigrants who want to make the United States their home.

Today, few politicians would openly advocate "open borders" and, in fact, the term is often used as an insult by conservative politicians to claim that Democrats are too soft on immigration. But in the past, the US border was essentially open to all European immigration, although entry for people from Asia, as noted above, was far more constrained.

For most of the nineteenth century, there were some state laws intended to bar poor European immigrants from entry—but even these laws were rarely enforced.[17] Rounding up immigrants and sending them home is a costly enterprise, and the government did not have enough resources to carry out many deportations.[18] Early on, states had the authority to deport immigrants on their own. Massachusetts and New York, which received large numbers of poor Irish immigrants after the Great Famine of 1845 to 1852, had laws allowing for impoverished immigrants to be deported—but few were in practice.

The first major federal law that restricted entry for some European immigrants was passed in 1891. The law defined certain categories of immigrants as "undesirable," forbidding their entry into the country, and authorizing their deportation if they did come. The list included criminals, the disabled, or immigrants carrying contagious disease, as well as impoverished immigrants who might become a "public charge" (a cost to taxpayers). Later, restrictions were extended to "undesirable" ideologies including anarchists, Communists, or labor organizers.

Despite the many categories of possible exclusion, there was either a lack of will or a lack of resources to support mass deportations in the early twentieth century. Fewer than one in one thousand immigrants were deported before 1910.[19]

One respondent to the survey we conducted on immigrant family history described how immigration officials back then were half-hearted in their examination of a family member who was technically subject to an exclusion rule. "One of my grandmother's sisters, Tillie, was disabled," our respondent said. She "could not hear or speak. Apparently the immigration officer processing the family detained them at Ellis Island, intending to hold them until Tillie spoke, and presumably intending to send them back if she revealed she couldn't. For some reason, he gave up and let them in anyway."

Descendants of European immigrants from this era do not think of their own families as rule breakers, and so they can be quick to draw a distinction between their own legal ancestors and undocumented immigrants today—but they don't always know their family's full story.

A particularly striking example of this dissonance occurred when Ken Cuccinelli, the acting director of US Citizenship and Immigration Services in the Trump administration, argued that the country should only welcome financially solvent immigrants "who will not become a public charge."[20] A genealogist later discovered that, ironically, Cuccinelli's great-grandmother, Maria Ronga, was detained for being a "likely public charge" (and thus subject to exclusion) when she arrived in the United States in 1903 with her widowed mother and three younger siblings. The family was only released when Maria's older brother Vincenzo, who was already living in New Jersey, arrived and vouched for them, arguing that he would be able to support them.[21]

The broad use of immigration control, including the requirement of a visa and passport , and the imposition of penalties for illegal entry, can be traced back to the 1920s, with the passage of restrictive immigration quotas.[22] Some of these systems had been set up years before, to enforce Chinese exclusion—including inspections at authorized entry points and patrolling the border for unlawful entry—and were expanded in the 1920s.[23]

Eileen Clancy filled out the survey we conducted on immigrant family history and told us that her grandmother was one of the immigrants in the newly created illegal category when she entered from Ireland after the 1920s quotas were in place. Eileen's grandmother had long kept this important detail secret from her grandchildren. "When I was a teenager, I heard a story from my grandmother for the first and only time at a family gathering—Thanksgiving, maybe," Eileen told us on our survey. "Her adult children—my aunt and uncles—tried to stop her from telling it, seemingly because they were embarrassed or maybe for legal concerns. She said that she entered the US illegally by crossing the Canadian border in New York State. I was *very* surprised to hear this. Possibly the most astonishing part: she said that she had *never* attained a legal status. So, no green card, not a citizen, nothing."

Even though Canada and Mexico were exempted from the immigration restrictions of the 1920s, the new laws expanded policing of the country's land borders—in part, to limit illegal immigrants from Europe like Eileen Clancy's grandmother. The first border patrol station opened in El Paso, Texas, in 1924. Before then, as historian Naomi Paik describes, "people crossed [the borders] without a marker, checkpoint, or border patrol officer in sight; for much of the country's history, people may not have been aware that they were even crossing a border."[24] Congress passed laws as early as 1907 requiring that Mexican immigrants pass through official ports of entry and pay a small immigration fee, but these conditions were rarely enforced.[25]

Annual immigration from Mexico increased fivefold over the 1910s, reaching nearly one hundred thousand entrants by 1920, due in part to the violence of the Mexican Revolution. Mexican workers were also seeking work in mining, agriculture, and some urban settings—jobs that otherwise would have been held by European immigrants now restricted by the quota system.[26] Throughout this era, Mexican immigrants were subject to periodic roundups and deportations, including one major campaign during the Great Depression and another in 1954 (the offensively named Operation Wetback), leading to the deportation of more than a million people.[27]

As unauthorized border crossings grew in the 1970s with the ending of the Bracero guest worker program, patrolling the southern border became a growing bipartisan priority—first in a grand bargain crafted by President Reagan, pairing a path to citizenship with added border security in 1986, then as part of the "get tough" approach of President Clinton, and eventually culminating in the recent Trump and Biden administrations. Heightened policing at the border, including border fencing and the use of military surveillance equipment, has been reinforced in recent years by expanding resources for interior enforcement, which includes detention and deportation of noncitizens. The United States has expelled more than fifty million immigrants since 1970, or around one expulsion for every immigrant currently living in the country.[28]

Despite the added barriers to entering the United States illegally, nearly one in three immigrants each year either arrives without a valid visa or overstays their current visa.[29] The demand for immigration simply outstrips available visas for legal entry.

THE "HUDDLED MASSES" THEN, THE EDUCATED FEW TODAY

It is hard to graduate from high school in the United States without reading the famous poem, "The New Colossus," that is embossed on a bronze plaque on the base of the Statue of Liberty. The poem makes a strong assertion about the type of immigrants that America attracts—or, at least, attracted at the time that the statue was dedicated in the 1880s. Even as schoolchildren, many of us could recite the words: "Give me your tired, your poor / Your huddled masses yearning to breathe free / The wretched refuse of your teeming shore / Send these, the homeless, tempest-tost to me / I lift my lamp beside the golden door!"

The poem is right that immigrants to America used to be the tired, poor, huddled masses. In the past, immigrants were indeed drawn from poor families from Europe. Men who could not read or who held low-paying jobs were more likely to have children who moved to America than men who had wealth, station, and high-paying work. Today, the opposite is true. Immigrants from all over the world tend to come from backgrounds marked with *more* wealth or education than others in their home country.

How do we know that immigrants in the past were from the poor, huddled masses, whereas immigrants today are the educated few? For immigrants today, it is relatively straightforward to measure wealth and education levels with large surveys such as population censuses.

Scholars have documented that immigrants to the United States from nearly every country of origin have more skills or resources than others in their home country.[30] Here are a few extreme examples. An astonishing 77 percent of Indian-born immigrants to the United States hold a college degree today, compared to only 8 percent of residents of India.[31] Nigerian immigrants are the most educated population in the United States, with 81 percent holding at least a college degree. In comparison, only 10 percent of the Nigerian population enrolls in further schooling after high school.[32]

Studying immigrant backgrounds in the past was far more challenging before it was possible to link historical census records back to childhood. In recent years, economic historians, including the two of us, have traced immigrants back to their childhood households using passenger records and the US census to determine in what sorts of families these immigrants originated. We found that Norwegian immigrants were more likely to come from families without assets or with fathers who held low-paying jobs; others have found the same for the Irish and Italians.[33] In the first peak of mass migration (around 1900), men whose fathers were illiterate or poor were more likely to move to the United States than those with fathers who were literate, owned some land, or held a white-collar job.[34] Similarly, immigrants from Italy were more likely to move from the country's less-developed southern provinces than from the wealthier, more industrialized north; interestingly, immigrants from both Italian regions were also shorter than men who stayed behind, suggesting that the immigrants were more likely to have suffered from malnutrition during childhood.[35]

The differences in who has come to the United States over time are—in part—an outcome of US immigration policy. With all of the immigration regulations on the books today, getting into the United States is much harder than it used to be, and having education and skills can help. Most obviously, these rules favor immigrants with

higher degrees through student visa programs and explicit visa categories for people with specialized and technical skills.

Beyond the overt preference for skilled immigrants, the very fact
of having immigration restrictions and quotas for entry almost certainly advantages immigrants with resources over immigrants without
them. Moving to the United States now requires added costs beyond
the price of an airplane ticket. Many immigrants pay thousands of
dollars for the services of an immigration lawyer, or a smuggler to help
them navigate an illegal border crossing. These high costs price out
the world's poorest residents from moving to the United States today,
and favor those with more resources.

That's a stark contrast to a century ago: when even poor European immigrants were allowed to enter the United States without
restriction, the only cost of immigration was the price of a transatlantic shipping ticket, around the same amount (in adjusted terms) as
a plane ticket today. As a result, even the tired, poor, huddled masses
could afford the trip, especially since many of them arrived on pre-
paid tickets funded by friends or family members. In fact, Europeans
without literacy or a trade often had the most to gain by moving to
the United States, where wages for manual work were higher than in
Europe, and therefore many made the journey.

We have heard numerous stories of the years and sometimes decades that it can take to plan for immigration to the United States
these days. In the past, many immigration journeys were more spontaneous. Consider the fairly typical story of Signe Tornbloom, the
eighteen-year-old daughter of hardscrabble farmers from Dalsland,
Sweden, who moved to the United States on her own in 1916. When
asked as part of the Ellis Island Oral History Project why she made
the trip, Signe said that she made up her mind soon after receiving
a letter from a friend in America. What did the letter say? Simply:
"Well, you'd better come over here. Everything is much better than
it is at home."[36] Such an easy, spontaneous decision to immigrate to

the United States is nearly unheard of today, a time of much tighter controls and significant red tape.

The bottom line is that a century ago America indeed attracted the poor, huddled masses from Europe, and today America is attracting the richer and more educated from almost every country. And yet, despite this and other major differences between immigrants who came to the United States in the past and those who come today, immigrant populations then and now fared well and to a strikingly similar degree, as we show in the following chapters.

4

CLIMBING THE LADDER

The Rags-to-Riches Myth

A<small>N IMMIGRANT'S EXPERIENCE IN THE</small> U<small>NITED</small> S<small>TATES IS</small> more of a thick novel than a short story. The first part of the novel starts in the home country. By leaving poorer home countries to move to the United States, immigrants often vastly improve their prospects, both in the past and today. The second part of the novel might open in a city like New York or on a farm in rural Minnesota and tell the story of how the heroine struggles to make her way in a new country. By the third section, our main character's American-born children would have stories of their own—tales of how they succeeded despite, or because of, their parents' struggles.

Many Americans have the impression, born of nostalgia, that a century ago the protagonist of this novel would have arrived penniless at Ellis Island and within a few pages would have quickly ascended from rags to riches.

What we find in the data is that this idea has always been a myth. At the heart of this legend is a person who starts with nothing and quickly makes good, but the evidence shows that both parts of this myth are wrong. First, on the whole, European immigrants who arrived in the United States a century ago were not penniless. A good number of immigrants arrived with job skills and other resources already in hand. And second, those immigrants who *did* start out with low-paying jobs were not able to catch up quickly, and most of them continued to lag behind even at the end of their work lives.

By overturning the rags-to-riches myth, we find that the immigrant experience in the past was marked more by *persistence* of initial rung than by rapid mobility up the ladder. Immigrants who held higher-paying jobs than the US born when they first arrived tended to stay ahead thirty years later, and immigrants who held lower-paying jobs upon arrival continued to lag behind throughout their lives. In other words, these initial earnings gaps, whether positive or negative, persisted over time.

The story of immigrant progress today is remarkably similar. Just as in the past, immigrants often double their income (or more) when leaving their home country for America—and, once in the United States, newcomers move up the ranks slowly, at much the same pace as European immigrants did a hundred years ago. Persistence is more common today than mobility: immigrants who hold low-paying jobs soon after arrival typically never fully catch up to US-born workers, and immigrants who arrive for a graduate degree or to work in high-paid professions end up earning more than the US born throughout their careers. For all the similarities between now and then, there is one major difference, though. Immigrants today typically earn less than immigrants in the past did because immigrants tend to come from poorer countries. As a result, immigrants tend to earn less than the US born nowadays, both upon arrival and by the end of their working lives.

ONE RAGS-TO-RICHES STORY

How did a national myth of rapid success among European immigrants a century ago first form? This narrative can be traced back to widely shared stories like that of Rocco Corresca, an orphan from Italy who moved to Brooklyn around 1900.

For his first months in the United States, as the story goes, Rocco lived in a room with fifteen other Italian men, collecting rags, bottles, and other discarded items on the street to be resold. By the age of nineteen, he reported saving $700 working as a shoeshine man (which would be around $20,000 today) and boasted of his plan to soon open a "bootblack" parlor shining shoes. Rocco recounts of himself and his roommates that "we had said that when we saved $1,000 each [or $30,000 in today's dollars] we would go back to Italy and buy a farm, but now that the time is coming we are so busy and making so much money that we think we will stay."

Rocco enjoyed a busy social life with a vibrant group of other Italian immigrants. Together, they attended a church where homilies were given in Italian, and gathered to relax after a long working week. "On Sundays we get a horse and carriage from the grocer and go down to Coney Island," he reported, and "other evenings we go to the houses of our friends and play cards."[1]

The story of Rocco's life survives because it was written down and published by Hamilton Holt, a Progressive Era reformer and publisher. In his magazine, the New York *Independent*, Holt featured a number of sympathetic personal narratives of immigrants at the turn of the twentieth century. In 1906, just as the debate about closing the border was intensifying, Holt published a compilation of these upbeat accounts as *The Life Stories of Undistinguished Americans as Told by Themselves*. Because of his interest in supporting open immigration, the stories Holt selected didn't include immigrants who stumbled: those who never tried to learn English or who grew disillusioned with their new homeland. For that matter, his stories also excluded those who arrived in the United States with a lucrative trade or family pedigree. Instead, Holt picked the now-classic stories of immigrants starting with nothing in their pockets and rising quickly through hard work and hustle.[2]

Rocco's story is not the only one in the collection to have an optimistic arc. Another chapter in *The Life Stories of Undistinguished Americans* is the tale of a man referred to only as "the Greek peddler," who recounts coming to America with only a few dollars and a drive to build a new life. "I got work immediately as a push-cart man," the Greek man recalls. "There was six of us in a company. We all lived together in two rooms down on Washington Street and kept the push-carts in the cellar." From these humble beginnings, the Greek peddler found success. "[I] got down to business," he says, "worked hard and am worth about $50,000 today." That sum would make the peddler a millionaire in today's dollars.[3]

Is the speed with which Rocco claims to make it in his adoptive home accurate? We have reason to think it is not. We were able to locate Rocco in the census manuscripts. We suspect that we found the right man because our Rocco, like the one in Holt's book, reports working as a bootblack and arriving from Italy in the right year.[4] According to the official documents, Rocco's life was successful in many ways. Rocco married and had a child. In 1920, at the age of thirty-six, Rocco managed to open his own bootblack parlor, nearly twenty years after first expressing his dream of opening one. In his forties and fifties, Rocco reports being a cashier at a shoe store—perhaps his own. Eventually Rocco was able to reach his dreams, but it took him far longer than the boastful young newcomer expected.

The published version of Rocco's story is one of rapid success in America, leaving readers to come away with an overly rosy view. Stories like Rocco's give rise to the myth that immigrants back then climbed the ladder to success in America faster than immigrants to-day. Our data provides a less rosy view: past European immigrants often struggled when they first arrived, and most of them did not succeed in reaching the American Dream within their lifetimes. European immigrants did make strides toward economic success, like Rocco saving up to open his own store, but the process took time.

A TRUE STORY OF INCREMENTAL PROGRESS

Once we found the much more down-to-earth pattern of immigrant success in the data, we were able to uncover stories of this slower and more incremental success everywhere we looked. Here's one coming-of-age story that is much more representative of the patterns we uncover in the data. Louis Bilchick left behind dire poverty in a small Eastern European village at the turn of the twentieth century to take a job hauling ice in New York City. He started on the bottom rung of the ladder in America and did not climb very far over the course of his work life. His older sons left school early to help make ends meet, working in a shirt factory and as drivers around the city, but one of his younger sons, Kalman (later known as Charles Beller), finished high school and moved up from a simple clerical position to eventual ownership of an advertising agency.[5]

Before moving to America, Louis lived with his wife and five children in a village named Kartuz Berezer in the Russian Empire. "We had a home, and a stable with a horse and a cow, and a little garden plot," his son Charles told interviewers for the Ellis Island Foundation many years later. But the family didn't own much else. "We didn't have any inside toilets or anything, so you had to go to an outhouse. And Lord help you in the wintertime, it was very cold." After Louis left for America in 1904, leaving his family behind in the village, life for his family was even harder than before. "We raised some vegetables and things like that. . . . And, occasionally, my father would send a few dollars, so we could save enough money to buy the steamship tickets in order to take us to the United States."

His father, Louis, settled in New York City, where he went into the ice and coal business—an important trade at a time when no one had refrigerators or electric heat. "In the summertime he would sell you ice for the iceboxes," his son Charles remembers. "He'd cut off a piece of ice from a big cake, bring it up in the tenement houses there, put it in the icebox, and get paid for that. In the wintertime, wood and coal was needed for the stove. Pot-bellied stoves or straight ovens, that's the way the people got warm."

When the family finally saved up enough to join Louis, the cost of the steamship tickets left them destitute. "When you say you came over without a penny in your pocket, you could say that about us," Charles recalls. "What you could carry on your backs and the like, that's about it. We came with practically nothing. . . . Give us a plain piece of bread, with a piece of herring or a potato and we'd be very happy."

From an early age, Charles and his brothers had to work odd jobs to help the growing family make ends meet. (Two new children were born in the United States.) Charles started working at nine years old, assisting a harness maker every Sunday. "I'd go into the stable with him in the morning," Charles remembers. "He would load me up like a horse" with harnesses that needed to be repaired. At the end of the day, Charles would deliver the finished product to stables around the neighborhood.

Charles was the only sibling of his seven brothers and sisters to graduate from high school, an education that paved the way for a successful career in advertising. Retired and reflecting back on his life, he told an interviewer: "Starting down at the bottom, working up through a few departments, finally winding up as assistant manager, manager, part-owner, one-fifth owner, one-fourth owner, one-half owner . . . when [people] say, you know, 'from janitor to owner,'" it is exactly stories like his they have in mind. Charles's story ends happily, in true American fashion: "I never dreamt I'd be in Florida—here," he said. "My wife thinks I'm the happiest man in Florida."

The Bilchick family moved up, but only in the second generation. Louis Bilchick was typical of first-generation immigrants at the time. He took a low-paying job when he arrived in the United States and remained in that job until he died in 1929, two weeks before the stock market crash. All of his children surpassed him, representing the mobility typical of the second generation, which we discuss in the next chapter. Charles, with his educational opportunities, became the most successful of all.

Few of the many immigrant stories that make up our nation's history are compelling enough on their own to make it to the pages of a newspaper or a novel. But with our newly collected data in hand, we can follow millions of immigrants like Rocco and Louis to tell their families' stories of economic progress and cultural assimilation over time.

EVIDENCE UNDERMINES THE RAGS-TO-RICHES MYTH

When we turn to the data, we find that Louis's story of slow, incremental progress is more typical of the immigrant experience than Rocco's dramatic ascent. Many immigrants—particularly from poorer countries like Norway or Portugal—worked in manual jobs when they first arrived, making less than most US-born workers. Contrary to the rags-to-riches myth, these poorer immigrants remained in lower-paid jobs throughout their lifetimes, never quite catching up with US-born workers.

The data also reveals another surprise: on average, past immigrants actually had similar jobs US-born workers, even upon first arrival. When we look at the occupations of *all* the immigrants of the earlier era—including the poorest of the poor—we find that even recently arrived immigrants tended to have similar skills/occupations to workers born in the United States. This pattern is at odds with the many stories we hear about immigrants like Rocco or Louis who arrived "with practically nothing." The reality is that not every immigrant started out "in rags." Instead, we see that plenty of immigrants—particularly from rich countries like England and Germany—arrived with skills that enabled them to quickly find high-paying jobs and outearn US-born workers.

How did we discover this new and surprising fact about the past? We started with hundreds of thousands of immigrant workers whom we first observed in the United States in the 1900 census, and followed them through the censuses of 1910 and 1920, comparing their work lives with the lives of US-born workers.[6] Unfortunately, this data doesn't include wages or annual earnings because the Census Bureau did not add questions about income until 1940. Instead, we focused on tracing immigrants from job to job to chart their occupational mobility. We also tried to infer immigrants' incomes in earlier years from all of the relevant information that the census did record: occupation, age, state of residence, and country of origin (or state of birth), taking advantage of the fact that we know, for example, how much the typical forty-year-old Italian carpenter living in Illinois earned in 1940 and then using this value to assign likely incomes to immigrants in earlier years. That way, we created a good—but not perfect—proxy of the earnings of immigrants relative to US-born workers before 1940.[7]

The data quite firmly rejects the first part of our national myth: that most European immigrants during the Age of Mass Migration arrived in poverty. That being said, there were still many immigrants like Rocco and Louis who started on the bottom rung of the ladder. These poorer immigrants remained in lower-paid jobs like farmhands, dockworkers, and manual laborers, tending to never quite catch up with US-born workers. Some coal miners, like James

Alexander (whom we introduced in Chapter 2), eventually became foremen, but few of them jumped into higher-paid office work or business ownership.

Of course, over the course of thirty years, the fortunes of most of the workers in our dataset improved—both immigrants and the US born—because workers tend to get promotions and earn more as they age. And immigrants' annual earnings did rise at a slightly faster pace than the annual earnings of the US born, which makes sense because immigrants earn more as they learn English and expand their network. But despite this earnings growth, immigrants who started out in low-paid jobs *still* earned less per year than the US born even at the end of their working lives, closing only around one-third of what was initially a $2,000 per year earnings gap in today's dollars (around a 10 percent gap).[8] Immigrants from Mexico in this period fared even worse, either holding pace or falling behind US-born workers, exhibiting no sign of catching up.[9]

This earnings comparison does not adjust for the many differences between immigrants and the US born. For example, immigrants were less likely to live on farms and more likely to live in cities, where wages are typically higher, suggesting that immigrants can "undo" some of their earnings penalty by choosing locations with higher earnings potential. Indeed, when we compare immigrants and US-born workers in the same state, the earnings gap between immigrants and the US born is larger than what we find nationwide. We return in the next chapter to the importance of immigrants' locations as one way of getting ahead.

What we document in the data matches many of the stories we found of immigrants narrating their lives in their own words. Louis Daiberl, who came to the United States from Germany in the 1920s, describes remaining in basic construction positions from his first arrival in the country. As he explained to the interviewers in the Ellis Island Oral History Project, this Louis found work right away. Not a day had gone by after arriving in a small town in Florida when "three, four German guys came down" to offer him a job. "Where you want to work? Want to go on the farm?" they asked. "I says, 'Hell, no. I'm not going back on no farm again.' . . . They all were bricklayer, [carpenter], masons, cement worker. So they got me with some Polish guy, a little contractor, only about three, four men." For this work, Louis was paid around twenty dollars a week, which he says "was tremendous to me." Over time, he secured better construction jobs, moving up dollar by dollar. "Every week he raised it a dollar, till it was up to twenty-three dollars. That was my best wage that I got down here."[10] This Louis is one of the immigrants who started out working in low-paying jobs when they first arrived and continued to hold relatively low-paid positions even by the end of their working lives—consistent with other evidence of persistence.

On the other side of the ledger are immigrants who arrived with skills, wealth, or other resources. These immigrants—often from richer countries like England and Germany—started out in the professions or as managers, holding jobs that paid around $2,000 more per year (in today's dollars) than US-born workers. What's more, these successful immigrants were able to maintain their earnings advantage over their lifetimes, earning around 10 percent more than the US born throughout their working lives. Jewish immigrants, whom we identify in the census using names and language spoken at home, also tended to work in relatively high-paying trades in the garment industry or in factories. One of Ran's American relatives, Jacob (Yankel in Yiddish), fits this pattern. He moved from Poland and became a skilled worker, working as a spotter, or someone who looks for imperfections in women's silk garments. He earned a decent middle-class income, eventually investing in the stock market and buying an apartment building that the family lived in.

Another such skilled immigrant was Karl Ingvald Strand, a Norwegian dentist who moved to the United States around 1890 and went on to work as an oral surgeon in Minneapolis. (Karl's education surpassed that of most of his Norwegian countrymen at the time.) Karl's great-grandson was one of the respondents to the survey that we conducted at a California teachers' conference and on Twitter. Karl's career illustrates how immigrants who started out ahead managed to stay ahead. Eventually Karl moved to Southern California and founded his own advertising company. "His entrepreneurial spirit continued late into his life," his great-grandson reported on our survey. "While convalescing in a hospital from an illness, he noticed an orderly struggling to sweep under his bed with a mop. He then patented the swivel-headed mop, and founded the Perfection Mop Company."

Karl is one of the many immigrants who arrived with a trade or skill in hand, and was able to find high-paying work right away. His story fits with the two new facts about the Age of Mass Migration that we have discovered—that fewer immigrants arrived penniless, and that those that did arrive poor took time moving up the ladder.

IMMIGRANTS TODAY ARE MOVING UP AT A SIMILAR PACE

These new facts might surprise Americans from all sides of the political spectrum. For all of their differences, recent presidents Barack Obama and Donald Trump have one thing in common: a firm belief that European immigrants arrived poor but managed to contribute to the country through their own hard work and ingenuity. President Obama praised Italian immigrants, saying that they "often came here with nothing" but overcame their challenges to succeed in every walk of life.[11] Trump made headlines around the world by praising European immigrants of yore—he put in an especially good word for Norwegians—in contrast to recent immigrants who he claimed were less likely to get ahead. "Why do we want all these people from 'shithole countries' coming here?"

Trump famously asked in a closed-door meeting, referring to countries like Haiti and Nigeria.[12]

But are immigrants these days really that different from immigrants in the past? In fact, during the Age of Mass Migration, Norway was one of the poorest countries in Europe. Norwegian immigrants tended to settle in rural places in Minnesota and the Dakotas, and to work in fishing, logging, and farming—the classic "Norwegian bachelor farmers" of Garrison Keillor's *A Prairie Home Companion*.[13] In our data, Norwegians were among the lowest-paid immigrant groups in the early twentieth century, earning $4,000 less annually than US-born workers (in today's dollars) and failing to make up much of this earnings gap even after thirty years in the country. When we discussed this gap with a colleague, the great-grandson of Norwegian immigrants, he jokingly decided to add the Norwegian vowel ø back into his last name on his résumé to show how far he had been able to rise from this humble background.

These days, just like in the past, some immigrants arrive with little education and hold low-paying jobs. These immigrants do not catch up with US-born workers within one generation. But other immigrants arrive with the skills and education that allow them to outearn US-born workers, even upon first arrival.

A stark example of this second group is the case of wildly successful immigrant entrepreneurs. These entrepreneurs might appear to be a self-made lot, but a closer look shows that they tend to come from families with high initial levels of wealth, education, or both. In fact, it is rare to find a captain of industry with a real rags-to-riches story. Pierre Omidyar, the founder of eBay, is from an Iranian family; his father is a surgeon who worked at Johns Hopkins University and his mother has a PhD in linguistics. Sergey Brin, cocreator of Google, was born in Moscow; his father is a professor of mathematics and his mother is a NASA scientist. The multidimensional entrepreneur Elon Musk was raised in South Africa by an engineer father who once co-owned an emerald mine in Zambia. Eric Liu, an activist and former White House speechwriter, wrote in his memoir of his family's immigration from Taiwan, *A Chinaman's Chance*, that his parents "arrived with more advantages of station and education than is typically acknowledged"[14]—an apt statement about the success of many immigrants who arrive with considerable resources today.

Immigrants who arrive with higher degrees and business connections are highly visible today, but they are not the majority. The majority start out well behind US-born workers—pulling down the average earnings for all immigrants so much that the average gap in earnings between the US born and all immigrants today is about 30 percent. In other words, if you include all the Elon Musks and Sergey Brins in your calculations—as we did—you find that immigrants still earn, on average, only seventy cents for every dollar earned by US-born workers. This earnings gap is three times wider than in the past. (Recall that the earnings gap during the Age of Mass Migration was only 10 percent.)

That may paint a bleak picture of present-day immigration, but if you take a longer view the news is good: with time spent in the United States, today's immigrants catch up to US-born workers at the same pace as in the past. Like European immigrants back then, immigrants from around the world today (particularly those who arrive earning less than the US born) increased their earnings over the course of their working lives, although they were not able to fully close this earnings gap in the first generation.[15] Yet immigrants do close a portion of this gap, which shrinks from 30 percent upon arrival to 16 percent twenty years later.

Immigrants switch jobs regularly, constantly keeping their eyes out for new opportunities. But the set of jobs open to many immigrants is relatively narrow, so they make limited progress during their working lives. My Le, an immigrant from Vietnam, might hold the record for the most job hopping: seventy-five jobs over a single decade, the 1980s. My told his story to Ellen Alexander Conley for her book *The Chosen Shore*. "My first job in this country," he says, "was at a nursing home washing dishes. Once I learned a little English, I went to the floors and helped the patients pick good food from the menu. I have had a total of seventy-five jobs over here during the last seven years. I have worked at Roy Rogers and 7-Eleven. I worked all the time except for the times I was in school."[16]

In order to be able to observe immigrants over the course of their careers, studies often focus on immigrants like My who arrived in the 1970s and 1980s, many of whom are now nearing retirement age. More recent research, on immigrants who arrived in the 1990s, suggests that this pattern of earnings growth has continued today—despite the higher number of undocumented immigrants.[17] We return to the topic of undocumented immigrants and their children in the next chapter.

RAPID SUCCESS IS A DATA ILLUSION

If immigrants don't quickly catch up in earnings to the US born—neither today nor in the past—then where did the myth of rapid immigrant mobility come from? One possibility is that boosterish stories like Rocco's tale of quickly rising in America have been accepted uncritically, especially in how Americans view the past. As time goes by, family stories also soften into myth, with the immigrant generation remembered as penniless—arriving with "a goat and one Bitcoin," as the comedian Desus put it. With distorted memories suggesting a lowly start, any later success seems all the more impressive.

Another possibility is that immigrant success was a genuine hallmark of an earlier era, before the Age of Mass Migration, and that this national myth stuck.[18] Scholars have found that the last time that rapid immigrant mobility was a feature of the American economy was before the Civil War. Immigrants who arrived in the 1840s and 1850s, soon after the invention of the steamship, actually *did* move up the occupational ladder faster than the US born.[19]

But there's a third possibility that we want to suggest here: the nostalgic view of immigrant success a century ago persisted for so long because we simply didn't have the data necessary to check the facts. What's more, the data that *was* available to researchers led scholars to draw the wrong conclusions from what they saw in the numbers. Once we got access to all the records—and, crucially, once we were able to follow individual immigrants over time—we found that the rags-to-riches story is nothing more than a data illusion.

To begin to understand this illusion, you need to remember that the most accurate way to measure upward mobility requires following a person over time—from childhood to adulthood or from the beginning of his career to its end. And that requires being able to link data across censuses. But previous generations of researchers did not have the linked data because of census privacy rules. (Recall that the Census Bureau releases identifying information such as first and last name only after seventy-two years.) Researchers were also unable to digitize what amounted to literally millions of census manuscripts.

Without access to linked data across censuses, scholars tried to learn as much as possible from the data that they did have. The most famous study of this type concluded that immigrants could rise quickly from rags to riches by comparing immigrants in the 1970 census who had arrived in the United States in different years. The data seemed to show that immigrants who recently arrived in the country earned a lot less than the US born, but that immigrants who had spent thirty or more years in the United States had not only caught up to the US born but surpassed them, earning around 15 percent more than the typical US-born worker.[20]

When we think more carefully about that study, it's easy to see that its conclusions are unwarranted. In 1970, many recent arrivals were immigrants from poor countries in Latin America, Asia, and the Caribbean who arrived after 1965. Long-standing immigrants who arrived in the 1930s and 1940s were part of the small cohort escaping from Europe at the outbreak of World War II. It doesn't seem plausible that a low-paid Mexican farmworker, say, would reach the earnings of a German scientist, even after twenty-five years go by.

Subsequent research noted that this study was essentially comparing apples to oranges. Comparing a low-paid apple to a high-paid orange creates the illusion of earnings catch-up in the data: comparing immigrants from a single census (inherently imperfect data) supported the idea that immigrants start with little but quickly catch up and even overtake the earnings of US-born workers. A better alternative is to follow a group of immigrants who arrive at a moment in time (say, immigrants who arrived after 1965, or immigrants who arrived in the 1930s); doing that enables one to follow the same cohort of immigrants over time, an apple-to-apple comparison. This approach still generated evidence of catching up, but at a much slower rate than when comparing immigrants from a single census.[21]

Immigrants who eventually return to their country of origin also contribute to this data illusion, in a way that even following a group of immigrants who arrived at the same time couldn't dispel. These return migrants (as scholars call this group) are included in the data on recent arrivals, but they disappear from the data after five or ten years, when they return home. Many immigrants return home because they struggled to find a good job in the United States. Others have no trouble finding high-paying work, returning only after saving enough money to afford a more comfortable lifestyle in their home country. On the whole, though, return migrants are more likely to have worked in lower-paying jobs. Once those working in lower-paying jobs leave the United States and return home, they disappear from the census, leaving only immigrants with high-paying jobs—creating the false impression that immigrants did better than they actually did.

Using the new linked data that follows individual immigrants over time, we were able to obtain much more accurate data, eliminating the illusions that distorted past research and contributed to the myth that immigrants in the past caught up quickly to US-born workers. The reality is that although immigrants do make up some ground as they spend more years in the United States—both in the past and today—the pace of progress is dramatically slower than originally thought.

RETURN MIGRANTS FIND SUCCESS BACK AT HOME

Immigrants who return to their country of origin can muddy the waters when it comes to analyzing the success or failure of immigrants as a whole. Return migrants are, however, an interesting group in their own right, and one that we, as Americans, usually forget about. It's a case of "out of sight, out of mind." The percentage of immigrants returning home has remained steady over the past century: around 25 to 30 percent of immigrants returned home to Europe in the 1910s, and a similar percentage have returned home over the past twenty years.[22]

Our datasets that follow individual immigrants over time don't include return migrants who cease to appear in the census once they leave the United States. When return migrants leave the United States and disappear from the census data, they also vanish from the minds of American policymakers. But from a global perspective interested in whether immigration contributes to human flourishing more broadly, the fate of return migrants is an important part of the picture.

During the Age of Mass Migration, return migrants usually returned home in triumph. Of 400 immigrants returning to Europe who were interviewed in 1911, only 104 were out of work; the remainder had been saving up money for a planned return.[23] In fact, some of these savers had been planning their return from the outset.

"Dear brother," wrote one Polish immigrant, Francis Tychewicz, to his brother still at home. "You wrote that your harvest has not been too good and that it is difficult for you, so if you want to come to America, then come. You could remain for two years in America, earn some money so that you could pull yourself out from under that misery and be a man."[24] Francis was writing from Reynoldsville, Pennsylvania, a small town in coal country, today a two-hour drive from Pittsburgh. At the time, Reynoldsville was replete with jobs, home to a silk mill, brick and tile works, and a tannery. As best we can tell, Francis saved up for a few years and went back to Poland because we find no later trace of him in the US census records.

These Polish brothers are far from an exception: the same story has been reconstructed from interviews and letters with Bulgarians, Slovenians, Ukrainians, Hungarians, and Italians. According to one old Italian saying, "he who crosses the ocean can buy a house," referring to the idea that saving up in America allows returnees to buy land back in Italy.[25] Spending some years as a temporary migrant may have been an especially attractive option in the late nineteenth and early twentieth century, when the limited banking sector in many European countries made it hard to borrow money to buy land on credit.[26]

In our research, we were able to study the path of a large sample of return migrants: those who moved to the United States from Norway and then returned to Norway by 1910. Men who moved to the New World came from the lower strata of Norwegian society, and we find that immigrants who spent some time in the United States and then returned to Norway were, in fact, among the poorest of the poor when they set off for America. They typically stayed in the United States for no more than three to five years, earning wages that were often twice as high as wages for similar work in Norway. As a result, these immigrants did remarkably well after returning to Norway. Many moved back to their home village, got married, acquired land, and worked as owner-occupier farmers. Strikingly, return migrants were actually more

likely to live in their home village than men who never left Norway
at all: return migrants were able to use their savings to move home,
whereas many nonmigrants moved to cities like Oslo or Bergen, presumably to find better jobs than they could in their villages.[27]

Not only did return migrants better their own lot by saving up to
marry and buy land, but they also brought back ideals and ideas they
had absorbed during their time in America. The Norwegian Immigration Commission marveled at the farming practices that return
migrants imported with them from the United States. "The rural districts are scarcely recognizable," the commissioners wrote. "All those
who come from America begin to till their soil better than it was tilled
before. . . . Crop rotation is introduced, machinery is acquired, . . .
more rational dairy methods are practiced, and gardens are laid out."[28]

Return migrants to Norway and beyond also became involved in
politics, inspired by their experience with American democracy. In
one study of Sweden, economists found that cities that sent more return migrants to the United States had higher voter turnout, more
membership in labor unions, and a greater share of votes for left-
wing parties. It seems that exposure to American standards made
workers unwilling to accept low pay and poor working conditions
in Sweden, prompting them to push for change.[29] Many European
politicians spent some time in the United States, working in manual labor—including Prime Minister Johan Nygaardsvold of Norway,
Prime Minister Oskari Tokoi of Finland, and Prime Minister Kārlis
Ulmanis of Latvia.

The latest numbers suggest that the return migration rate is just as
high now as it was in the past. Many immigrants plan to return home
one day, in some cases because they arrive on a temporary student or
employment visa. But months can become years and these immigrants
often find themselves staying in the United States more permanently.
There is a famous Israeli joke about a woman who asks her friend,
who is living in America, when she plans to return home. "When

my son graduates from college," she replies. "That's great news," the first woman exclaims. "How old is your son?" The immigrant's answer: "He's two!"

᭺

MOVING UP THE ECONOMIC LADDER HAS NEVER BEEN A RAPID process. Even in what many think of as the golden age of immigration in the late nineteenth and early twentieth centuries, few immigrants disembarked and immediately found a path to prosperity, let alone discovered streets paved with gold. But these new arrivals did make steady progress up the socioeconomic ladder, closing some of the income gap with US-born workers over the course of their working lives. Many fear that today's immigrants from non-European countries like Mexico and El Salvador will not be able to replicate the past successes of European immigrants. But we find that today's immigrants are climbing the ladder of economic mobility at the same pace as immigrants did in the past. And, as we show in the next chapter, background is not destiny: the children of immigrants are remarkably successful, both in the past and today, regardless of where their parents once came from.

5

BACKGROUND IS NOT DESTINY

Children of Immigrants Rise

In April 2020, the *New York Times* ran a special feature called "I Am the Portrait of Downward Mobility." The article told the stories of Americans nearing middle age who despaired of ever reaching their parents' level of prosperity. "It used to be a given that each American generation would do better than the last," the piece began, "but social mobility has been slowing over time."[1]

Lauren Bruce and Melissa Haddock are two of the women profiled in the piece. Lauren was raised in Madison, Wisconsin, by two US-born college graduates. Growing up, her parents always had money for extras—home repairs or a summer vacation—but today her own finances feel far more precarious. "My financial situation is vastly worse than that of my parents," she says. "They always owned houses and had new cars, never worried about seeing a doctor, benefited from solid pensions and preached that college was the secret to their success." Lauren's parents believed in a ladder to success—climb up the right way, rung by rung, and you are guaranteed financial security and at least moderate prosperity. "I'm not sure that ladder exists any more," Lauren frets. Melissa feels the same way. Her mom and dad were working class, a waitress and a mechanic in rural Alabama. Now, as an adult, Melissa has a sense of treading water against the current. "My parents very much believe that you can pull yourself up by your bootstraps," she confides. "And that's great when you have the resources to do that. But what about when [you] don't?"

In paging through the profiles, we couldn't help noticing one group of Americans who defy the trends, one group who express a sense of optimism for the future: the children of immigrants. Sonya Poe was born in a suburb of Dallas, Texas, to parents who immigrated from Mexico. Her parents came to the United States "so their future children could have a better life—and we have," says Sonya. "My dad worked for a hotel. He would work overnight, and he worked a lot of hours. . . . Their goal for us was always: Go to school, go to college, so that you can get a job that doesn't require you to work late at night, so that you can choose what you get to do and take care of your family. We're fortunate to be able to do that." Sonya was the first in her family to go to college. "We are very thankful and blessed to not worry about money kind of at all," she says. "I always feel guilty saying that because my parents are always so stressed about money. My husband has a good job. I have a good job. We're kind of in a better position."

The dream that propels many immigrants to America's shores is the possibility of offering a better future for their children. Using millions of records of immigrant families, we find that the children of immigrants surpass their parents and move up the economic ladder both in the past and today. If this is the American Dream, then immigrants achieve it—big time.

One pattern that is particularly striking in the data is that the children of *poor* immigrants make substantial progress by the time they reach adulthood. For reasons that we explore later in the chapter, the children of first-generation immigrants growing up close to the bottom of the income distribution (at the 25th percentile) are more likely to reach the middle of the income distribution than are children of similarly poor US-born parents.[2]

What's more, no matter which country their parents came from, children of immigrants are more likely than the children of the US born to surpass their parents' incomes when they are adults. This pattern holds both now and in the past, despite major changes in US immigration policy, from a regime of nearly open borders for European immigrants to one of substantial restrictions. Children of immigrants from Mexico and the Dominican Republic today are just as likely to move up from their parents' circumstances as were children of poor Swedes and Finns a hundred years ago.

Not only does upward mobility define the horizons of people's lives, but it also has implications for the economy as a whole. Some voters worry that poor immigrants will drain public resources, but this concern doesn't take into account the very real possibility of upward mobility. A 2016 National Academies of Sciences, Engineering, and Medicine report found that first-generation immigrants use more public services than they pay into the system in terms of taxes, in large part because of the cost of educating their children in public schools. "However," the report concludes, "as adults, the children of immigrants (the second generation) are among the strongest economic and fiscal contributors in the U.S. population, contributing more in taxes than either their parents or the rest of the native-born population."[3] Even immigrants who come to the United States with few resources or skills bring an asset that is hugely beneficial to the US economy: their children. The rapid success of immigrants' children more than pays for the debts of their parents.

Children who arrive without papers face more barriers to mobility than other children of immigrants. Fortunately, this group is relatively small: only 1.5 million—or 5 percent—of the 32 million children of immigrant parents today are undocumented. Indeed, this number is small because many children of undocumented immigrants are born in the United States and thus are granted citizenship at birth. This small group of children without papers are one exception to the hopeful story of economic mobility that we tell in this chapter—and not because they put in any less effort, but because they encounter obstacles all along their path. The children in our data from countries like Mexico and El Salvador whose parents benefited from an earlier legalization effort in the mid-1980s are doing well now, and their counterparts today have this potential as well. With a stroke of a pen, politicians can make that happen, providing work permits and a path to citizenship for immigrants who arrived as children without papers. This is one policy question for which we don't see many downsides.

TINO'S STORY

We didn't have to walk far from our office doors to find a wide array of stories that highlights how the thirty-two million children of immigrants can rise. The novel telling the story of Tino's family unfolds in three parts. In the first part, a rural shepherd moves from the Mexican interior to a city on the Mexican side of the US-Mexico border where he meets and marries a local woman. In the second part, this shepherd's son gets a lucky break—a chance to immigrate to the United States—finding work first as a Spanish teacher in a California border town and then as a professor in the California State University system. In the third part, the shepherd's grandson (our hero, Tino) graduates from Harvard and ascends to the California Supreme Court. This spectacular story is just one data point—but it illustrates the pattern we find in our wider dataset: that children of immigrants are poised to rise.

Tino Cuéllar was born in the Mexican city of Matamoros, mere biking distance from the city of Brownsville, Texas. The two cities are nestled on the Gulf of Mexico. South Padre Island, a popular spring break destination for college kids, is just off the coast. Today, Matamoros is one of the spots where children and their families wait for an asylum hearing for a shot at entering the United States.

"What was so powerful for me about the experience" of growing up on the border, Tino says, "is that the US was so close and so far. . . . You can visit but if you think 'I'd do better as an American,' you can't move there, even though it's fifty meters away."

That Tino's parents eventually made their way to the United States was the result of a number of improbable strokes of luck. Despite his relatively short stature, Tino's father became a basketball recruit at a school on the US side of the border. "When my father was probably about sixteen, he became very good at basketball, which is remarkable because he's not that much taller than me—he's probably around five foot eight," Tino says. "But he was good enough that he was playing basketball for a Catholic school just on the other side of the border."

Going to school in the United States widened Tino's father's horizons. Both of Tino's parents enrolled in college as part of the Mexican government's big push to train a generation of teachers. There, Tino's father had his second lucky break. "When my father was in school, he decided to apply for a Rotary Club scholarship," Tino explains. "He didn't get it—he was the runner-up. But because the person who got the scholarship had a girlfriend who didn't want him to go abroad, the scholarship was given to the second best, and that was my father. He ended up studying at the University of Alabama just before I was born."

Tino's mother got pregnant with him in Alabama, and Tino could very well have been born an American citizen if his parents hadn't decided to drive the fifteen hours home to give birth in Mexico, which they thought was the patriotic thing to do. As a young kid, Tino attended the same Catholic school on the US side of the border where his father had once played basketball. Many residents of Matamoros had border crossing cards allowing them to shop on the US side. Tino and his brother used these cards to get to school.

"When I was twelve or thirteen," Tino recalls, "my parents became very disillusioned with Mexico. I remember conversations when they thought they were not advancing professionally, they thought it was very corrupt." His parents' dream was to find work as educators on the US side of the border. "What happened at the consulate, it was like something out of a novel," Tino says. "The consular official said to my mother and father, 'You two know English, you have some education. I'll give you visas and a limited amount of time to find a job in the US. But your children have to stay behind in Mexico until you find a job.' We were basically the security for our parents. I honestly don't know to this day how much this plan bore a relationship to accepted policy. At the time, I felt terrible about it because I thought our family was being split up, but I now understand we were being given an extraordinary opportunity."

Tino's father found work in another border town, this time on the US side, first teaching high school Spanish and then at a small university campus. The family settled in Calexico—the name is a blend of the words California and Mexico—a small desert town six blocks from the border. "San Diego and its temperate weather were two hours away, and felt a world away," Tino recalls. "Most kids (about seventy percent when I was there) were limited English proficiency, and many of my friends and classmates were the children of farmworkers and agricultural laborers. Many found it challenging to make it to a four-year college."

Now that Tino lived in the United States, he realized that he had a chance to apply for financial aid to go to college. Tino went on to earn his undergraduate degree from Harvard and later added a law degree and PhD in political science. From there, he took a faculty position at Stanford, where he met Ran. Today, Tino—better known to the world as Mariano-Florentino Cuéllar—was, until recently, a justice of the California Supreme Court, one of the most prestigious positions in the legal system. He now heads the Carnegie Endowment for International Peace.

As young Tino was biking back and forth between Matamoros and Brownsville, another child of immigrants—Lucy Koh—was riding the bus to a predominantly African American public school in Mississippi. Her mother, Eunsook, held a professorship at Alcorn State and her father, Jay, owned a string of small businesses in the area. Eunsook and Jay grew up in South Korea after Eunsook escaped on foot from North Korea at the age of eleven with her uncle and cousins. Eunsook vividly remembers pretending to be a local child at the many inspection stations her family encountered along the route, all the while harboring a few precious documents and a packet of South Korean currency under her clothes. A week into the journey, she contracted malaria and her uncle and cousins took turns carrying her over a mountain pass. Eventually they reached the South and their guide told them to "speak freely and loudly!" A few decades later, Eunsook and Jay moved to the United States and settled in Mississippi, an unlikely location for an Asian family in the 1970s. Their daughter Lucy grew up, went to law school herself, and soon after met and married Tino. She is now a US District Court judge, the first of Korean American descent.

CHILDREN OF IMMIGRANTS ARE MORE UPWARDLY MOBILE THAN CHILDREN OF THE US BORN

We present the stories of Tino and Lucy not to suggest that every child of immigrants will succeed as dramatically as they have. Some children will flourish beyond their wildest dreams in America, and others will stumble. In reaching the very top of their professions, Tino and Lucy are obvious outliers. How do the lives of more typical children of immigrants unfold?

When we analyze records for the population as a whole, we find more modest, but still remarkable, social mobility. All children—of both immigrants and US-born parents—who were raised at the bottom half of the income distribution tend to move up toward the middle of the distribution in the course of their adult lives. But, most strikingly, we find in the data that the children of immigrants from nearly every country of origin tended to move further up the economic ladder than the children of US-born fathers. This pattern has been constant over the past century.

Let's start by thinking about children in an average immigrant family. As we saw in the last chapter, immigrants typically don't earn as much as the US born so, on the whole, children of immigrants tend to be raised in poorer-than-average families. Yet, by the child's generation, we find complete catch-up in earnings between the children of typical immigrants and the children of US-born parents.

Particularly striking is the finding that the children of immigrants tend to catch up even if their parents did not earn very much. In the parental generation, immigrants from China or the Philippines earned almost as much as workers born in the United States, while immigrants from Vietnam or the Dominican Republic earned quite a bit less. Yet, we find that the earnings of children from all of these immigrant groups reached the earnings of the children of US-born parents by the time they were old enough to have their own careers. The same pattern holds in the past for the children of immigrants from poor countries like Sweden and Finland: immigrant parents from these countries tended to earn less than US-born workers in the late nineteenth or early twentieth centuries, and yet their children managed to catch up.[4]

That children of immigrants catch up after having been raised in poorer families is already impressive. Now consider what happens when we compare children raised in families with similar earnings. What we find in this apples-to-apples comparison is truly striking: the children of immigrants are able to move beyond the economic position of their parents more so than the children of the US born. This mobility advantage shows up in every historical period and from *nearly every country of origin*, and is particularly strong for the poorest families.

To conduct an analysis that compares children raised in similar circumstances, we need data that links children to parents so that we can pinpoint a family's resources during childhood. For the historical data, we used census records to link sons living in their childhood homes to census data collected thirty years later when these young men had jobs of their own. We picked the years 1880 and 1910 to observe childhood households: the first year includes many Northern and Western European immigrants, and the second includes many Southern and Eastern European immigrants. Our modern data is based on federal income tax records instead. The tax records allow researchers to link children to their parents as tax dependents in the 1980s, and then observe these children in the tax data as adults in the 2010s.[5]

One thing to keep in mind is that the tax records only include immigrants with a valid Social Security number, which will exclude children with undocumented parents. We don't think that this limitation rules out very many households in this period because most undocumented immigrants living in the United States in the early 1980s (when the children in this sample were born) were able to legalize their status in a 1986 immigration reform. We consider later in the chapter how these conclusions may change for children born in the 1990s or 2000s, some of whom were raised by undocumented parents or are themselves undocumented.[6]

Our research investigated children from all backgrounds, but the four charts in this chapter focus on children from poorer backgrounds—

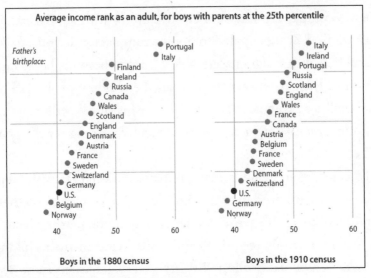

Average income rank as an adult, for boys with parents at the 25th percentile

Boys in the 1880 census

Boys in the 1910 census

FIGURE 6A AND 6B. In the past, sons of poor immigrants experienced more economic mobility than the sons of white US-born fathers. These figures compare the income rank of sons raised at the 25th percentile of the income distribution by fathers born in various European countries or in the United States. The sons were observed in their childhood homes in 1880 or 1910, and then in adulthood in 1910 or 1940, where we measure their rank in the income distribution. The underlying data are linked census files. CREDIT: Illustrations by Patti Isaacs, based on Ran Abramitzky, Leah Boustan, Elisa Jáncome, and Santiago Pérez, "Intergenerational Mobility of Immigrants in the United States over Two Centuries," *American Economic Review* 111, no. 2 (February 2021): 580–608

specifically, children raised at exactly the 25th percentile of the income distribution, which would be around $31,000 a year today (roughly equivalent to two adults working full time for the minimum wage).[7] Each gray dot represents the earnings of sons raised by fathers from different countries of origin—sixteen European countries for the past (Figure 6a and 6b) and forty-five large countries around the world today (Figure 7a)—compared to earnings of sons raised by US-born fathers (black dot). We can also examine the earnings of daughters of immigrants in Figure 7b for the modern period.

In both eras, the average earnings of children of US-born parents who were raised at the 25th percentile of the income distribution reached the 40th to 45th percentile of the income distribution in adulthood, moving somewhat beyond their parents' station.[8]

FIGURE 7A AND 7B. In the modern era, sons (Panel a) and daughters (Panel b, next page) of poor immigrants achieve more economic mobility than the sons and daughters of white US-born fathers. These figures compare the income rank of sons raised at the 25th percentile of the income distribution by fathers born in various countries or in the United States. The sons were born around 1980 and we observe their parents' outcomes in 1994–2000 and the childrens' outcomes as adults in 2014–2015. The data underlying these images come from income tax records and were provided by the Opportunity Atlas team. CREDIT: Illustrations by Patti Isaacs, based on Ran Abramitzky, Leah Boustan, Elisa Jáncome, and Santiago Pérez, "Intergenerational Mobility of Immigrants in the United States over Two Centuries," *American Economic Review* 111, no. 2 (February 2021): 580–608

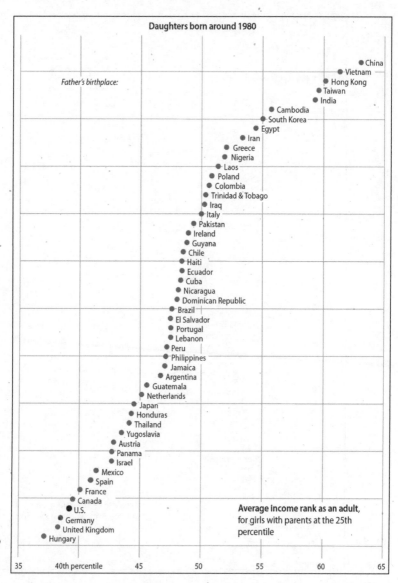

Panel b

The first striking takeaway is that, as a group, children of immigrants achieve more upward mobility than the children of US-born fathers, reaching the 51st percentile of the income distribution on average. We focus on the children of white US-born fathers in these charts because the children of Black fathers tend to have lower rates of upward mobility. So the mobility advantage that we observe for the children of immigrants would be *even larger* if we compared this group to the full population.[9]

The second notable takeaway from these charts is that even children of parents from very poor countries like Nigeria and Laos outperform the children of the US born raised in similar households. Even the children of immigrants from Central American countries—countries like Guatemala, El Salvador, and Nicaragua that are often demonized for contributing to the "crisis" at the southern border—move up faster than the children of the US born, landing in the middle of the pack (right next to children of immigrants from Canada!).

We emphasize here the comparison between children of immigrants and children of the US born. But we also find substantial variation in children's outcomes by parental country of origin. Although the children in these charts were all raised at the 25th percentile of the income distribution, some groups reach only the 40th percentile of the income distribution in adulthood and others reach the 65th percentile. We discuss possible causes of this variation below.

Our third finding is that the mobility advantage of the sons of immigrants is just as strong today as it was in the past. What's more, some of the immigrant groups that politicians accused long ago of having little to contribute to the economy—the Irish, Italians, and Portuguese—actually achieved the highest rates of upward mobility.[10]

Today, we might not be that surprised to learn that the children of past European immigrants succeeded. We are used to seeing the descendants of poor European immigrants rise to become members of the business and cultural elite. Many prominent leaders, including politicians like President Biden, regularly emphasize pride in their Irish or Italian heritage.[11] But at the time, these groups were considered the poorest of the poor. Many of the Irish-born fathers in our first historical sample, for instance, escaped the Great Famine, a catastrophe during which one of every eight Irish residents died, and another one in eight left the country.[12] In their flight from disaster,

Irish immigrants are not too dissimilar from immigrants who flee hurricanes, earthquakes, or violent uprisings today.

Although the three striking findings portrayed in these charts focus on children raised at the 25th percentile of the income distribution, our research looked at children raised at all income levels. Children of immigrants who were raised at the top of the income distribution also enjoy a mobility advantage over the children of US-born parents, but this advantage is smaller at the top. There is less scope for upward mobility—at least in relative terms—for children raised in affluence. After all, it's hard to rise beyond the top 1 percent. Like a joke one of our friends tells, "you know, there hasn't been much upward mobility in my family for generations—my father was a doctor, I am a doctor, and my son is now in medical school."

As a society, we share more concerns about how poor immigrants will fare and whether their children will get trapped in low-paying jobs or dependent on government support. But our data sleuthing should lay these fears to rest. The children of immigrants do typically make it in America. And it most often takes them only one generation to rise up from poverty.

WHY DO CHILDREN OF IMMIGRANTS RISE?

What enables the children of immigrants to escape poor circumstances and move up the economic ladder? When we raise this question with friends at a dinner party (yes, we are fun at parties!), the answer we hear most often is that immigrants have a better work ethic than the US born and that immigrant parents put more emphasis on education. In this view, because immigrants have "the drive, ambition, courage, and strength to move from one nation to another," as one sociological study put it, the children of immigrants are "the children of exceptional parents"—and so it's not surprising that they are doing well themselves.[13]

We agree that the special features of immigrant families could be part of the story. Yet when we crunched the numbers, we found something more nuanced: what jumped out of the data are two special attributes of immigrants that explain much of their children's phenomenal success.

First, immigrants tend to move to locations in the United States that offer the best opportunities for upward mobility for their kids, whereas the US born are more rooted in place. Second, immigrants often do not earn what their true abilities would allow, but they nevertheless can transmit education and skills that allow their children to move up the income ladder.

Let us elaborate. Our first finding is that geography matters—a lot. Generations of social science research has confirmed that where children grow up influences their opportunities in life. Economists have found that certain locations, like San Francisco and Providence, are associated with high upward mobility: if families move to these areas when their children are young enough, they get some of the advantages of living in the area and their children are better able to rise above their parents' station.[14]

What's new here that pops out of our data is that immigrant parents are more likely than US-born parents to settle in these high-opportunity areas, which are flush with good jobs and offer better prospects for mobility in the next generation.[15] In the past, immigrant parents chose to live in parts of the Northeast, the upper Midwest, and some parts of the West that coupled industrial job prospects with newly opened public schools available to all. Conversely, immigrants were very unlikely to settle in the South, which around 1900 was primarily agricultural, not offering much opportunity for advancement.

As striking proof that geography matters, we find that children of immigrants outearn other children in a broad national comparison, but they do *not* earn more than other children who grew up in the same area. In terms of economic fortunes, the grown children of immigrants look similar to the children of US-born parents who were raised down the block or in the same town. This pattern implies that the primary difference between immigrant families and the families of the US born is in where they choose to live.

One implication of our findings is that it is very likely that US-born families would have achieved the same success had they moved to such high-opportunity places themselves. In fact, we find that the children of US-born parents who moved from one state to another have higher upward mobility than those who stayed put: their level of upward mobility is closer to (but not quite as high as) that of the children of immigrants who moved from abroad. So you might ask: Why don't US-born families move out of a region when job opportunities dwindle?

J. D. Vance poses this question in his bestseller *Hillbilly Elegy*, about growing up in Middletown, Ohio, only forty-five minutes from the border with Kentucky, the state where his family had lived for generations. For Vance, moving up the ladder meant moving out of his childhood community, a step that many Americans are unwilling to take. He went on to enlist in the Marines, and then attend Ohio State and Yale Law School. "Though we sing the praises of social mobility," he writes, "it has its downsides. The term necessarily implies a sort of movement—to a theoretically better life, yes, but also away from something."[16]

Vance is hitting on the *cost* of attaining upward mobility for children of US-born parents. Many of the children of US-born parents grow up in areas where their families settled long before, so economic mobility for them is often coupled with the costs of leaving home. By contrast, immigrants already took the step of leaving home to move to America, so they may be more willing to go wherever it takes *within* the country to find opportunity. In other words, US-born families are more rooted in place, while immigrant families are more footloose.[17]

Another barrier to moving between locations in the United States is that the areas that offer the best opportunities for upward advancement also have the highest costs of living, particularly high rents and housing costs.[18] Of course, both immigrants and the US born face these costs. But one interesting study finds that immigrants are more willing to live in high-wage/high-cost-of-living cities (think: San Francisco) because they do not spend as much of their household budget locally and instead send some of their money to family at home in the form of remittances.[19] As a result, immigrants value the high wages in these markets more than they worry about the high cost of local products. Immigrants also tend to live in smaller apartments and are more likely to double up with two families in one unit, and so they may be better able to navigate the high housing costs that are the price of entry into the most productive markets.[20]

Now let's return to the second reason we find for the tendency of children of immigrants to rise in the United States: their immigrant parents tend to "underperform" in the labor market relative to their true ability. Immigrants often arrive in the United States without speaking fluent English and lacking local job networks. Highly educated immigrants may also face other barriers—if, for example, they do not have the proper degree or certificate to enter an occupation that they would otherwise be qualified for.[21] Think about the proverbial Russian scientist who ends up driving for Uber: his earnings don't fully reflect his true talents and abilities. But when his children graduate from an American school and speak English without an accent, they can quickly catch up and surpass their peers raised in families with similar earnings, presumably because their parents transmitted other values or skills that money can't buy.

Jay Koh, the father of Tino's wife, Lucy, is a classic example of the "under-placement" that many immigrants experience when they arrive in the country. In 1965, Jay moved to the United States alone to study at American University. His wife, Eunsook, who had escaped from North Korea when she was young, followed him a few years later. Eunsook started a graduate program at the University of Maryland, where she hid her third pregnancy under a white lab coat so that she wouldn't miss an opportunity to complete her thesis experiments.

It was soon clear that two student stipends would not be enough to support a family of five. So Jay left school and opened a convenience store, putting in fourteen-hour days, while Eunsook finished her PhD and tended to the three kids. A string of small businesses followed—a wig store in Vicksburg, Mississippi, a liquor store in Oklahoma City, and eventually work as a manager at a Burger King in Norman, Oklahoma. Meanwhile, Eunsook held academic positions at Alcorn State and the University of Oklahoma. If Jay didn't have to start earning money right away, he, too, may have become a professor like his wife, or maybe a lawyer like his daughter Lucy. But, as did many immigrants before him, Jay found steady work to support his family, earning less than his true abilities would otherwise have allowed.

Jay and Lucy's story illustrates one of our findings. Relative to the jobs that her father actually held, Lucy appears to have had a meteoric rise. But relative to what her father *could have* earned, given his talents and training, Lucy's upward mobility might not seem quite as surprising.

Our data supports this idea that the children of immigrants appear to move up quickly in part because their parents were under-placed. We test out this theory by comparing the children of immigrant fathers who themselves arrived in the United States as children (and thus likely went to American schools and became fluent in English) versus the children of immigrant fathers who arrived as adults.[22] Immigrant fathers who arrived as adults face more potential language and networking barriers and thus are more likely to be under-placed in their ultimate job. As we would expect, we find the most rapid upward mobility for the children of fathers who arrived as adults, confirming that a parent's under-placement can leave room for a child to rise.

One popular theory for immigrant mobility these days is that immigrant parents put more emphasis on education. Just think back to the passersby interviewed by Desus and The Kid Mero on the street corner in Queens, all of whom commented on their parents' (at times unrealistic) expectations for their rise into the professions.

Our historical census data contains information about educational attainment for parents and their children (we do not have this data in the modern tax records). At least for the past, we find that differences in schooling do not explain the rapid economic mobility of second-generation immigrants. If anything, the children of immigrants were *less* likely to stay in school than the children of US-born parents at the same point in the income distribution. Children of immigrants were ten percentage points less likely to be enrolled in school as teenagers in 1910 (around 80 percent versus 90 percent), and were five to ten percentage points less likely to graduate from high school by 1940. So, contrary to the explanation that education drives success, the children of immigrants were able to move up the income ladder in the past despite receiving fewer years of schooling.[23]

Today, though, the story could be quite different. Education is an increasingly important part of what it takes to get ahead, with the association between education and earnings far higher now than it was in the past.[24] As the US economy has shifted away from agriculture and manufacturing toward technology and services, the income benefits associated with staying in school are higher now than in the past. And immigrants of all means have high aspirations for their children's education. Some of the mobility advantage that we document for the children of immigrants today is likely due to a stronger emphasis on education in immigrant families.

Many respondents to our survey described their immigrant parents' focus on education as the key to their own success. Rafael Rojas, a child of working-class immigrants from Mexico, told us that his mother showed the kind of concerned (and sometimes overbearing) parenting that is often associated, colloquially, with the stereotype of the Asian Tiger Mother. "She would tell us that if we failed or got into trouble in school that we would see the consequences," Rafael wrote. "Many a day I remember my sisters and I had our asses whupped or took a beating for failing a class or having a teacher tell her that we were not focused and a problem in school." Now that time has gone by, he appreciates the discipline and resiliency his mother instilled, crediting these qualities with helping him and his sisters do well in school.

Immigrant parents from all backgrounds put a strong priority on education today. Cher Vang, a poor immigrant from Laos, enjoyed limited economic success herself. As she explained to the interviewer for the Hmong Oral History Project, "I have a home. I have a car. I think that's all I ask for." But she has bigger dreams for her children. "We send them . . . to different kinds of classes. . . . Maybe next five or six generations, they will be in the upper class, but if you don't think ahead this will not be."[25]

Although immigrant parents have lofty goals for their children, many—particularly those from poorer countries—often do not have the language skills or institutional knowledge to navigate the school system. Cuban American artist Edel Rodriguez moved with his family to Miami as part of the Mariel boatlift in the early 1980s. He describes doing well in school with his parents' blessing, but without the assistance that many children of US-born parents take for granted. "When I came here I got into studying," he says. My parents "wanted me to be good, but they weren't that involved. They didn't go to open house at school or anything like that. . . . I could see that it would probably be difficult for them to relate to and communicate with a lot of Americans. I ended up doing a lot of things myself."[26] Sometimes the emphasis that immigrant families place on education pays off, but aspirations are not always enough.

WHY SOME IMMIGRANT GROUPS
DO BETTER THAN OTHERS

Every dot on our economic mobility charts represents a rich story of immigrants from specific countries of origin moving up in America. Although we can't do justice to the many individual immigrant stories that underlie these averages, we can try to explain why the children from some immigrant backgrounds do better than others *as a group*. So far, we have focused on one aspect of the mobility charts—namely, that the children of immigrants surpass the children of US-born parents. But the mobility advantage is not uniform across parental country of origin.

Children of Asian immigrants do spectacularly well, while those from Caribbean countries tend to lag behind. Keep in mind that we are focused on children who were raised at the bottom of the income distribution (25th percentile). On average, sons of immigrants from China, India, and Hong Kong in this position reach the top third of the income distribution in adulthood, while sons of immigrants from Jamaica, Haiti, or Trinidad and Tobago do not reach the middle. In between these two groups are sons of immigrants from European countries (around 57th percentile), the Middle East and North Africa (around 55th percentile), Latin America (around 53rd percentile), and then Central America (around 50th percentile).[27] The pattern for daughters is broadly similar, but the daughters of parents from Caribbean countries do far better than their brothers, while the daughters of parents from Europe do worse.

Why do the sons of Caribbean immigrants from Jamaica, Haiti, and Trinidad and Tobago lag behind the children of (white) US-born parents? These countries are majority Black, and so the children of immigrants from the Caribbean may be held back by discrimination at school or in the workplace in the same way that children of Black US-born parents often are. But the story is more complex than race alone.[28] After all, the daughters of immigrants from the same three countries do remarkably well, moving up the ladder faster than the daughters of white US-born parents. What's more, sons of fathers from other majority Black countries in our data, like Nigeria, are more upwardly mobile than sons US-born fathers. So although race does matter for upward mobility in the United States, it intersects with gender and country of origin in complicated ways.[29]

Children of West Indian parents are not that surprised to learn that daughters rise faster than sons. They point out that their parents were always more watchful of daughters, keeping them close to home. "We weren't allowed to play outside," said one daughter in a Caribbean family growing up in New York City. "I think it's that typical kind of West Indian immigrant thing. You don't mix with the Americans and all that foolishness." Another daughter of Jamaican parents agreed. "Boys being boys . . . it is okay for them to stay out late. But if you are a girl, you've got to be home by 8:00."[30] Particularly in poor neighborhoods, staying close to home under the watchful eye of a parent can help ensure that children finish school and stay on a path to success.

Crime and law enforcement are another factor. Caribbean neighborhoods tend to be both more dangerous and more over-policed. A quarter of sons in West Indian families, but only 5 percent of daughters, have faced arrest.[31] This pattern is compounded by racial profiling. "If the police officer discriminates, it is on the basis of race," rather than immigration status or country of origin, says one team of sociologists. "A police officer rarely has a basis for knowing if a young man on a public street is African American or West Indian."[32] Men with a record of arrest or incarceration have a harder time finding work or moving into well-paid jobs later on.[33]

On the other end of the spectrum, children raised in poor families headed by immigrants from China, India, and Hong Kong tend to move many steps up the economic ladder as adults. It is tempting to attribute this success to the fact that many immigrants from these countries tend to work in high-skilled positions and earn high wages. But remember that we compared children whose families were equally poor when they were young, so we cannot explain immigrant children's success by their high family income. One possibility is that poorer Chinese and Indian families benefit from higher levels of resources in their ethnic communities—what some scholars have called "ethnic capital."[34] Even immigrants working in lower-paid jobs, like dishwashers or home health aides, are likely to have friends and relatives working in higher-paid positions as engineers or computer programmers, and may be able to draw on these connections for help.[35]

Tina Cheuk was raised in one of these working-class Chinese homes. Even though Cheuk's parents were not highly educated, she remembers being part of a wider network of Chinese immigrants, many with professional jobs. "My parents, both with barely a middle-school education, were off to a new land, not speaking a lick of English," she told us. They "had chosen to fly to Chicago because another family from their village of Wenzhou, China had found domestic work (e.g., cleaning house) there. My parents overstayed their visas (as planned) and worked cleaning houses and cooked for rich people. My parents were not part of the educated doctors and engineers who were many of my classmates' parents," she reports, but she had her horizons widened by meeting a diverse set of immigrant families. Today, Cheuk is a college professor, studying how immigrant students learn English, just as she herself had done.

Another possibility is that poor Chinese and Indian parents have higher levels of education than their earnings suggest. One respondent to our survey, a child of immigrants from China, described how her mother had "a master's degree in science, but initially worked as a waitress, a housecleaner, in a hotel, in a sewing factory, as a freelance seamstress, and a number of other odd jobs to help support us.

I remember that both my parents worked really long hours for many years." Later, the family's position improved. "My mom was able to transition back into science, and she's been working in labs ever since. Money was not very plentiful, but it was a stable environment. I ended up going to a private high school on scholarship, and I went to an Ivy League university for undergrad, mostly paid for with financial aid." This respondent may have grown up close to the 25th percentile, when her mother was working in low-paying jobs, but she also had the advantage of being raised by parents with higher degrees, which might have helped her on her own path to the Ivy League.

Members of what sociologists call the "1.5 generation," or children of immigrants who themselves arrived as immigrants, are included in our larger datasets, but their story is somewhat unique: as children, most still have memories of the home country, so they have to go through an acculturation process of their own at a young age.[36]

Some members of the 1.5 generation, like Tino whose story we heard earlier, are remarkably successful, matching the outcomes of the second generation. Others mirror the slower progress of their immigrant parents. What determines the path for members of the 1.5 generation? One factor is the age at which these young immigrants arrive in the United States. Those who arrive as older teenagers (closer to adulthood) are twice as likely to drop out of high school than immigrants who arrive as young children.[37]

Some members of this special generation can be held back by a combination of weaker language skills and—more profoundly—the experience of living one's formative years in a recently arrived immigrant household. The first few years in the United States can be chaotic and challenging as parents seek their first jobs and start their slow climb up the ladder, and members of the 1.5 generation can be caught up in that turmoil.

Boua Cha, who arrived at the age of ten from Laos as a refugee from the Vietnam War, is a poignant example. Her story appeared in a landmark study of the children of immigrants, *Legacies*, conducted by sociologists Alejandro Portes and Rubén Rumbaut. (Rumbaut is also the scholar who coined the term "the 1.5 generation.") Within a few years, Boua spoke English "effortlessly and without an accent" and she graduated from high school with honors, before being admitted to the local state university with some financial aid. But Boua had spent much of her teenage years juggling her schoolwork with "the responsibility of shopping, cooking, cleaning, and other duties that her mother would have managed." She ended up eloping with a man from her ethnic community, dropping out of college, moving into a "modest home," and starting a family.[38]

One of our colleagues in economics, Alex Imas, represents the other path for children in the 1.5 generation. Back at home in Moldova, his father had dreamed of being a doctor and his mother of being an artist. Because they are Jewish, no university would accept them. So his father became a carpenter and his mother a bookkeeper. "Arriving in the Bronx in the '90s was a huge culture shock," Alex reports. "I still remember evenings where my whole family would go down to the streets of New York City to look for furniture, bike parts, and other useful things people left out in the trash. Our entire apartment was filled with other people's garbage, but for us it was some of the nicest furniture we'd ever had." After some time in the United States, Alex's parents retrained and moved up the ladder. "My parents ended up going to night school to learn basic programming while learning English and cleaning houses during the day. . . . They are now both computer programmers and sent my sister and me to the same top-ten university. We still regularly talk about how amazing all of this is."

UNDOCUMENTED CHILDREN

Our findings for the typical children of immigrants may not hold for the children of undocumented parents living in the United States today, many of whom face unique challenges. The children in our modern data were born in the early 1980s, and so it is likely that many of their parents (even if they arrived without papers) were able to take advantage of the 1986 Immigration Reform and Control Act (IRCA), a law that granted amnesty to undocumented immigrants, giving them an opportunity to become legal citizens. As a result, most of the children in our data were raised by permanent residents or full-fledged US citizens, and likely had the opportunity to become citizens themselves. In this way, the modern data that we have been using throughout the chapter reveal what would be possible today for the children of undocumented parents if they had a path to citizenship.

But this one-time amnesty has not been repeated, so children born in the 1990s or 2000s who arrived without papers may not be faring as well because they lack the authorization to work legally.[39]

It will take another ten years or so for these children to grow up and enter the labor market, so we don't yet have data to tell how mobile these children will be, but we do have clues. Children without a green card or citizenship can face substantial barriers to getting ahead. Although going to school does not require legal residency, most adult pursuits—like driving, voting, or working outside of the cash economy—do. As a result, many of these children don't see the point in finishing high school.

Those who persevere against the odds will find that applying to college and funding a college education can be an enormous challenge. That was the experience of Jose Antonio Vargas, author of the memoir *Dear America: Notes of an Undocumented Citizen*. "I felt like the all-American kid," he recalls, "riding my bike to high school, joining the newspaper, drama club, and choir, feeling proud of my English and my grades, and excited about the future." But then "at age sixteen, a storm hit. . . . I reached that terrible moment in every undocumented child's life, the moment of realizing the import and impact of one's immigration status."[40] Jose patched together a college education at San Francisco State on scholarship and then, using falsified papers, found full-time work in journalism. Years later, in 2011, he came out as an undocumented immigrant.[41]

But Jose's combination of persistence, ingenuity, and luck is the exception, not the rule. Sociologist Roberto Gonzales followed about 150 undocumented children from Mexico through adolescence and early adulthood. He found that staying in school—even earning a college degree—could not lift these children above their parents' station. "I graduated from high school and have taken some college credits," one immigrant, Margarita, told Gonzales. "Neither of my parents made it past fourth grade, and they don't speak any English. But I'm right where they are. I mean, I work with my mom. I have the same job. I can't find anything else." She continues: "It's kinda ridiculous, you know. Why did I even go to school?"[42]

Regardless of their education, undocumented children tend to work in low-paid, temporary jobs in light manufacturing or in private services like landscaping, housekeeping, or cleaning. Gonzales tells the story of Jonathan and Ricardo, a "study in contrasts," who are both working on an assembly line in Los Angeles. Jonathan is an affable high school dropout; Ricardo is an intense and driven college graduate with a master's degree in management. Yet the two men are working side by side at the factory. "Doors stopped opening" for Ricardo when he finished school, and so he found himself working in the same place he would have been if he had quit school in his junior year of high school.[43]

Quantitative research studies underscore the point that Gonzales often heard from his interview subjects: legal status can be destiny. One study compared brothers and sisters from the same family, in which one sibling was born in Mexico while the other was born in the United States. Siblings who were born in Mexico and arrived without papers were less likely to finish school than their US-born counterparts. Even within the same family, these US-born siblings knew that their citizenship would help them find work and make sure that their schooling paid off.[44] According to another study, after the Obama administration announced the Deferred Action for Childhood Arrivals (DACA) program in 2012, which provided access to working papers, undocumented children increased their rates of high school completion, cutting the gap between citizens and noncitizens nearly in half.[45]

One thing to keep in mind is that this group of immigrants who arrived as children without papers is relatively small, numbering only 1.5 million out of the 32 million children of foreign-born parents living in the US today. This number is low because the majority of immigrants are documented (around 75 percent), and the majority of the children of undocumented immigrants are born in the United States and so are themselves citizens (73 percent).[46] Because their numbers are small, including undocumented children in the sample does not change our broader conclusion about the rapid upward mobility of the children of immigrants. We find a similar rate of upward mobility in the General Social Survey, a representative survey of the country that covers both the documented and the undocumented.

Undocumented children represent wasted talent and unnecessary anguish, facing challenges that are entirely within our power as a society to resolve. DACA improved the situation for some undocumented children, but the program's status is always at risk of being overturned because it was announced by executive order rather than passed into law. Associated legislation, known as the DREAM Act (short for the Development, Relief, and Education for Alien Minors), was first proposed twenty years ago, but has been narrowly defeated in Congress multiple times since. Many policy issues seem complicated, involving various interest groups and incentives. President Truman was said to ask for a "one-handed economist" because economists like us are known to see multiple sides of every policy issue. But this issue seems simple to us. The barriers that undocumented children face are stumbling blocks of our own making. We, as a society, can remove these obstacles and enable children who arrived without papers to flourish in the United States, just as the many other children of immigrants have flourished.

More broadly, we think that immigration policy should take the long view, acknowledging that upward mobility takes time, and is sometimes measured at the pace of generations, rather than years. Children of poor immigrants from nearly every country in the world make it to the middle of the income distribution by adulthood and so the fears of creating a permanent immigrant underclass are entirely misplaced.

6

BECOMING AMERICAN

O N OCTOBER 5, 1908, PRESIDENT THEODORE ROOSEVELT sat captivated by the action onstage at the Columbia Theatre in Washington, DC. It was opening night for Israel Zangwill's play *The Melting Pot*. The first object on the stage to draw the eye was an American flag, alongside framed portraits of Christopher Columbus and Abraham Lincoln, in the corner of the shabby living room set. But then, in the gloomy afternoon light, the audience could also spy a painting of Jews wrapped in prayer shawls at the Wailing Wall and bookshelves crowded with "moldering Hebrew books" (all according to Zangwill's stage directions).[1]

The Melting Pot takes place in an immigrant neighborhood of New York City, an updated and Americanized version of *Romeo and Juliet*, but with a happy ending. Through twists of fate, the young lead, David, who fled to America after his parents were killed in the 1903

Kishinev pogrom, falls in love with Vera, the Christian daughter of the very same Russian official who'd ordered the massacre. David and Vera's love stands in for the promise of America, a land that Zangwill believed would sweep away ancient hatreds and erase old identities.

Amid the romance, the action paused from time to time for characters to deliver solemn odes to the country's promise. America is "God's Crucible," David declared, "the great Melting-Pot where all the races of Europe are melting and re-forming!" "A fig for your feuds and vendettas!" he continued. "Germans and Frenchmen, Irishmen and Englishmen, Jews and Russians—into the Crucible with you all! God is making the American."[2]

These pronouncements were music to Roosevelt's ears. At the patriotic finale, as David and Vera declared their love, the chorus of "My Country, 'Tis of Thee" swelled up from the orchestra. Roosevelt later wrote to Zangwill that "that particular play I shall always count among the very strong and real influences upon my thought and my life."[3]

Teddy Roosevelt believed that America was the "great Melting-pot." Immigrants should be welcomed on American shores, he thought, but only if immigrants jettisoned their old identities and allegiances in favor of a wholly new American self. Openness to immigration, he wrote, "is predicated upon the [person]'s becoming in every facet an American, and nothing but an American. . . . There can be no divided allegiance here. Any man who says he is an American, but something else also, isn't an American at all. We have room for but one flag, the American flag."[4]

Nowadays, with immigration on the upswing, immigrant stories are again a fertile ground for theater, novels, and film. But the melting pot—an industrial basin in which individual metals (read: ethnic groups) dissolve and merge together to make a stronger new American alloy—no longer feels like the right metaphor. The imagery of the melting pot has been replaced by one of a mélange of separate parts—a salad bowl, maybe, with individual vegetables combined to form a single dish, or a kaleidoscope, a mosaic, or a tapestry. The humor and the emotional center of immigration narratives these days is the tension that immigrants feel as they retain parts of their old identities while adopting new American habits as well.

One hero typical of today's immigrant narratives is eleven-year-old Eddie Huang. Eddie is the fly-on-the-wall narrator to his family's own assimilation story. On the pilot episode of the beloved sitcom *Fresh Off the Boat*, which first aired in 2015 and was loosely based on the real-life celebrity chef Eddie Huang's memoir, Eddie rolls his eyes at his father Louis's wholesale embrace of American culture. Louis "loved everything about America," he says. "Full-on bought into the American Dream." To Eddie, the aspiration to fully blend into American culture was a goal worthy of gentle mocking.

The series centers on Louis's decision to open a steakhouse called Cattleman's Ranch, a choice that is hyper-American while, at the same time, following in the footsteps of many Chinese American restaurateurs and small businessmen before him. The rest of the family takes a similar mix-and-match approach to becoming American. Eddie brings Chinese food from home to the lunchroom, but dresses in oversized jerseys favored by early 1990s hip-hop stars. Eddie's mom adopts the Anglicized name Jessica, but the show portrays her as the classic (often stereotypical) Chinese immigrant: she pushes her kids to excel in school and worries that she has failed her mother-in-law, who lives with the family and speaks only Mandarin.

❦

ROOSEVELT'S VISION OF IMMIGRANTS BECOMING "NOTHING BUT American" is no longer in fashion, often replaced by an appreciation of the many ways to meld immigrant culture with American identity.

But, despite ongoing revisions of what it takes to become truly American over the past century, the data we have compiled reveals that actual immigrant behavior has remained much the same from Roosevelt's day until the present.

What do we mean? Both in the past and the present, immigrants arrive in the United States holding distinctive cultures and identities. Many do not speak English. They eat ethnic foods, celebrate their own religious and national holidays, and are more likely to marry others from their country of origin. In their first years, they cannot vote in US elections and rarely participate in the political process. But as immigrants spend more time in the country, they change their habits, attitudes, and behaviors in many ways, acting more and more like the US born. Immigrants learn English. They leave immigrant neighborhoods. They marry spouses from other ethnic groups. Even when marrying within the same ethnic group, they choose to give their children less foreign-sounding names as they spend more time in this country.

What's particularly striking is that immigrants shift toward the behaviors of the US born at much the same pace in the past and the present. The melting pot of the past was not as blended as we might think, and today's mélange of immigrant cultures is not as disjointed. The similarities of the two eras overturns a widely held belief that immigrants in the past more readily joined American society. After all, the myth goes, immigrants in the past were from European countries that shared a common cultural basis with their adoptive home, whereas immigrants today are from a more diverse set of countries with very different cultures. But, despite these differences in country of origin, we find a remarkably similar pattern of social and cultural assimilation then and now. Furthermore, immigrant groups most often accused of a lack of assimilation are actually among the quickest to assimilate—a pattern we find among Southern and Eastern Europeans in the past and Mexican immigrants today.

WHAT DOES IT MEAN TO "ASSIMILATE"?

Milton Gordon, the son of Jewish immigrants, was born in a small town in central Maine in 1918. He grew up playing in the neighborhood with the children of Yankee farmers and French Canadian factory workers. Gordon had little interaction with the broader Jewish community until his parents divorced and he moved with his mother to Portland, Maine.[5] Perhaps this early experience of trying to fit into a Protestant and Catholic America led Gordon to pursue a doctorate in sociology, focusing on the immigrant experience. Gordon's research culminated in his book *Assimilation in American Life*, published in 1964, which outlines what he saw as a fixed set of stages that all immigrants must pass through to join American society.

Gordon imagined that immigrants climb a ladder into the mainstream, which he associated—at the time—with the white Protestant middle class. According to his theory, immigrants start on the first rung with a process of "acculturation," learning English and adopting American customs. Next, they participate in local institutions (perhaps universities or churches), then marry US-born spouses, and finally identify themselves as Americans. Gordon believed that, by completing these stages, immigrants would start to blend in and eventually lessen the prejudice and discrimination that they might otherwise experience from the US born.[6]

Gordon's model makes assimilation sound straightforward, but the reality is that, in such a diverse country, assimilation can take many paths. In Gordon's theory, American culture can be conceived as one common ladder, and all that immigrants need to do is to climb up, rung by rung. But what if there are *many* ladders starting in different neighborhoods and leading to different end points? Immigrants from the Caribbean or Latin America who initially settle in heavily Black neighborhoods might adopt the speech patterns, dress, and foods of their African American neighbors. Even if they never adopt white Protestant folkways, these immigrants do converge to the behavior of some segment of the American population. Sociologists call this segmented assimilation.[7]

We agree that there are many ways for immigrants to join American society. And we have been struggling with the use of the word "assimilation" ourselves. When we discuss assimilation in public forums, audience members often express discomfort with the concept for two reasons. First, "assimilation" makes it sound like immigrants have to reject their distinctive ethnic culture in order to become American. After all, one of the most potent references to assimilation in pop culture is from *Star Trek*, in which an alien enemy forcibly "assimilates" other societies into the collective, draining them of their distinctive nature. Second, the history of the word "assimilation" has often come alongside the idea that there is a hierarchy of cultures, and that immigrants have to leave behind their inferior culture to join the better American one.

But, in the end, we concluded that any word to describe the process by which immigrants join a new society—such as "acculturation," "amalgamation," and "incorporation"—can have negative associations. We believe that immigrant groups can assimilate into US culture while retaining some of their unique cultural markers. Our assessment is that the word doesn't matter as much as the behaviors and attitudes we are trying to describe.

So when we use the term "assimilation" in this chapter, we simply mean the process by which the behaviors and attitudes of immigrants grow more similar over time—or converge—to those of the US-born population.[8] We like the definition of assimilation proposed by sociologists Richard Alba and Victor Nee: assimilation is the "decline of ethnic distinction."[9] By this definition, ethnic distinction might decline as immigrants spend more time in the country, but some distinctiveness often remains. This definition also takes into account the fact that assimilation is a two-way street: immigrants adopt behaviors that they learn from their neighbors in America, and the US born find their tastes and attitudes shaped by immigrants they meet. (We talk about immigrants' many contributions to American culture in the next chapter.)[10]

Eric Liu, the former Obama administration official we mentioned earlier, offers in his memoir one example of how an immigrant family can become American while retaining many elements of their home culture. When Eric's Taiwanese American relatives celebrate Thanksgiving, they forego turkey in favor of "spareribs and steamed fish and fried dumplings and Chinese greens." "We would all crowd around a great circular dinner table," Eric reminisced. "After we'd slurped up the last grains of rice from our bowls, the kids would play Sorry! and Candyland while watching holiday specials in the basement playroom. We ate Wise potato chips and Chips Ahoy cookies. Upstairs, the adults ate orange slices and Chinese peanuts and date-nut candies and played mahjong and talked urgently about the state of things—their work, their families, the situation in Taiwan."[11]

We want to make another point clear: we are interested in studying assimilation as social scientists observing the way the world *is*, rather than as cultural critics declaring how the world *ought* to be. We realize readers may have strong views about whether immigrants should or shouldn't be encouraged to assimilate. Some political philosophers who think about how to build a good society argue that immigrants have an obligation to integrate into their adopted societies, even if this means they need to "shed some of the cultural baggage they bring with them."[12] Our goal is instead to assess the historical record alongside modern data, providing a sense of what immigrants actually do and have done to become Americans at various points in time. We do not necessarily think that immigrants *should* assimilate culturally into US society in every respect—indeed, part of what makes a society flourish is its openness to cultural diversity. Although some aspects of social and cultural assimilation (such as learning English) do offer clear financial returns, we trust that immigrants themselves can make the right trade-off between the benefits and costs of assimilation.

There have been voices throughout US history warning that immigrants do not want to—or cannot—become truly American. In the past, this accusation was leveled at Southern and Eastern Europeans; today, it has been turned on Mexicans and Central Americans. We show that this concern is wrongheaded. As best we can measure it, immigrants have always taken steps to join American culture and society—and still do so today. Of course, we acknowledge that the process of becoming American is far deeper than we can capture with measures like where immigrants live and who they marry. For example, immigrants these days are *more likely* than the US born to express patriotic sentiment and faith in American institutions.[13] In 2019, 75 percent of immigrants (and 77 percent of their children) report being "proud to be American," compared to only 69 percent of the US born. Immigrants are likewise more confident in Congress, the presidency, and the Supreme Court these days. Unfortunately, we do not have attitudinal surveys for the past. We tried as much as possible to find measures of assimilation that we could use to compare immigrants then and now. When we do, we find that today's immigrants from around the world are just as likely to assimilate as were European immigrants in the past.

IMMIGRANTS JOIN AMERICAN SOCIETY JUST AS QUICKLY TODAY AS THEY DID IN THE PAST

It is a widely held belief, both on the left and the right, that immigrants today are slower to embrace American culture than European immigrants of the past. Right-wing pundits like the late Rush Limbaugh valorize earlier immigrant groups as being "Americans first, not Italians first" who "changed to fit into what America was," in contrast to immigrants today, whom are described as holding fast to their own culture and making little effort to become American.[14] Politicians on the left instead celebrate the cultural differences of America's many immigrant groups today and argue that immigrants do not need to let go of their culture to become American. Liberals often agree with conservatives that today's immigrants are slower to assimilate than in a past that was marked by conformity and forced Americanization: they just don't see this pattern as a problem.

What these commentators on both sides of the aisle lack is clear data about how immigrant behavior has changed over time. We find in the data that immigrants today are no more likely to retain their home culture than were immigrants in the past. Both then and now, immigrants take active steps to embrace American culture—and at much the same pace. At the same time, immigrants do preserve certain aspects of their original identities, even after spending many years in the United States, and so immigrants never completely adopt the traits of their US-born counterparts.

One challenge in measuring immigrant convergence to the broader American society is that data on many cultural practices— things like food, dress, and accent—are not systematically collected and can be hard to measure. For example, there's no good data on whether immigrants wear saris or pantsuits, or if they've replaced Bollywood movies with Hollywood fare. However, other measures of social and cultural assimilation are readily available, including data on learning English, leaving immigrant neighborhoods, marrying US-born spouses, and adopting Americanized names for themselves or their children. So that's the data we draw upon for our research on rates of assimilation.

Each measure captures a different feature of the assimilation process. Learning English can have high financial value in terms of access to jobs. Leaving immigrant neighborhoods and marrying a spouse with a different ethnic background are two signs that immigrants have grown comfortable with the broader culture, although they are by no means a necessary step for cultural assimilation. People can certainly marry within their own ethnic group or stay in an immigrant enclave and still be assimilated along other dimensions. The names that immigrants choose for their children encapsulate the trade-off that immigrants face between retaining elements of their own culture and wholly embracing the wider American culture around them.[15]

LEARNING ENGLISH

Assimilation takes many forms, but the one behavior that most Americans believe is essential for true assimilation is speaking English. A majority—72 percent—of respondents to a Gallup poll say that it is "essential" for immigrants living in the United States to learn English.[16] Tomás Jiménez, a sociologist at Stanford, conducted extensive interviews with US-born residents around the San Francisco Bay Area. Speaking English was the one behavior that his respondents—"regardless of age, ethnic and racial background [or] socioeconomic status"—described as a necessary step for becoming American. For the people interviewed, "English was the only key in which it was possible to sing the national tune."[17]

Immigrants can reap tremendous benefits from learning English, particularly in the modern economy. Experimental studies typically find that immigrants who have learned the destination country language earn around 20 percent more than similar immigrants who have not.[18] For example, immigrants to Denmark who were granted refugee status after 1998 were given extra language training, but earlier refugees were not. Immigrants who received language training ended up earning more and working in more communication-intensive jobs than similar refugees who arrived in earlier years.

Despite the strong economic advantages to learning English, prioritizing English can come at a cultural and social cost. Some immigrants fret that their own children prefer to speak English and worry that they will become unmoored from their heritage. Mexican American journalist Alfredo Corchado laments in his memoir that "the younger generation in my life is losing the mother tongue," saying that at times he pushes back "by blasting 'Despacito,' hoping a Luis Fonsi song with Justin Bieber will at least make my nephews curious about their grandparents' native language."[19]

The late Polish American poet Czeslaw Milosz may have put it best when he said, "Language is the only homeland." Milosz grew up in Vilnius, a city that had been passed back and forth between Russia and Poland for centuries, becoming a land of many languages. Polish was, to Milosz, "an everyday language," the language of family. Russian was the language of the state, "the language to make jokes in, whose brutal-sweet nuances were untranslatable." In his memoir, he recalls that when he was a child, his Jewish friends were just like everyone else when they were playing tag or climbing trees—until their mother leaned over the balcony railing and called them in for supper in Yiddish, putting a halt to the similarity. Years later, when Milosz fled Poland during the Cold War, eventually settling in Berkeley, California, the Polish language was all he retained to remind him of home.[20]

Much of what we know about immigrants' fluency in English comes from a "yes or no" question on the census asking immigrants if they speak English. It's a crude measure of English fluency, but it's a start and it allows us to compare immigrants in the past and present. In 1920, at least 80 percent of immigrants from every country of origin answered yes to this question of English proficiency.[21] Today, 87 percent of Latino immigrants and 95 percent of Asian immigrants would be classified as speaking English by this measure, right in the middle of this historical range. Around a quarter of immigrants who report speaking English today further answer that they do so "not well."[22] The same was likely true in the past, but the survey used back then did not ask that detailed question.

Survey questions are too coarse to pick up the nuances of fluency. We would like to know a lot more about how immigrants speak, both now and in the past. How deep is their English vocabulary? How complicated are their sentences? Do their accents give them away as foreign?

One way to get such detailed measures of vocabulary or accent would be to record immigrants talking, either in conversation or in a structured interview. We are fortunate that the Ellis Island Oral History Project—the same one we've been drawing on for stories throughout this book—contains transcripts and audio files of twelve hundred in-depth interviews with immigrants who moved to the United States before 1940. Immigrants were asked to talk candidly about their childhood in Europe, their transatlantic journey and experience at Ellis Island, and their new life in the United States.

Working with an interdisciplinary team of colleagues, we treated these transcripts not as personal stories, but as raw material for building a dataset, offering a first window into English attainment in this period.[23] Unfortunately, we don't have a comparable dataset with hours of recorded speech for immigrants today, so we can't directly compare the speed by which immigrants become proficient in English then and now.

Our dataset covering immigrants from Europe in the first part of the twentieth century makes it possible for us to assess immigrants' vocabulary, sentence complexity, accent, and other measures of English fluency in the past. Each one of these measures requires a bit of explanation but they are very intuitive because we are used to (implicitly) judging these aspects of conversation on a daily basis.

Let's start with vocabulary. One indication of a word's complexity is the average age at which a native speaker adds that term to her vocabulary. For example, we pick up simple words like "fight" as children but learn more complex synonyms like "altercation" or "scuffle" later in life. Linguists have determined the "average age of acquisition" for many words in the English language.[24] By keeping track of whether speakers use words learned at younger versus older ages, we can get an overall measure of the complexity of a person's vocabulary.

Beyond vocabulary, we measured sentence complexity based on a simple metric—sentence length. More complex sentences tend to be longer, containing more dependent clauses and conjoined ideas. The average sentence for immigrants in our sample was twelve words long. (That's precisely as long as the previous sentence!)

Finally, we measured the accentedness of immigrants' speech by asking research assistants to listen to the audio files of these oral history interviews. We used a nine-point scale from most to least accented to code immigrants' speech.

Immigrants coded by all these measures as having "low proficiency" clearly speak in a less sophisticated form of English than the immigrants coded as having "higher proficiency." If you'd like to judge for yourself, take a look at these two stories from immigrants in our sample. Both immigrants are speaking about their family's departure from Russia under duress, and both had been living in the United States for many years by the time they gave their interviews, but the words they choose to describe this experience are very different.

Paul Deutsch uses plain words and simple sentence structure to describe his family's escape: "My father went away from the army," he said. "The Russian Army with the Japanese Army was fighting at that time. He was a soldier in the Russian Army and he didn't want to stay there, and he came over here in 1905, my father. Then after a couple, two years more, so he took my mother and three boys up, you understand, three brothers."

Mory Helzner uses far more elevated vocabulary and complex sentence structure with extra clauses and asides: "And, of course, at that time the Revolution was brewing," he said. "I was born in 1914. I think it's important that I indicate the date, March 22, 1914. And it was prior to the Russian Revolution and things were becoming very hectic. And, and all of a sudden the Revolution comes, in 1917, and we're all in a state of upheaval, a terrible hunger ensured that thousands of people were just dying like flies. And I could witness all this. How we survived is still considered a miracle by me. But fortunately we did."

These detailed measures give us a new window into how immigrants assimilate by learning English. We think about immigrants in the data who arrived as young children as close to the "second generation," in the sense that they were raised and went to school in America. Not surprisingly, we find that immigrants who arrived as young children from any country of origin achieved near unaccented speech, used more elevated vocabulary, and spoke in longer, more complex sentences. So full English fluency takes at most a single generation. We also found some differences in English proficiency by country of origin: immigrants from Britain or Ireland scored highest (not surprisingly, since they arrived speaking English), with immigrants from Germany and Austria not far behind. Italian immigrants had the lowest levels of English fluency back then. But all these differences dissipate as immigrants spend more time in the country.

English proficiency was also associated with economic success. We can see that immigrants who developed a better vocabulary or spoke with less of an accent also reported earning more on their 1940 census form. You could imagine that English proficiency is just picking up other aspects of an immigrant's background—his level of education or his father's occupation back in the home country. But even after accounting for these factors, English proficiency had a direct relationship with earnings in this period, just like in the modern studies. This finding supports the idea that some aspects of social or cultural assimilation have clear financial benefits for immigrants as well as for the country more generally.

ANOTHER FASCINATING PATTERN THAT EMERGES FROM THIS data on English proficiency is that refugees integrated more fully than other immigrants by this metric. European refugees in the first part of the twentieth century actually developed *stronger* English proficiency by the end of their lives than other European immigrants. And better English proficiency was, in turn, associated with higher earnings.

Refugees have been an easy target for anti-immigration politicians in recent years, sometimes described as charity cases who offer little in exchange for the nation's hospitality. In his last year in office, President Trump set the annual cap for refugee approvals at 15,000, down from the more common figure of 70,000. President Biden promised on the campaign trail to raise this limit to 125,000, but has so far wavered on the pledge.[25] Emergency approvals for what might amount to 50,000 Afghan refugees after the withdrawal of US troops is a recent exception.[26] One assumption behind this aversion is that refugees are less likely to be employed or to be able to integrate into American society. But this assumption turns out to be false.

Most datasets, even today, do not distinguish refugee arrivals from other immigrants. The oral histories that we used to code measures of English proficiency gave us a way to gather data on historical refugees. The interviewers at Ellis Island asked immigrants about their lives before moving to the United States and why they chose to leave their home country. Although the United States did not establish a formal refugee or asylum system until 1980, we used immigrants' answers to these interview questions to figure out who came as refugees rather than for other reasons. We define immigrants as "refugees" if they described their journey as a flight from persecution or as occurring under duress (for example, due to war). Non-refugee immigrants, on the other hand, instead talked about moving to the United States to seek economic opportunity or to follow family.

It is easy to pick out the refugee immigrants from the oral histories because most refugees had harrowing things to say about their lives before moving to the United States. Emilie Adams, a World War I refugee from France, remembers at the age of five avoiding being shot by soldiers by having to "take . . . a white flag, and . . . we had to put that flag out before we could come out of the house." Another refugee, Wadih Zogby, lived in Lebanon through the same war. "One third of the population of Lebanon died of starvation or diseases that came after starvation," he recalls. "Once the [sea lanes] opened, about 1920, my brother, who was here [in the United States], kept on writing to us, 'Please come, please come.' And we were very happy to be out, because we suffered like blazes during the First World War."[27]

Many refugees survived their perilous circumstances through sheer luck and found that they had no country to go back to. A World War II refugee named Alice Fishman describes moving to America with her mother and father after staying alive for two years in the Buchenwald concentration camp, while two of her sisters survived the war by hiding in a convent in France. Her survival was a matter of chance. "We were on line one day to get our numbers," she recalls. "The tattoo. Somehow there was an air raid or . . . some loud noise went off, maybe a bombing. . . . But then we dispersed back to our own areas, and we never went back on line for the numbers. That's the only way we were saved. . . . But the smell of death was everywhere."[28]

Refugees are the immigrants most likely to settle permanently because they fear further violence if they return home. And learning English is an investment: immigrants need to spend time building up their vocabulary and their fluency, and they do so in the hope that the investment will pay off in terms of better job opportunities in the future. Indeed, we found that refugees were more likely to be fluent in English by the end of their lives than other immigrants from the same religious group and country of origin. That might seem counterintuitive, but better language acquisition and better economic outcomes among refugees are actually both consistent with economic theories about how immigrants invest in new skills.[29] Refugees have a counterintuitive incentive to invest in learning English than immigrants who come for economic reasons, some of whom don't plan to stay in the United States for very long.

Another possible explanation for refugees' stronger English fluency is that refugees might arrive with more education, which would make it easier to learn a new language. War and persecution might push residents across the economic spectrum to flee, while other immigrants in the past tended to be from less literate backgrounds.[30] Azra Hodzic, a modern-day refugee, told the story of abandoning her stable, upper-middle-class life in the 1990s in Bosnia, where her husband had worked as a mechanical engineer. "We've tried to regain what we had in Bosnia," she said. Her husband's first job interview in the United States was at "a factory that made lamps. He was supposed to spray some metal plates and then scrub them really hard. He took the job. . . . He was there for almost a year, and eventually he moved up to the engineering department."[31] Similar stories are common for refugees from Syria and Afghanistan today.[32]

It's certainly possible that arriving with more education helps refugees learn English more easily. But our data shows that this isn't the whole story: we find an association between refugee immigration and English proficiency even after adjusting for the immigrant's occupation (or the immigrant's father's occupation) in the old country.

The upshot of this research is that far from being a burden upon American society, refugees—at least in the past—made stronger efforts to contribute to the economy by learning English and finding a foothold for their families. In more recent years, refugees have hailed from a wide set of countries—including Communist countries like Cuba and the former Soviet Union, and war-torn areas like Iraq and Somalia. Recent refugees follow a similar pattern to that of refugees from the more distant past, learning English faster and experiencing faster wage gains than immigrants who moved to follow family or to find a job.[33] So not only is there no evidence that refugees should be singled out as unable to assimilate, but refugees seem to make more progress than other immigrants do.

IMMIGRANT NEIGHBORHOODS

Speaking English allows immigrants to build cultural ties with friends, neighbors, and coworkers who were born in the United States or who immigrated from elsewhere. One sign of being socially integrated is living outside of an ethnic neighborhood. What we find in the data is that immigrants are just as likely to live outside of ethnic neighborhoods today as in the past.

Immigrants live in many different circumstances. Some immigrants live in outlying suburbs where only a few other fellow residents are born abroad, some live in mixed neighborhoods, and still others live in heavily immigrant enclaves, in which perhaps 75 percent of the residents are also born outside the United States. One summary number that captures the most common neighborhood experience for immigrants is called the "isolation index." The isolation index tells us, for the representative immigrant, what percentage of his or her neighbors were also born abroad. The isolation index considers all of those cases and constructs an average across them, providing us with one summary number.

Here's one striking fact based on the isolation index: immigrant integration was nearly identical in 2020 to the degree of residential integration a century ago. In 1920, the immigrant isolation index stood at 45 percent. A century later, the index value again sits between 45 and 50 percent.[34] These values mean that, in both eras, the typical immigrant lived in a neighborhood in which around half of their neighbors were also born abroad. If immigrants were equally spread throughout all neighborhoods, we would expect that figure to be closer to 15 percent. So immigrants clearly live in clustered areas, but no more so now than in the past.

With historical census data, we can get an even more precise snapshot of who lived next to whom. Census takers used to go door-to-door to fill out the survey, so the households listed next to each other on a census manuscript were often next-door neighbors.[35] One measure of segregation is living near others from abroad. By this measure, almost every immigrant group has had the dubious distinction of being the most segregated group at some point in the past. For example, in 1860, Irish immigrants living in industrial cities like Lowell and Lawrence, Massachusetts, were the most segregated immigrant group in the country. In 1880, this distinction went to Chinese immigrants in San Francisco. By 1910, it was the Italians in Providence, Rhode Island, and in 1930, it was Mexicans in California and Texas.

Many immigrant neighborhoods form because immigrants choose to live close to others from their home country, seeking help from each other if they need it. Immigrant enclaves can grow up around a few immigrants who choose a neighborhood simply because it is close to work or because housing is plentiful, rather than because of the presence of other immigrants. These pioneers can act as a magnet, attracting fellow immigrants to settle nearby.

Flushing, Queens, a vibrant business district and large residential community, is the heart of Indian American life in New York City today. The founding of this ethnic community can be traced back to a few immigrants who moved into the area in the 1960s. One of these early arrivals was Naresh, who was recently interviewed by a historian about his early life in the area. When Naresh moved to New York in 1966, "all Indians then lived in Manhattan," he recalls. Naresh himself opted for the less expensive borough of Queens. "I was satisfied with Flushing because the Number 7 subway line provided an easy commute . . . ," he remembers, "and the apartment rents were quite cheap. . . . At that time, every third plot in Flushing was vacant."[36] Naresh became one of the original anchors to the neighborhood, helping newcomers find a place to live. Initially, there were no Indian shops or cultural centers in Flushing. Residents had to cart groceries on the subway from Manhattan. Yet, by the 1980s, a block of Indian shops opened—grocers, restaurants, clothing stores—and later another block and then another.

Similar immigrant clusters emerged a century ago as immigrants from Europe settled in American cities. Henry Lorch spoke to the Ellis Island Foundation about growing up in Hudson, New York, about one hundred miles north of New York City. As Naresh was to the Indian community of Flushing, Henry's uncle was to the German community in Hudson. Henry's family was a magnet that drew other German immigrants to town and helped them get settled in America. His family regularly hosted new immigrants in their big boarding house, so much so that Henry later recalled that he was about twelve years old before he ever saw just his own family sit down at a table together. "There was always boarders, we always had to eat in the kitchen and the boarders ate in the dining room," he recalled. Henry's uncle owned a small factory and would help newcomers find work. "Whoever came over from the old country, from Germany," he said, "they would stop at our place and stay with us until they found their own apartment."[37]

Although some immigrant groups faced barriers in the wider housing market and lived close together out of necessity, a substantial body of evidence—both qualitative and quantitative—shows that immigrants themselves prefer to live in ethnic communities, at least when they first arrive in the country.[38] When sociologists present research subjects with a hypothetical choice of places to live, immigrants tend to choose neighborhoods with many other immigrants of their own ethnic group.[39] Economists have pointed out that if immigrants are not welcome in some areas, leaving immigrants with fewer choices of where to rent, landlords should, in theory, take advantage of that scarcity and charge immigrant families more in the few neighborhoods open to them. Yet that's not what happens in practice: instead, researchers have found that immigrants pay *less* for housing in more segregated cities. These rental patterns suggest that the formation of immigrant neighborhoods is not driven by a lack of other options—rather, immigrants seem to prefer to live close to others from their home country, at least until they find their footing.[40]

Politicians and commentators tend to assume that living in an ethnic neighborhood is a sign that immigrants are not trying to fit into American culture and that they will be held back economically. Research suggests that the reality is more complicated: some immigrants can use the networks they form in an ethnic neighborhood to get ahead. But other immigrants who live in ethnic neighborhoods find themselves isolated from outside opportunities.

Korean Americans are one example of an immigrant community that has flourished from tight network connections, including large residential areas near major cities. Many Korean-owned businesses avoid banks altogether in favor of community resources. "From a Korean's standpoint," explained one shop owner, banks are "such a hassle. So much paperwork. You have to give them two years' financial records. You have to give them a business plan of what you want to do for the next three to four years. You have to give them business projections. And it's a lot of things that Koreans don't want to hassle with because there are other avenues to get money, other avenues that are 100 percent guaranteed that you get it instead of going through the Small Business Administration."[41]

But sustaining a shadow banking system is not easy. What if the borrower runs away with the funds? Or what if a hapless businessman tries his best to get off the ground but his business fails? Often there are no written contracts at all, just a borrower's word, so it is hard to collect on loans that go bad. So lending within immigrant networks requires a high degree of trust and community oversight. That's where neighborhood connections come in. When lending within the community, lenders reduce their risk through the implicit threat of

excluding defaulters and their families from future business contacts—
and possibly also from marriage and other opportunities open only
to those in good standing. In fact, the tighter the bonds that an immigrant borrower feels to her own community, the higher the cost of
failing to repay loans from the group.[42]

Small businesses within the Korean community are also a primary
source of employment for new arrivals. Sociologist Illsoo Kim writes
that "most Korean businesses, especially labor-intensive retail shops
such as green grocery businesses, fish stores, and discount stores, want
to hire, and actively recruit, Korean immigrants."[43] Hiring immigrants
from one's own ethnic group is a widespread practice beyond the Korean community; the practice can produce a more trusted set of em-
ployees or can serve as a form of favor trading that pays off for the
employer.[44]

As helpful as the ethnic economy might be for some new arrivals,
many immigrants do not want their kids to be reliant on such ethnic
connections forever. Even for local business owners, a mark of having
"made it" in America is often that their children don't have to take
over their shop or restaurant in the old neighborhood. When asked
by a sociologist if he would take over his father's jewelry store, one
Chinese American already working in the finance industry sputtered
indignantly that his father "doesn't hate me enough to ever want me
to take over his business. The reason he worked so hard is so that we
wouldn't have to live that kind of life."[45]

Indeed, we find evidence in our own research that Jewish immigrants who left large enclaves experienced *faster* earnings growth for
themselves and their children than neighbors who stayed behind.[46]
In particular, we focused on immigrants who participated in an early
twentieth-century mobility program with the slightly Orwellian
name Industrial Removal Office (IRO). Participants agreed to leave
New York City—which, at its high point, had more than 250,000
Jewish residents—for other cities and towns around the country.[47]

Two such men were Samuel Klein and Jacob Roskin, neighbors on the Lower East Side in 1900. Samuel accepted a small amount of assistance to leave the city through the IRO—not much more than a $9 train ticket—and relocated eventually to California. Meanwhile, Jacob stayed behind, eventually moving with his family to the Bronx.

We found Samuel's and Jacob's families in the census records in 1940. By then, Samuel's oldest son, Saul, had graduated from college, a rarified status in that era, when only around 10 percent of young men had any college education.[48] Saul reported a salary of $3,000 on the 1940 census (the equivalent of $55,000 today) and lived in a new suburban development in Studio City, California. Along with his young wife, Saul was well on his way to the dream of a white picket fence.

Back in the Bronx, Jacob's son had finished high school, but never went to college. Instead, the younger Roskin followed in his father's footsteps, selling bedroom sets at the Jacobson Brothers store on the Grand Concourse, with annual earnings of only $730 (or $13,000 today).

We find this pattern repeated in the wider dataset. Although the gap between the incomes of Samuel's and Jacob's sons is larger than most, in general we see that the Jewish men who left New York with the help of the IRO as well as their sons earned around 5 to 10 percent more than their neighbors who stayed behind.

We can't completely rule out the possibility that men like Samuel Klein who accepted help from IRO program officers were already different somehow—maybe more adventurous or more talented—than men like Jacob Roskin who did not. But we do find that, within the IRO program, men who had more years of exposure to life outside of New York (because they moved earlier in the program's history) ended up gaining the most. Each year spent outside the enclave seems to be economically useful, which suggests that there is a real benefit to living in a more integrated neighborhood or municipality.

INTERMARRIAGE

We started the chapter with the (fictional) story of David and Vera, the lovers at the heart of the play *The Melting Pot*. You might recall that David's parents were killed in an anti-Jewish riot in the old country, and that Vera's father was the Russian officer who'd ordered the massacre. Yet in America, they met and married, a plot point that playwright Israel Zangwill saw as a classic sign of immigrant assimilation. Fifty years later, the theme of immigrants as star-crossed lovers returned in more tragic fashion in *West Side Story*, which paired a young Puerto Rican woman with her US-born love interest.

These stories reflect hopes and anxieties about one form of assimilation—relationships that cross ethnic lines, particularly the prospect of intermarriage. Intermarriage has been a traditional measure of cultural assimilation, particularly in sociology, going back at least to Milton Gordon's assimilation ladder in the 1960s. The idea is that marrying a US-born spouse is a sign that immigrants have adopted American customs and been embraced by "mainstream" society.[49] These days, the concept of intermarriage has been expanded to include marrying anyone outside of an immigrant's own ethnic group: by this measure, a Mexican immigrant like Tino Cuéllar assimilated by marrying Lucy Koh, even though she is a second-generation Korean American immigrant herself.

Like the other measures of social and cultural assimilation in this chapter, we find that intermarriage rates for first-generation immigrants are strikingly similar in the past and present.[50] In the past, the share of immigrants married to a spouse from a different national origin ranged from 10 percent to 60 percent, depending on the country of origin. Today, intermarriage rates are somewhat higher, ranging from 20 percent to 85 percent.[51] Thus, if anything, marriage rates imply that cultural assimilation is *faster* now than it was in the past.[52]

Intermarriage rates vary significantly across immigrant groups. Immigrants from English-speaking countries like England, Scotland,

and Wales in the past and the UK and Canada today post the highest rates of intermarriage, perhaps because they speak a common language with the US born.[53] Immigrants from Southern and Eastern Europe—Italians, Portuguese, and Russians (mostly Jews)—had the lowest rates of intermarriage in 1930, even though, as we show in the next section, these immigrant groups were quick to shift toward American-sounding names for their children. The difference could be that picking a name is entirely up to you, as a parent, whereas finding someone to marry requires that that person is also willing to marry you. Given the anti-immigrant sentiment at the time, the US born may have been especially unwilling to marry Southern European immigrants. Haitian immigrants have the lowest intermarriage rates today, followed by various Asian groups (Filipinos, Koreans, Vietnamese), which may again be an indication of the preferences and biases of the US born.[54]

The facts that we discuss here are drawn from the censuses of 1930 and 1980. In these years, census questions allow us to focus on immigrants who got married after they arrived in the United States. (Not surprisingly, almost all immigrants who got married before moving to the United States have spouses from the same country of origin.)

Some elements of assimilation occur within an immigrant's own lifetime (like learning English), while others (like intermarriage) take place across the generations. As we would expect, the children of immigrants are more likely to intermarry than are immigrants themselves. Immigrants who arrived as children (the 1.5 generation) are somewhere in between. For example, in 1930, only 20 percent of all immigrants from Ireland were married to a non-Irish spouse. This value rose to 45 percent of Irish immigrants who had arrived in the United States as children (the 1.5 generation) and to 65 percent of the US-born children of Irish parents.

The whole subject of dating, relationships, and marriage is a common source of tension between immigrant parents and their children.

Sarah Lee, who grew up in a Korean family, told her story of dating a Latino man to Ellen Alexander Conley for her book *The Chosen Shore* and we reproduce part of the story here. "It was really hard in the early stages when I felt like I had to make this huge choice between my boyfriend and my family who has raised me all my life," she admits. But she decided that moving out of her parents' house is what it means to be truly American. "I started to realize that . . . I'm not in Asia anymore where the culture forces the parents to break every bone in their body to help you get an education. [In Korea,] once you graduate from college, you live with your parents until you get married, and once you get married, you help out your family by marrying into a nice family. But the fact is that I'm moving out when I graduate." Despite Sarah's determination, cultural differences still complicate the relationship. Her boyfriend has a good job as an accountant and put himself through college, a fact that is a point of pride for him but appalls her own Korean parents. "My parents think that a responsible family should put their children through college right away, even if a parent has to get six jobs. . . . They don't understand when I tell them my friends are paying for their own schooling. They think automatically that they have bad parents."[55]

Sometimes, getting permission or grudging acceptance for marrying outside of the immigrant community is simply a matter of waiting. The authors of *Inheriting the City*, a sociological study of the children of immigrants, found that "the longer children remained single, the more their parents relaxed their criteria. Many Russian respondents said that their parents' initial line was, 'They can be purple, blue, seven feet tall, anything, but they're Jewish.' By the time the children were in their mid-twenties, it was, 'They're already like giving up on me, so they'll take anybody at this point.'" The children of Asian immigrants agreed. "A Chinese respondent said, 'At 21 my parents wanted me to marry someone Chinese. I waited till I was 32, and by then they were just happy I married anyone at all!'"[56]

Slowly but surely, across the generations, immigrants marry outside of their own ethnic group, both then and now. Although intermarriage is surely not a necessary step to join US society, these patterns reinforce what we see in an array of other measures—that immigrants and their children take active steps both in the past and today to become Americans.

WHAT'S IN A NAME

The names that immigrant parents choose for their US-born children can be one potent symbol of fitting in. Republican senator David Perdue, when running for reelection in Georgia in 2020, emphasized then Senator Kamala Harris's foreign parentage by intentionally pronouncing her name Ka-MAH-la (rather than KA-ma-la), as if to say that her name is so strange and alien that it would be impossible to think of her as one of "us."[57]

Immigrant parents make careful decisions in choosing names for their children in the United States, reflecting their attitudes to and knowledge of American culture as well as their attachment to home. Vice President Harris was born around five years after her parents arrived in the United States, her mother from India and her father from Jamaica. Kamala, a Hindi name, is rare in the United States. Kamala's younger sister, born three years later, was given the relatively common and ethnically ambiguous name Maya.[58] Shifting from a name like Kamala to a name like Maya may have reflected her parents' growing awareness of the nuances of American naming practices, or a stronger connection to the multicultural kaleidoscope of American culture.[59] Parents may also shift away from ethnic names to avoid teasing or bullying on the playground, or to prevent discrimination by employers later on.

Ran and his wife, who are both immigrants from Israel, tell a similar story about naming their three children. Their first son—Roee—

was born a few years after they arrived in the United States. Roee is
a common Israeli name that means "shepherd" (as in "The Lord is
my shepherd; I shall not want," from Psalm 23), but most Americans
have never heard the name. Ran and his wife even chose the name's
spelling—Roee with two *e*'s—to avoid confusion with the American
name Roy. Yet babysitters and teachers were still perplexed.

As they spent more time living in the United States, Ran and
his wife learned about American naming conventions and chose their
other kids' names accordingly. For their second son, born a few years
later, they tried to find a name that would be easier for Americans to
pronounce, so they chose the name Ido. It's so short, they reasoned.
How could it be mispronounced? But when the doctor's office left a
voice message with an appointment reminder for "I do," Ran's family
realized that their second son would also face confusion—and possibly even discrimination—due to his name. When their third son was
born, they named him Tom, a name that means "innocence" in Hebrew but also sounds completely American. You can almost imagine
hearing an announcer at the ballpark calling out, "Leading off and
playing second base, Tom Abramitzky."

Based on Ran's personal experiences, we hit on the idea that the
names that immigrants choose for their children—and how these
names shift as immigrant parents spend more time in the United
States—are useful measures of cultural adaptation. Giving a child an
American-sounding name is a free-of-charge way to identify with US
culture, making it an option available to both the rich and the poor.

Of course, the fact that naming is free of charge does not mean it
is completely free of *personal or social cost*. If, for example, Ran chose
the very American name Logan for his son to help him fit in—a name
that, according to our data, is very infrequently given by immigrant
parents—his mother would probably be puzzled about how Logan
has anything to do with Israeli heritage (and Ran himself might feel
some loss of connection to his home culture). The pull between the

social benefit of integrating into a new society and the social cost of loosening ties with the old country is precisely why the names that immigrants choose for their children are a meaningful measure of assimilation. When parents choose a name for their children, they need to make a trade-off between maintaining their original cultural identity and fitting into their new society.

Some immigrants use their name choices to reject their home culture entirely, signaling a full embrace of American society. One ethnographic study of the Soviet Jewish community in New York City interviewed a teenager, Igor, who changed his name to Nicky. It was just one way the boy turned his back on his Russian heritage. "He refused to answer his parents when they called him by his given name, told new friends that he was Italian, and took to wearing the same clothing that he saw on his Italian-American schoolmates."[60]

For other immigrants, using an Anglo name can be wrenching, leading to acute feelings of identity loss. Reyna Grande, the celebrated author of the immigration memoir *The Distance Between Us*, felt like she was losing a piece of herself when her teacher in Los Angeles expected her to use a single last name, contrary to the Mexican convention of using both parents' surnames: "'But I'm Rodríguez, too,' I said. 'It's my mami's last name.' . . . I wanted to tell him that I had already lost my mother by coming to this country [from Mexico]. It wasn't easy having to also erase her from my name. *Who am I now, then?*"[61]

For some immigrants, mixing and matching Anglo names with ethnic customs is one way to assimilate into America while retaining other aspects of immigrant culture. Writer Wajahat Ali, the son of Pakistani immigrants, grew up with a foreign-sounding name that he says inspired "childhood mockery." He heard all kinds of taunts on the playground, epithets like Whatchamacallit?, Waja-the-Hut, and Warbalot. These days, his Pakistani American friends are selecting crossover names for their children—"lots of little Aidans, Rayans and Adams, Sarahs, Laylas and Sophias"—while continuing to welcome them into the Muslim community with birth announcements proclaiming: "ALHAMDULILLAH, by the greatest blessings of God, we are overjoyed to announce the birth of our beloved new baby son."[62]

Unlike other personal behavior, which does not leave a trace in the data, shifts in the names that immigrant parents give to their children can be tracked through public records, and these shifts tell a story about how newcomers balance the desire to stay connected to their roots with the wish to embrace their new home. To track these shifts, we collected the names of millions of children from census records in the early twentieth century, and from California birth certificates for the present (we have data from 1989 to 2015). We focus on California because it is one of the only states that allow researchers to use data that reveals children's names (with proper precautions for privacy).

Some names may sound foreign—names like Wajahat or Igor—while others are stereotypically American. But sometimes it's not clear. In any case, we didn't want to just take a guess for each name. We needed a more systematic way to classify names as foreign- or American-sounding. So here's what we did. With our data, we were able to count the number of US residents with each given name by their place of birth. We found that some names are ten times more likely to be found in immigrant households: names like Hyman (a Yiddish name) or Carmela (Italian) in the past or names like Juan (Spanish) or Yazmin (Arabic and Farsi) today. Other names are instead ten times more likely to be given by US-born parents: in our data for the 1990s and 2000s, these were names like Logan and Ashley. And yet other names—like John and Elizabeth—are very evenly balanced between immigrants and the US born.

Using these name counts, we constructed a "foreign name index," a measure of the relative probability that a name was held by an immigrant or a nonimmigrant. Names like Hyman would get close to the maximum score of 100 on our index, meaning that almost every resident named Hyman was born outside the United States; names like Logan would instead be very close to zero, indicating a very low probability of being born abroad.

We use a separate index for each era because naming trends change over time. For example, Eric and Kurt have high index scores in the past, when most men with these names were immigrants from Scandinavia or Germany. Today, these names are widely popular and, if anything, are more associated with US-born parents than immigrant parents. We also made country-specific versions of the index to check whether immigrants shifted away from names associated with their own ethnic group toward *any* other name, even if those names might not be particularly popular among the US born (like, would an Italian-born mother shift away from names like Carmela toward names like Yazmin after meeting immigrants from other cultures in the United States).

We found in the data that, when immigrants first arrive, they give their children distinctively foreign-sounding names. US-born moms gave their children names with an average score on our index of around 35. Immigrants who had a child within the first three years of arriving in the United States selected names with higher scores (around 55). But as they spend more time in the United States, the names selected by immigrant parents start to look closer to the names picked by US-born parents. Eventually, immigrant parents close about one-half of this "naming gap" with the US born, both in the past and today. Immigrants also shift away from names associated with their own country of origin to pick from a wider pool of ethnic names from around the world.

Immigrants rarely go all the way to naming their kids Logan or Ashley, but as they spend more time in the United States they are much more likely to name their kids neutral names like John or Elizabeth. This convergence of the names chosen by immigrant and US-born parents is suggestive evidence for the process of cultural assimilation. But the fact that immigrants don't fully adopt the naming patterns of the US born implies that many immigrants value retaining their distinctive cultural identity, as well.[63]

Even more surprising to us when we first uncovered this pattern was the fact that the shift in name choices happened for immigrants from Latin America and Asia today just as much as it did for European immigrants in the past. After all, European immigrants have been widely valorized as eager to join American society, whereas many voters today worry that immigrants are no longer making an effort to assimilate. What we find is squarely at odds with that narrative. What's more, immigrant groups most often accused of a lack of assimilation are actually among the quickest to assimilate in terms of their naming practices. In the past, Russian Jews and immigrants from Portugal, Austria, and Finland were fastest to assimilate by this metric. Today, it is Mexican immigrants who shift toward American-sounding names at the fastest rate.

Choosing American names for their children can be a defensive reaction to real or perceived discrimination against immigrants or specific ethnic groups. Immigrants react to historical events that increase anti-immigrant bias—such as discrimination against Germans during World War I, the internment of Japanese Americans during World War II, and the 9/11 terrorist attack for Muslim Americans—by redoubling their efforts to blend in. According to research from some of our colleagues, following these stark events, immigrants in targeted groups shifted toward more American-sounding names for their children.[64] One son of South Asian immigrants who responded to our survey told a bittersweet story of intentionally absorbing American culture as a defensive posture. "As a kid in the Bronx," he remembers, "I thought that if ever confronted, I could prove that I was a 'real American' by reciting the New York Yankees' 1978 batting lineup—which I still know by heart to this day: Rivers, Randolph, Munson, Jackson, Piniella, Nettles, Chambliss, White, and Dent."

Parents may also believe—rightly or wrongly—that names that are perceived to be too foreign will hold their children back at school or in job interviews. Some research backs up this concern. One study sent out thousands of identical résumés to firms in Toronto, manipulating only the name of the prospective job seeker. Résumés topped with Indian or Chinese names garnered fewer callbacks, even when advertising identical levels of education and work experience.[65] To prevent these setbacks, children can also change their own names or choose to go by a nickname at work. "[I am a] brown guy named Usama in Texas" announced one child of immigrants interviewed on the segment of the *Desus & Mero* show we mentioned at the beginning of the book, to which the comedian Desus responded, "We can stop right there." Hasan Minhaj added that "I got to give you props, you never did the name change." Nope, but he and Hasan both laughed at how they know a few Usamas who now go by Sammy.

But many immigrants can't hide their ethnicity forever. Even if an Igor or a Wajahat could suppress his name on a résumé and get past the initial screening for a job interview, his identity would be revealed later and, if an employer is bent on discrimination, he might never get hired at all. Ideally, we could find data that would indicate whether workers with foreign names are less likely to get a job, rather than simply less likely to get an initial employer call. But unfortunately such data can be very hard to collect today.

The good news is that our historical data allows us to follow kids' names to adulthood, tracking their economic progress in relation to the foreignness of their names. We discovered through simple comparisons between men with foreign-sounding names like Hyman and American-sounding names like John that having a foreign name is associated with a series of economic disadvantages, including higher unemployment rates and lower earnings. Men with names like Hyman were also more likely to marry within their own ethnic community.

These patterns might seem to confirm the résumé studies, showing that kids with foreign names are beset by obstacles.

But a deeper analysis shows otherwise. When we zeroed in on families, comparing brothers raised by the same parents, we found that the effect of foreign names on earnings disappears. For example, a man named Hyman did not have lower earnings or higher unemployment rates than his own brother named John, nor was he more likely to marry within his own ethnic group. On its own, having a more foreign name did not seem to hold back the children of immigrants. Instead, we suspect that a comparison of men with different names is picking up the difference between children raised in more or less assimilated families. Parents who choose names like Hyman differ on other dimensions—they may be less aware of US culture and speak a foreign language at home, for example—than parents who choose names like John, and their children may therefore have a different life path.[66]

SUPPORT ASSIMILATION, BUT DON'T FORCE IT

Overall, our findings provide confirmation that immigrants assimilate quickly into the broader US culture. Immigrants start on the process of cultural assimilation within a few years after arrival. Assimilation can be measured in years, not in generations, with immigrants' identification with US culture growing stronger with more time spent in the United States. Both in the past and today, immigrants from all over the world learn English, leave immigrant neighborhoods, and marry US-born spouses. Furthermore, today's immigrants do not assimilate any more slowly than past immigrants, and they adopt American-sounding names for their children at similar rates to those of European immigrants during the Age of Mass Migration. When we turn to the data, we can see that the widely held, nostalgic view that European immigrants made more of an effort to join American society than immigrants do today is simply wrong.

These findings carry a lesson for today's highly fraught immigration debate: far from consigning themselves to permanent outsider status, as many fear, immigrants and their descendants participate in a broadly shared American culture and adopt deeply felt identities as Americans.

The common pace of cultural assimilation then and now is even more remarkable when we consider that, in the past, policymakers imposed explicit attempts to "Americanize" immigrants and their children, whereas today there is a growing acceptance of immigrant cultures. Indiana and Ohio went so far as to ban the German language in the aftermath of World War I.[67] Public schools in the past were conducted entirely in English, and some politicians worry that the bilingual education programs offered today will hold immigrants back.[68] Yet, despite these different approaches toward assimilation policy, immigrants pick up English at a similar pace and find ways of joining American society on their own.

These days, the United States has very few policies designed to address immigrant assimilation. But this hands-off approach seems to be working. So we encourage policymakers to stay the course here, allowing immigrants the time to join US society at their own pace.

7

DOES IMMIGRANT SUCCESS HARM THE US BORN?

S UPPORTERS OF BORDER RESTRICTION ARGUE THAT IMMI-grants steal the jobs and reduce the wages of US-born workers. At a heated press conference during the Trump administration, presidential advisor Stephen Miller defended a proposal not only to crack down on illegal immigrant entry, but also to cut slots for legal immigration as well. "If you just use common sense," he asserted, it's clear that immigration restriction would help the working class. "Companies want to bring in more unskilled labor . . . because they know that it drives down wages and reduces labor costs."[1] The United States already has 150 million workers, give or take. If you add another million from abroad each year, Miller argued, companies can offer lower wages for the same work because there are more workers to choose from.

This argument is easy to understand and sounds reasonable. If there were a fixed number of jobs, then more immigrants would necessarily mean fewer jobs for the US born. But the number of jobs is not fixed, and by contributing to innovation and starting new businesses, immigrants often create new employment opportunities for others. Think: everything from big tech giants like Google and eBay to small local businesses like dry cleaners and restaurants. And immigrants need new housing and consumer products themselves, all of which helps put Americans to work.

These days, the contributions that immigrants make to the labor force are more important than ever. If not for immigrants, who will be the workers of the future? Fertility rates have been low for more than a decade. The US-born population is getting older.[2] In fact, population growth was lower in the last decade than at any time in nearly a century, and without immigration, this number would decline further.

Some workers who do the same jobs as immigrants (often past immigrants) stand to lose from immigration. The evidence, however, does not support the idea that immigrants lower wages of less-educated US-born workers overall. At first it may sound surprising that less-educated people from other countries do not lower wages for existing workers without a high school degree. But immigrants tend to concentrate in tasks that don't require English language skills (like landscaping or construction), while the US born are more likely to hold jobs that require interacting with customers or the public. What's more, immigrants often fill positions that many US-born workers would not take at wages that consumers are willing to pay, such as picking crops or taking care of the elderly.[3] In this way, immigrants create markets for certain products that otherwise might not exist.

The presence of immigrant workers can also make US-born workers more productive. In research labs, immigrants from around the world share new ideas with US-born coworkers, and in service settings, immigrants and the US born tend to specialize in different tasks—consider: an immigrant dishwasher and a US-born waiter working together at a restaurant.[4] Immigrant-provided services like cooking, cleaning, and childcare can also free up time for US-born workers so they can be more productive in their own jobs.[5] Many American voters agree: according to a recent opinion survey, two out of three Americans think that "immigrants strengthen the country because of their hard work and talents," as opposed to burdening "the country because they take jobs, housing and health care."[6]

Voters who oppose immigration aren't concerned only about economic competition: many also fear that immigrants weaken their communities and are prone to crime. Donald Trump infamously opened his presidential campaign in 2015 with the egregiously false statement that Mexican immigrants are "bringing drugs, they're bringing crime, they're rapists" and regularly held press events with members of "angel families" whose loved ones had been killed by immigrants.[7] Yet the data shows that immigrants are less likely to be arrested or incarcerated today relative to the US born.

In this chapter, we will show that evidence from the past and today demonstrates that immigrants do not steal jobs from US-born workers, nor do they commit more crimes than the US born. Immigration contributes to a flourishing American society.

In order to learn about the effect of immigration on the economy, scholars would ideally be able to compare two parallel Americas, one with high levels of immigration and one with low levels. These days, around 15 percent of the US population was born abroad. It would be helpful to know how the economy would change if that number was closer to 5 percent or as high as 25 percent. But it goes without saying that we can't rerun history twice to try out this experiment. Here is where the past can be useful. At a few key moments in history, the United States conducted very similar experiments through the normal political process. As economic historians, we can go back and see what happened when the border closed in the 1920s and reopened in the 1960s.

HOW IMMIGRATION QUOTAS IN THE 1920S AFFECTED THE ECONOMY

Consider this tale of two cities. In 1890, the state of Ohio had two major cities: Cleveland, on the shores of Lake Erie, and Cincinnati, on the southern border with Indiana and Kentucky. The two cities were just shy of three hundred thousand residents.[8] In each city, 11 percent of the population was German born and another 3 percent was born in Ireland.[9]

Cleveland was also home to a small population of immigrants from Southern and Eastern Europe, while Cincinnati was not. As immigration from countries like Hungary, Austria, and Poland exploded from 1890 to 1920, so too did the immigrant communities of Cleveland. And then suddenly, Congress passed a set of strict immigration quotas that particularly targeted Southern and Eastern European countries, leading immigration to Cleveland's ethnic communities to grind to a halt. Meanwhile, Cincinnati did not go through this boom-and-bust cycle, but instead continued to receive a steady (albeit lower) inflow of immigration from Ireland and Germany.

So what happened to Cleveland after the immigration restrictions, when its steel industry could no longer rely on a steady immigrant workforce? Did Cleveland's factory owners suddenly start hiring workers born in the United States to operate the rolling machines and the furnaces? Did Cleveland's workers have an easier time finding jobs, and did their wages rise as a result?

When digging into the data on hundreds of cities and towns like Cleveland and Cincinnati, we find that the border restrictions had some surprising and counterintuitive effects. The idea that closing the border automatically benefits US-born workers turns out to be another myth in need of debunking.

In fact, the passage of the Emergency Quota Act in 1921 was one of the most dramatic changes in immigration policy in American history. For the first time, the total number of immigrants allowed to enter the country was limited by statute. The numerical targets set in the 1920s—first put in place in 1921, and then modified in 1924 and 1929—were far below the number of unrestricted entrants just a few years before. From over a million entrants a year in the late 1910s, annual immigrant arrivals were eventually set at 150,000.

What's more, immigration quotas were intentionally set to keep out immigrants from Southern and Eastern Europe but allow space for immigrants from Northern and Western Europe. Entry slots were assigned by country of origin according to the number of immigrants from each country living in the United States, first using the 1910 population and then rolling the figures back to 1890. Lawmakers deliberately chose 1890 because it came before the mass immigration from Southern and Eastern Europe, ensuring that more than 90 percent of entry slots went to Great Britain, Ireland, Germany, and countries in Scandinavia.[10]

The 1920s quotas were the outcome of a long process of building a political coalition against immigration.[11] The Dillingham Commission, convened by Congress in 1907, proposed a sweeping set of new immigration restrictions, including strict limits on immigrant arrivals and quotas by country of origin. The "science" of eugenics, which was ascendant in the 1910s, further bolstered support for these ideas. Practitioners like Harry Laughlin, director of the Eugenics Records Office at Cold Spring Harbor (today home to one of the leading cancer research centers), argued that certain "races" of people (what we would today call national origin groups) were of inherently sturdy or industrious stock, while others were feebleminded or servile.[12] Immigration policy should be crafted, according to this view, to maintain the good breeding of the original American settlers from Northern and Western Europe and to keep out groups that might dilute the purity of the population. After decades of organizing, the anti-immigration coalition ultimately prevailed in the waning days of World War I, passing a literacy test for entry in 1917 over President Wilson's veto.

As the push for immigration restriction picked up steam, economists and other policy experts debated the likely consequences of cutting off immigration. The debate would sound familiar to us today. Jeremiah Jenks, a Cornell professor and member of the Dillingham Commission, argued that immigrants stole manufacturing jobs from US-born workers and lowered wages for everyone. As immigrants poured in, Jenks wrote, "a large proportion of native [born] Americans . . . have left certain industries," including coal mining and metals manufacturing. Wages remained steady, but Jenks concluded that immigrants "prevented the increase in wages which otherwise would have resulted" from America's manufacturing boom.[13]

Other scholars suspected instead that immigrants boosted the productivity of their coworkers by taking the hardest and most dangerous positions in factories or mines, working together with the US born who often served in supervisory roles. "No considerable groups of native [born] Americans are bewailing the fact that they cannot find work in the mines," asserted Edward Steiner, a professor at Grinnell College.[14] The American Farm Bureau Federation agreed, arguing that immigrants performed simple farm labor tasks and allowed American farmers to move into managerial positions.[15]

In 1927, a few years after the legislation passed, the American Economic Association hosted a panel to discuss how the restrictions had affected the economy so far. The gathered experts noted that, even though immigration had dropped by hundreds of thousands, the wages for manufacturing work in US cities did not seem to be rising by much. Harry Jerome, the director of the National Bureau of Economic Research, took to the podium to explain why. Rather than raising wages, firms had been turning to other sources of labor, including "negro migration to northern industrial districts . . . Mexican emigration to the United States, and . . . movement from rural districts to the cities." It's too simplistic, he argued, to assume that when immigration was shut off, everything else would remain the same. As European workers stopped coming to cities, other workers took their place.[16]

One hundred years have passed since the border closed. With the benefit of hindsight, we should be able to figure out who was right: Professor Jenks, who expected that wages would rise and white US-born workers in industrial cities would return to manufacturing jobs, or Professor Jerome, who imagined that new migrants—from Mexico, from the South, from rural areas—would move to industrial cities to take jobs previously held by immigrants from Europe.

The challenge, even now, is how to isolate the effect of immigration restrictions from other economic trends in the 1920s. In 1920, nearly any European immigrant could enter through Ellis Island. By 1922, restrictive quotas were in place. So the simplest approach would be to compare the wages and job opportunities of American workers in the years before and after the national quotas were imposed (say, comparing 1920 to 1922). Indeed, economist and eventual US senator Paul Douglas did exactly that, documenting that real manufacturing wages jumped by 30 percent between 1915 and 1925 as immigration started to slow down.[17] However, the wage increase does not coincide perfectly with the timing of immigration: while wages increased steadily, starting in 1915, immigration fell during World War I (1914–1918), rebounded strongly from 1919 to 1921, and then declined again with the quota law in 1921. We see no evidence that the wage growth slowed during the years with an immigration rebound.

So it seems unlikely from a single national wage trend alone that immigration restrictions can be credited with these wage gains. Keep in mind that the economy was changing in many ways during the

Roaring Twenties, an era marked by advances in automobiles, aviation, communication (radio, telephone), and electrification. Do we really have immigration restriction to thank for all this progress? Or is there more to the story?

In general, economists are leery of drawing conclusions from a single before-and-after comparison. That's why we tend to look for multiple dimensions of comparisons through which to draw conclusions. For example, one thing we realized in our own research into the economic impact of immigration restrictions is that the quotas affected some US regions more than others: in particular, a major port of entry like New York City experienced larger immigration slowdowns than smaller outlying towns. That's a good start—but comparing big cities to small towns is inconclusive because other economic trends might have affected these areas differently.

What we found out was this: the quota policy was much more restrictive for immigration from some countries of origin than for others. Spots were reserved for nearly every Northern and Western European who wanted to enter the United States, but only one in ten Southern and Eastern Europeans would have the same opportunity. Add to this insight the fact that some cities (like Cleveland) had large Southern and Eastern European enclaves, while others (like Cincinnati) had older communities of Northern and Western Europeans, and we can make some progress in studying the quota policy.

Immigrants tend to settle in areas that already have an existing community from their home country.[18] As a result, cities like Cleveland had been receiving large inflows in the 1900s when immigration was unrestricted, and then experienced significant cutbacks in immigration in the 1920s, after the border closed, while cities like Cincinnati had steady (and lower) immigrant inflows over the period.[19]

We compare cities like Cleveland that were strongly affected by the national immigration restrictions to cities like Cincinnati that were not, before and after the policy change. This type of analysis is known as a "difference in differences." The first difference is before and after the legislation passed in cities like Cleveland, and the second difference is between cities that were more or less affected by the policy. The benefit of this approach is that cities like Cleveland and Cincinnati experienced many of the same economic trends during the heady years of the Roaring Twenties, yet only Cleveland was strongly affected by the national quota policy. So any difference we see in Cleveland (compared to Cincinnati) is more likely due to the quota policy.

What we find in analyzing the data is more complex than the "common sense" idea that blocking immigration results in higher wages for the existing workforce. Here's what happened instead. In the short run, workers living in cities like Cleveland may have enjoyed higher earnings.[20] But soon enough, firms found ways to avoid paying these higher wages. These firms replaced European immigrants with two groups of new workers: immigrants from Mexico and Canada (countries not subject to the quotas) and US-born workers who moved in from other areas, including rural-to-urban migrants.[21] Many of the new arrivals were young men, lured into the city by the new job openings. Moreover Black workers in the South began migrating north in large numbers only after the border restrictions choked off immigration from Europe.[22]

In rural areas, the loss of immigrants as farm labor did not open up jobs for US-born workers. Instead, immigrant workers on farms were replaced by machines, rather than by new pools of workers from elsewhere. As John Steinbeck famously lamented in his 1939 novel *The Grapes of Wrath*, tractors "throw men out of work," sending "families scamper[ing] on the highways, looking for crumbs." When immigration dried up, farms in places like North Dakota bought more tractors to make up for these losses. Farms in neighboring Manitoba, Canada, still had immigrant workers coming in and so did not buy tractors at the same rate.[23] Farmers also shifted toward planting wheat, a less labor-intensive crop than the corn they'd been planting when immigrant labor was abundant.

Thus, in both cities and rural areas, even the most sweeping immigration restriction in American history had only mixed effects on the existing workforce. Some US-born workers were able to find better jobs, particularly young men from farms and small towns who were able to move to cities to try their hand at factory work. But the benefits to workers were far smaller than one might think because employers are highly adaptive. They don't necessarily turn to the "worker next door" to offer that worker a job when immigration slows down, but instead search for other pools of labor. Or they buy new machines, if they can be had more cheaply. As it turns out, newcomers from Europe were just one item on a long menu of production possibilities.

Today, the menu items may have changed, but the idea of substitutions remains the same. If the United States stopped admitting foreign-born doctors, for example, many of the diagnostic services might be outsourced to physicians working remotely from overseas.[24] And without immigrants to hold factory jobs, firms might invest in expensive robotic arms or other automation technology. The immigration restrictions of the 1920s teach us that the idea of closing the borders to aid American workers is too simplistic for the messy complexity of the real economy.

HOW REOPENING THE BORDERS AFFECTED THE ECONOMY

The immigration quotas of the 1920s remained the law of the land for forty years. Throughout the Great Depression, World War II, and the beginning of the Cold War, America was closed to most European immigration, except for the few immigrants who entered through the quota system and a small number of postwar refugees. During these forty years, the United States welcomed up to half a million Mexican guest workers a year through the Bracero Program, primarily to work in agriculture, but these entrants were not allowed to settle permanently.

Since the border reopened in 1965, there have been several cases of abrupt policy changes or major events abroad that allow for further careful study of the effects of immigration. Economists have studied all of these episodes: In 1964, the Bracero guest worker program came to a sudden end. In the early 2000s, the H-1B program designed to host temporary, highly educated immigrant workers expanded in size for a few years, allowing more workers to qualify. The border fence constructed under President George W. Bush in the mid-2000s also had the potential to reduce illegal entry. The most famous of the foreign events is the Mariel boatlift of 1980 that dropped 125,000 Cubans into Miami—a metropolitan area of three million residents—over a period of a few months.

As we will see in the next few pages, these studies find that increasing the number of less-educated workers did not have much effect on the wages or employment prospects of US-born workers. Instead, as with the quotas of the 1920s, workplaces turned toward automation or other sources of labor, rather than to the existing workforce, when immigrant workers were no longer available. When the Bracero Program ended, farms shifted to harvesting machines. Miami was particularly slow to automate compared to other cities after receiving an infusion of new immigrant workers. By contrast, cutting off highly educated immigrants suppressed innovation and even reduced job opportunities for the US born. So there is little evidence that less educated immigration harms US-born workers today, while several convincing studies have shown that highly educated immigrants can promote job growth.

BRACERO GUEST WORKERS

The Bracero guest worker program between Mexico and the United States started during World War II and ramped up in the 1950s.

"Bracero," which comes from the Spanish word for "arm" (*brazo*), de-
notes a manual laborer. From 1951 to 1964, around three hundred
thousand Mexican workers were authorized to enter the United
States each year, primarily to plant and harvest food in California and
neighboring states.

But in the early 1960s, as part of President Kennedy's and President Johnson's war on poverty in America, policymakers began to
wonder: Why let in so many workers from Mexico when there weren't
enough jobs for every unemployed American? Kennedy strongly believed that Bracero workers took jobs that US-born workers would
otherwise do, saying that the Bracero program was "adversely affecting the wages, working conditions, and employment opportunities
of our own agricultural workers."[25] After Kennedy's assassination,
President Johnson ended the guest worker program under the banner of his Great Society plans. "One of the basic goals of the Great
Society," Johnson said, is to guarantee "all Americans . . . dignity and
economic security. . . . We are now embarked on a major recruiting
effort to attract unemployed American workers to fill seasonal farm
jobs."[26]

Today, blaming immigrants for the poor job opportunities of
American workers would be perceived as nationalistic or right-wing.
But in the 1960s, the Democratic political establishment and the *New
York Times*, the liberal paper of record, agreed that canceling Bracero
contracts would make room for domestic farmworkers. The law abol-
ishing the Bracero Program would "convince large growers that they
can no longer count on limitless cheap labor from Mexico," the *Times*
opined, suggesting that letting the Bracero Program die would allevi-
ate the "chronic state of depressed wages and working conditions" for
American farmworkers.[27]

By the time the Bracero Program was on the chopping block, only
2 percent of prime-age US-born men worked as farm laborers. So as
soon as the program ended, California landowners began to complain

that few qualified US-born workers heeded their call for the harvest season. In Orange County, "workers were reported walking off jobs in citrus areas because they were not able to earn enough," wrote the *Times*.[28] Julie Benell, a food critic for the *Dallas Morning News*, wrote a personal letter to President Johnson fretting that farmers "bring these men up from Los Angeles or down from San Francisco, and they pick half a field of lettuce and walk off the job. They won't pick lemons because of the long thorns on the trees."[29] One might say: just pay the US-born workers a better wage and they will do the work. But in some cases, farming the product isn't profitable at a higher wage and so the farm would shut down.

The sudden shortage of farm labor did put workers in a good position to ask for higher wages. It's possible that the successful union campaigns of the United Farm Workers led by Cesar Chavez— including the Delano grape strike of 1965, which took place the year after the Bracero Program ended—would not have gathered steam if the guest worker program had continued.[30] It was also during this time that Congress voted to include agriculture workers under the federal minimum wage.

But other forces were at play in the 1960s, beyond the ending of the Bracero Program, that contributed to rising farm wages. A team of economists recently reevaluated this period and concluded that the Bracero Program was unlikely to have been responsible for the wage increases. The study compared states according to their initial reliance on Bracero farmworkers in their agricultural industry. In states like California and Arizona, Bracero workers made up close to half of the farm labor force, whereas states like Pennsylvania did not rely on farmworkers from Mexico to pick apples in their fruit orchards. Despite the large differences in reliance on Bracero workers, hourly wages for farmworkers inched up steadily during the 1960s in all states, with no notable acceleration in states that had been reliant on Bracero workers.[31]

So who worked the farms after the Bracero Program ended? For some crops, special waivers allowed Mexican workers to enter again on a short-term basis. Eventually, Mexican immigrants began crossing the southern border on their own, without a contract or other documentation. These new entrants, many of whom had been on Bracero contracts a few years before, are the same immigrants we call "illegal entrants" today. In other cases, farmers shifted away from crops like lettuce, asparagus, and strawberries that could only be picked by hand toward crops like cotton and tomatoes, for which harvesting technology was available. Tomato harvesters had been on the market for a few years—but their sales skyrocketed in the absence of a readily available Mexican workforce.[32]

In fact, the shift away from delicate, hand-harvested crops after 1965 may help explain why American palates were so bland in the 1960s and '70s. Rather than eating fresh produce in season, dinner in the 1960s was often served alongside frozen vegetables, particularly varieties like peas and corn that can be machine-harvested.[33] But decades later, with the growth of the H-2A visa program, a temporary agricultural visa not too dissimilar from the Bracero Program before it, the 2000s was an era of food rediscovery. Avocados! Microgreens! Organic berries! As much as these trends were about shifting tastes, they also reflected a return to temporary agricultural visas, and the lower food costs that go along with them.

A "BIG BEAUTIFUL WALL"

By 1975, the number of unauthorized border crossings from Mexico had reached the levels last seen during the heyday of the shuttered Bracero Program.[34] Many of these immigrants stayed in the United States temporarily, working for the harvest season before returning to family in Mexico. In that way, a formal guest worker program had been replaced by an informal (and illegal) one.

Undocumented immigration continued to swell in the 1980s and 1990s. Immigrants without papers moved beyond the farming sector into construction, restaurant work, and childcare and eldercare. Rather than living in agricultural barracks and returning to Mexico each season, these immigrants increasingly settled in cities and established roots. The number of undocumented immigrants estimated to live in the United States rose from around three million in 1990 to twelve million in 2005, before leveling off and even declining in recent years.[35]

The centerpiece of President Trump's 2016 campaign—his plan for a "big beautiful wall" on the southern border—was, in some sense, thirty years out of date.[36] First construction on a border fence began in 1990 near the San Diego-Tijuana crossing point. Then, after 9/11, President George W. Bush authorized construction of seven hundred miles of border fencing, leaving only the most inhospitable desert crossings without a barrier. Alongside these new physical barriers, the Border Patrol added more officers and equipment. Expenditures on border control increased tenfold since the 1980s.[37]

Do these barriers work to cut down on immigrant entry? And if so, do they help buoy the wages of US-born workers? It is hard to measure the number of unauthorized entrants, but the number of apprehensions at the border did start to decline in 2007.[38] The timing of this slowdown lines up with the first miles of border fencing built under the Bush-era Secure Fence Act of 2006. But as with the 1920s immigration quotas, economists worry about drawing too many conclusions from a naive before-and-after comparison. Sure, the mid-2000s was marked by the construction of border fencing, and so we might expect undocumented immigration to fall. But the years 2007 and 2008 were also the start of the Great Recession, an economic downturn that limited job openings in the United States and thus undoubtedly deterred new immigration.

One reason to suspect that the new fencing did not deter entry very much is that it only covered seven hundred miles of a two-thousand-mile border. When the San Diego-Tijuana crossing was fenced in the mid-1990s, apprehensions in San Diego dropped by 95 percent.[39] But the number of undocumented arrivals to the United States overall did not decline—instead, it rose rapidly. Building a wall in one city (such as San Diego) might dramatically reduce immigration through that port of entry while diverting immigrants to other points along the border.

A team of economists have found that the same type of diversion took place in the years following the Secure Fencing Act.[40] After the new barriers were constructed, Mexican immigrants avoided the newly fenced entry points in favor of less-barricaded (and often more dangerous) routes. Adding barriers "didn't stop people from crossing," said Claudia Smith, an attorney at the California Rural Legal Assistance Foundation. "It just forced them to cross in the deadliest stretches of the border."[41]

Overall, this study estimates that the new fencing discouraged fifty thousand entrants, out of around five million undocumented Mexican immigrants living in the United States—or around 1 percent of the total.[42] Of course, we don't know what would happen if the entire border—including the desert and the Rio Grande Valley—was fenced off. But we can see that every attempt in the past to create barriers has encouraged migrants to try to find work-arounds, often successfully despite the added costs and dangers.

Ironically, the harsh policies at the border intended to keep illegal entry low ended up increasing the size of undocumented communities within the country.[43] As crossing the border became more expensive and more dangerous, many Mexican immigrants decided to stay in the United States more permanently, rather than working for a season and returning home. Historian Ana Raquel Minian reports that many undocumented immigrants now refer to the United States as a cage of gold, or *jaula de oro*: work opportunities are better in the United States, but come at the expense of losing ties to family. When the border had been only lightly policed, many Mexican immigrants worked in temporary positions and returned home on a yearly basis, but as the border grew more fortified, immigrants came to feel that they needed to make a decision "once and for all."[44] In 1995, around a third of Mexican immigrants stayed in the United States for more than ten years; by 2018, this number had risen to 83 percent.[45]

No one wins from the border fencing policies. Immigration restrictionists aren't satisfied: they hope that barriers will keep illegal immigrants out of the country, not unintentionally trap them on American soil. And it is emotionally painful for Mexican migrants stuck on the northern side of the border. Yes, the higher wages offered in the United States can help migrants provide for their families, but these opportunities now come at the cost of permanent separation from their land of birth.

MARIEL BOATLIFT

Halting the Bracero Program and building a border fence are two American policies enacted to keep immigrants—particularly less-educated immigrants working in agriculture—out of the country. The Mariel boatlift, on the other hand, was a policy of the Fidel Castro government in Cuba that encouraged 125,000 Cubans to emigrate to the United States. Most of the newcomers did not hold a high school degree and sought work in fields like construction or domestic service.

The start of the Mariel boatlift came as a surprise to everyone involved. Here's one account of how the boatlift unfolded, which we believe captures the events accurately: On April 2, 1980, Manuel Morillo, a Cuban American salesman in New York City, got an urgent phone call from his mother. Breathlessly, she told him that the Cuban government had just announced that they planned to open the port of Mariel to emigration. The usually closed country was allowing anyone who could find a boat to pick up their family members and take them off the island. Go, she said, and rescue your sister. Manuel flew to Miami that night, and made his way to Key West. From there, he found a ship captain who would ferry him to Cuba.

The many Cuban Americans who rushed to the port of Mariel were then left to wait. Manuel brought only a week's provisions, but he ended up idling in the port for twenty-five days, buying extra food from circling boats at exorbitant prices. The system was capricious and disorganized. Manuel was eventually able to help seventy refugees (mostly Jehovah's Witnesses) to escape on his rented boat, but his sister was not among them. The Cuban government said he would be able to return later and fetch her, which he eventually did.[46]

Manuel was one of the thousands of Cuban Americans who helped family members leave the island, primarily in May and June of 1980. Around 3,000 of the 125,000 arrivals (called "Marielitos") had been released from jails—terrifying some American onlookers—but most were simply hoping to reunite with family and start a new life.[47]

Luis de la Paz, a chemical engineering student in Havana, made it to America on the boatlift. "You had to start from scratch," he remembers, even going so far as "finding [your own] spoon to feed yourself." But Luis had an education, and within a few years, he began writing for the Spanish-language press. Not every Marielito was so lucky. Luis recalls that Miami was unprepared to receive so many new residents in such a short time, and that the influx of refugees caused a shortage of housing and jobs.[48]

US-born workers immediately feared that Cuban refugees would undercut their pay in factories and on construction sites. One unemployed steelworker in Illinois griped that "pretty soon [refugees] will have all our jobs. . . . The Government is spending a lot of time and money to ship them all over the country while we, the backbone of this country, don't get any more consideration than this." Rev. Kenneth Acey, a Black minister in nearby Fort Wayne, Indiana, agreed, worrying that "we spend millions of dollars to help the refugees come to this country, while we have people that need homes, people who need to be fed, and people who need jobs. Blacks are being pushed over to the sidelines."[49]

Economists wondered if Rev. Acey's concerns were borne out in the data. Surely, they reasoned, the arrival of so many Cuban workers into one city over such a short period would depress wages or raise unemployment of US-born workers, at least temporarily. David Card of UC Berkeley started looking into this question in the mid-1980s, publishing his findings in what has become one of the most famous economics papers about immigration of all time. What rocketed the paper to fame were the unexpected findings: after the boatlift, US-born workers (including Black workers) in Miami did not seem worse off than in similar cities in terms of either earnings or unemployment.[50] Unemployment of the existing Hispanic workforce rose by 1.5 percentage points in Miami from 1980 to 1982, but it increased even more (3.4 percentage points) in comparable cities like Atlanta, Houston, and Tampa. The likely cause of this spike in unemployment, however, was not the Mariel boatlift but the fact that 1982 was the peak of a major recession when unemployment rates were going up everywhere.

The original Card finding has been scrutinized from every direction. Recently, one prominent critique argued that the boatlift caused large wage losses for a specific group of US-born workers: workers without a high school diploma, precisely the group most likely to compete with Cuban immigrants.[51] But others have defended the original paper, countering the criticism by arguing that the main dataset available to study this question—the Current Population Survey—contains too few high school dropouts to know for sure.[52] Furthermore, it just so happens that the survey began redoubling its efforts to include Black households in 1981, the year after the boatlift, making it appear that wages fell because average wages for Black workers are lower than average wages for whites.[53] After the dust settled, Card's original results suggesting that the Mariel boatlift had little effect on the local economy in Miami appear to stand.

How is it possible that 125,000 Cubans arrived in Miami in a two-month period without affecting wages for US-born workers? First, some workers—both existing city residents and new Cuban arrivals—decided to leave Miami to avoid facing heightened competition for jobs. Carlos Morales, who arrived on the boatlift, was one such worker. "I decided to go to a church to ask if they could help me settle in a different state," he recalls, because he found it very hard to find steady work in Miami. A few months later, he moved to Chicago, where he worked in a factory for five years and studied at night until he became a professional electrician.[54] Morales's experience was part of a larger pattern. Card found that the rate of population growth in Miami slowed after the boatlift, likely because current residents were moving away from the city while other prospective newcomers who would have moved to Miami chose to move elsewhere.

A second reason why wages did not fall in Miami after the boatlift relative to other cities is that businesses in Miami were slower than those in other cities to adopt new automation technologies—like self-checkout at grocery stores or ATMs at banks—that began replacing workers with machines in other areas. Firms in Miami had plentiful workers to do these tasks and did not find it as lucrative to invest in new machinery. In Miami, workers may have competed with Marielitos, but in other cities, workers faced competition from machines.[55]

If the Mariel immigrants had arrived in Miami and everything else had remained the same, then it is likely that wages for US-born workers in Miami would have fallen with new immigrant entry. But everything else did *not* remain the same. Some workers moved out of the area and some new machines failed to move in. Because the economy is so quick to adapt, even a large inflow of immigrants to a single area over a short period of time did not lower wages for US-born workers. The boatlift ended not with a bang, but with a whimper.

ATTRACTING SCIENTISTS AND INNOVATION

Around 30 percent of immigrants in the United States have a college degree.[56] These highly educated immigrants have a different effect on the economy than temporary agricultural workers or Cuban refugees. Many highly educated immigrants originally come to the United States on temporary student visas. After graduation, they can work for a few years for a US company on a program called Optional Practical Training (OPT). Another route to the country is the temporary H-1B visa program, available for occupations with "highly specialized knowledge," often in science and technology fields; after sponsoring workers on this temporary visa, employers help some of these workers enter the green card lottery for legal permanent residence.

Immigrants are nearly twice as likely as the US-born population to be scientists or inventors. In recent years, around 14 percent of the US population was born abroad. But these foreign-born residents contribute significantly to innovation, making up more than 20 percent of resident patent holders, nearly double the share that we would expect from their percentage in the population.[57] Immigrants who arrived on employment visas (like H-1B) or on student visas are especially likely to contribute to the high patenting rate.[58]

The H-1B program has long been subject to a cap of 85,000 workers a year, although universities and other nonprofit institutions can apply for H-1B visas above the cap. If you took a class with a young professor from another country, chances are she was an H-1B visa holder. The one exception to this cap was a short-lived increase from 85,000 to 195,000 slots under President Clinton in the late 1990s. By 2004, the H1-B cap was back to its 85,000 limit.

The typical image of a US-born worker "displaced" by immigration is the unemployed steelworker in Illinois or the working-class parishioners of the Black pastor in Indiana decrying the Mariel boatlift. But PhD economists like us, or workers in the finance or tech sectors that employ many of the graduating seniors who take our courses, may also face competition from educated immigrants.

As college professors, we interact with many students and colleagues holding either temporary visas or green cards. Ran himself became a naturalized US citizen a few years ago after originally entering the United States on a J-1 student visa and then starting his job at Stanford on an H-1B visa. On surveys, Americans report welcoming attitudes toward immigrants with a college degree.[59] Perhaps as a result, many of our graduate students and colleagues from abroad have found the United States to be a friendly and accepting place—especially in the bubble of the ivory tower.

We do not hear too many stories—at least in academia—about our foreign-born colleagues facing anger from their US-born co-workers or neighbors for "taking jobs away" from US citizens. But one colleague opened up to us recently because she knew we were working on this book. "I had two roommates during graduate school," she said, "and one of them [we will call her Megan] was an American. When I got a job, Megan didn't say anything. A day later, she came up to me in the hallway and said, 'It's not fair that you came here and you can just find a job.'" Megan, meanwhile, had graduated with her master's degree the year before and was still searching for work. Our colleague continued, saying it was hard to live with a roommate "who isn't happy that you are here, who thinks you are taking their opportunities. It made me feel like I was living in a dangerous environment." Thereafter, she always locked her bedroom door.

Megan's open resentment was not only frightening, but it was also likely unfounded because there is little evidence that highly educated immigrants steal jobs from highly educated US-born workers. Economists have studied the large increase in H-1B visas under President Clinton and did not find that US-born scientists lost out on job opportunities when additional highly educated immigrants arrived to take specific positions. Instead, high-tech firms in cities with many positions open for H-1B workers (like Seattle and San Francisco) increased their patenting activity in those years relative to similar cities that had not been hiring many H-1B workers, especially among scientists with Indian or Chinese surnames (the two most common H-1B countries). Hiring of US-born scientists in those cities did not dry up; if anything, it expanded as US-born scientists worked together with their new colleagues.[60]

Of course, there are some cases where competition is more zero-sum. One clear example are the coveted positions in organizations of a fixed size—for example, orchestras, sports teams, or academic departments at US colleges and universities. After the collapse of the Soviet Union in 1991, nearly three hundred thousand residents of the former USSR claimed political asylum in the United States; many of them were scientists and engineers. Soviet academics particularly excelled in mathematics. One study found that PhD students in American mathematics programs who graduated in the early 1990s, after the arrival of Soviet mathematicians, were less likely to secure an academic position, especially in those subspecialties of math that had a strong Soviet presence. Facing competition from an influx of Soviet mathematicians appeared to harm the new crop of American-trained mathematicians.[61]

But even here, the story is more complicated. Some professors already working in American math departments benefited from new collaborations, enhancing productivity. When productivity increases in an industry like tech, new products are launched, output can expand, and employers hire more workers. But in a nonprofit like academia, the number of professorships is fixed, so each Russian superstar took a slot away from another mathematician.[62] This pattern may not be very representative of the employment dynamic in the rest of the economy.

Where did these thwarted US-born math PhDs go? Many went into private industry or worked on Wall Street as traders in investment banks. Russian mathematicians also helped to fuel the emergence of quantitative hedge funds, which rose from nonexistence in 1990 to 13 percent of the investment market today. As the *Wall Street Journal* declared recently, "the quants run Wall Street now."[63] The expansion of opportunities in math did seem to take place, just not in the ivory tower.

Just as the arrival of highly educated immigrants through the H-1B program or with the collapse of the Soviet Union spurred innovation, the border restrictions of the past had the opposite effect. Economists estimate that close to twelve hundred scientists from Southern and Eastern European countries were excluded from entry to the United States by the immigration quotas of the 1920s.[64] Some of the excluded scientists moved elsewhere—to the UK or Canada or Palestine—and were able to continue their research careers. But others were excluded from immigration altogether, and some of their ideas were lost to science. When the quotas were temporarily relaxed to provide entry permits to more than one thousand Jewish scientists dismissed by the Nazi government—including Nobel Prize winners like Albert Einstein—the United States gained, as patenting activity in key research fields resumed its earlier pace.[65]

IMMIGRANTS ARE NO MORE LIKELY TO COMMIT CRIMES

Immigration affects every facet of American life. As economists, we spend most of our time debating the effect of immigrants on the wages and job opportunities of US-born workers. But immigrants also contribute to the economy as consumers and as taxpayers, and they will help support an aging population as baby boomers retire. We end this chapter by busting two myths—that immigrants bring crime, and that immigrants weaken American culture.

Opposition to immigration is not simply a matter of economic winners and losers. Anti-immigration politicians rely heavily on messages about crime and drugs. The idea that immigrants are inherently criminal goes back at least as far as Senator Henry Cabot Lodge, one of the original architects of immigration restrictions in the early twentieth century. Lodge warned that some Italian immigrants were "members of the Mafia, a secret society bound by the most rigid oaths and using murder as a means of maintaining its discipline and carrying out its decrees."[66] References to the mafia were the early twentieth-century equivalent of scare stories about MS-13 and other Mexican or Central American gangs today.[67]

It's clearly hyperbole to think that most immigrants are involved with organized crime. Yet many voters worry that immigrants are more likely than their US-born neighbors to commit burglaries or assaults. The data tell a different story, however. Especially in recent years, immigrants are *less* likely than the US-born to be arrested and incarcerated for all manner of offense.

Studying the criminal behavior of immigrants is a challenge because arrest records don't include a suspect's place of birth or citizenship status. In recent years, though, law enforcement agencies have been compelled to share data with the Department of Homeland Security to search for undocumented immigrants. Researchers who were granted access to this linked data for the state of Texas found that— contrary to the common narrative—undocumented immigrants were *half* as likely as the US born to be arrested for violent crimes. For property crimes and drug violations, the gaps between undocumented immigrants and the US born were even larger. (The rates of criminal behavior for legal immigrants were substantially closer to, but still below, the rates for the US born.)[68] Similar patterns have been documented for the country as a whole, albeit with less complete data.[69]

The double penalty of jail time and potential deportation likely contributes to the low rate of criminal activity among undocumented immigrants. The fear of deportation might be an especially powerful deterrent. Of course, another possible explanation for the low arrest rates is that many crimes perpetrated by undocumented immigrants might go unrecorded; this seems plausible for crimes in which the victims are undocumented themselves and therefore reluctant to involve the police.[70] But this can't be the full story. Although some crimes—like home invasions—aren't always reported to the police, almost every murder is reported, and the data shows that homicide rates among undocumented immigrants are just as low as the rates for other crimes.

A century ago, immigrants were no more likely to be imprisoned, compared to the US-born population of the same age and gender (but immigrants were not less likely to be incarcerated, as immigrants are today). We do not have arrest records for the past, but there are some scattered data on incarceration. Immigrants were more likely to be young men, and young men are more likely to commit crimes, and so in the raw data—before adjusting for age and gender—immigrants in the past were indeed more likely to wind up in jail.

Why, then, is the myth of the criminal immigrant so pervasive? One possibility is that the media sensationalizes crimes perpetrated by immigrants. A team of economists found that newspapers in Switzerland were twice as likely to report on a crime with an immigrant culprit.[71] And for voters who are already prone to dislike immigration, even *one* immigrant offender seems like one too many. Even if immigrants were half as criminal as the rest of the population, population-wide crime rates suggest that they would still be responsible for one thousand murders a year, and each of these one thousand cases has the potential to be endlessly publicized depending on the victim and the circumstances.

Even if immigrants themselves are less likely to commit crimes today, it is still possible to imagine a scenario in which areas that receive more immigrants could also face rising crime rates. Why would this be? One possibility is that residents are less willing to fund public services—including the police—when they perceive the money going to "other people's" neighborhoods; if so, crime in immigrant neigh-borhoods could rise.

In the United States, at least, researchers have *not* found any such association between immigration to an area and local crime rates: there is no surge in crime after immigrants, undocumented or other-wise, arrive in a state.[72] Likewise, there was no association with immi-grant inflows and arrests for violent or property offenses in US urban areas in the past.[73]

In the European context, the evidence is more mixed. Scholars have documented small increases in property crime following immi-grant inflows in both the UK and Italy.[74] The European data linking immigrant arrivals to crime comes as a warning shot. If cities and towns pull back on funding local services because the voters resent spending on immigrant populations, crime rates may rise. In that way, fear of immigrants can become its own self-fulfilling prophecy.

GLOBAL DIVERSITY CONTRIBUTES TO ANERICAN CULTURE

In an earlier chapter, we described how immigrants join US society and become Americans. But cultural assimilation is a two-way street. Just as immigrants adopt American customs and practices, so too do immigrants reshape American culture, expanding the American palate and soundscape.

For the most part, Americans appreciate—and even revel in—the diversity of gastronomic options available on our shores. Gustavo Arellano, a writer for Southern California's *OC Weekly*, summed it up well: "Mexican food, if anything, that's the one thing all Americans like. You may not like the *Mexican*, but you sure love Mexican food."[75]

Each immigrant group to the United States has brought with them an important food tradition that we now think of as quint-essentially American. German immigrants planted hops for brew-ing lagers, now the most common (and sometimes scorned) form of

American beer.[76] Italian immigrants reimported tomatoes to the New World and brought with them recipes for sauces that would become an American staple on pizza and pastas.[77] Jews opened delicatessens and bagel shops; Greeks owned roadside diners offering an immigrant take on classic American burgers and fries. Today, American cities offer sushi, pho, tandoori, and tacos. Food and travel writer John Mariani crows that "as a result of more than 400 years of immigrant history, America has become . . . the richest gastronomy in the world—one that ravenously accepts from other food cultures while influencing them in return."[78] There is even research conducted by our colleagues in economics that quantifies the association between immigrant arrivals to an area and the diversity of ethnic restaurants (not surprisingly: more immigrants means a more diverse array of restaurants).[79]

The American music industry has also become the arbiter of global trends, in part because of the contributions of immigrants from all over the world. Music critic Howard Reich argues that the scaffold of American music is "built on the shoulders of immigrants," who have provided "a cacophonous merger of a thousand cultures thrown together like nowhere else on Earth."[80] Most recently, one could point to superstars from the Caribbean—Rihanna, Nicki Minaj, and before them Lauryn Hill and the Fugees—as infusing American hip-hop, rap, and R&B with an island sound. But this tradition of immigrant artists is far from new, stretching back to the Irish balladeers and Italian crooners of the early twentieth century. Even the most nostalgic, all-American fare—the song "White Christmas" and the orchestral suite *Appalachian Spring*—were written by Jewish immigrants.

Immigrants have made so many contributions to culture that it seems obvious—like second nature—that new arrivals will contribute to local cuisine, fashion, music, and the arts, creating a form of cultural fusion. Yet this outcome is not a foregone conclusion. If you travel today to a European country with the same share of foreign-born residents as the United States—say, Italy or Spain—you will primarily find Italian or Spanish restaurants. Maybe you'll find a few Colombian or Moroccan spots interspersed in the city center, and certainly some ethnic options in immigrant neighborhoods—but nothing like the range of choices you can find in all US cities, and even many of our small towns. So the special recipe to cultural fusion is not only immigration but also a society open to immigrants and willing to learn from the diverse experiences they bring.

How impossible it seems now to imagine rolling back time to America in 1840, before the mass migrations from Ireland began, before the waves of immigrants from all over Europe, let alone before the more recent immigrations from Asia and Latin America. What would Americans eat? Not pizza and beer, not hot dogs, not lo mein—and certainly not tacos. What would be on the airwaves? These topics are not often the subject of economic research on the costs and benefits of immigration, although together these cultural imports may have contributed more to our collective happiness than all of the wages slightly lowered or slightly raised.

8

A SECOND GRAND BARGAIN

The Long View of Immigration Policy

IN 1958, THEN SENATOR JOHN F. KENNEDY PENNED THE PAM-
phlet *A Nation of Immigrants* to celebrate the contributions of previous immigrants, primarily from Europe, to building the country.
Does the evidence support a similarly hopeful and welcoming story
today, in a way that also includes immigrants from countries like
Mexico, Guatemala, Laos, India, Nigeria, and Iraq?

Based on our own research, the answer is yes. We could imagine
rewriting Kennedy's pamphlet today. Both in the past and the present,
and no matter where their parents came from, the children of immigrants raised in poor households experience dramatic upward mobility. These children of immigrants can rise in large part because their
parents move to the states and cities that offer the most opportunity
for them and their children.

The common nostalgic view that European immigrants in the past moved up the economic ladder more quickly than immigrants from Asia and Latin America today is myth, not reality. The children of Guatemalan and Cambodian immigrants achieve the same degree of upward mobility as the children of poor immigrants from Britain or Austria did a century ago. In both eras, the children of immigrants are more upwardly mobile than the children of US-born parents. Not only that, but immigrants today are just as quick to assimilate into American society as their counterparts in the past. And the good news is that immigrants' success does not come at the expense of US-born workers.

Politicians often take a short-term perspective, with an eye toward the next election cycle. Given that there are short-term costs associated with new arrivals, particularly in paying to educate their children in public schools but also in other public programs, it might be tempting to only accept immigrants who already hold a higher degree or a highly paid occupation or to cut down on immigrant entry altogether.

But we have many sectors that need immigrant workers now. Who is going to take care of America's growing elderly population, or provide a wide range of other in-demand services?

An immigration policy that takes the long view, that is accepting of the fact that upward mobility takes time, will be more welcoming to immigrants of all backgrounds. And we argue in this chapter that politicians who take this bold stance may not be penalized by the electorate. In fact, we find in the data that attitudes toward immigration are more positive now than at any time in US history. Even though our systematic analysis of political speeches finds that views toward immigration are more polarized by party than ever before, there is a silent majority in favor of immigration today. After a careful look at the evidence, we come away thinking it is possible to craft a solidly pro-American and pro-immigration message that can bring in voters on both sides.

ATTITUDES TOWARD IMMIGRANTS ARE MORE
POSITIVE (BUT MORE POLARIZED) THAN EVER

It can be jarring to hear the messages of anti-immigration politicians these days. Some sentiments that would only be heard on the fringe a generation ago are now being shared in mainstream politics. To take just one example: Lauren Witzke, the 2020 Republican candidate for Senate in Delaware, tweeted, "Most third-world migrants can not assimilate into civil societies. Prove me wrong."[1] Even though Witzke lost handily to an incumbent Democrat in a blue state, she still garnered 39 percent of the vote.

But resistance to newcomers has always been part of our public discourse about immigration; it is only the target groups that have changed. Today, the "out groups" are Mexicans, Central Americans, and Muslims. In the past, the targeted outsiders were the Irish, and then Italians, Jews, and other Southern and Eastern Europeans—with a steady drumbeat of hate against the Chinese. The sentiment that Witzke expressed in 2020 is not so different from what the anti-immigration senator Henry Cabot Lodge declared more than a century before: "[Immigration] is bringing to the country people whom it is very difficult to assimilate" because immigrants are from "races most alien to the body of the American people."[2]

Despite the loud and increasingly emboldened anti-immigrant voices these days, we find that Americans are more pro-immigration than ever, even if sentiment toward immigration is increasingly split by political party. We have been collaborating with computational linguists at Stanford to systematically analyze the language used in congressional speeches about immigration over the last two centuries.[3] Our study uses the full corpus of speeches from 1870 to the present, more than eight million speeches in all, approximately two hundred thousand of which pertain to immigration.

Politicians like Henry Cabot Lodge no longer represent the majority view. In analyzing the *Congressional Record*, it's clear that, a century ago, anti-immigrant sentiments like Lauren Witzke's were expressed by a wide majority of representatives in the House and the Senate. But now anti-immigration politicians are a smaller faction, even though they represent an increasingly loud and emboldened minority.

The ability to analyze 150 years of congressional speeches in granular detail is a feat of modern computing. The first challenge we faced in putting this data together was figuring out which speeches were indeed focused on immigration. Our research team read through a sample of speeches that contained keywords like "immigration" to confirm that the content was immigration-related.

The second challenge was to determine whether each speech was positively or negatively inclined towards immigrants. Because there are far too many congressional speeches to have one person (or even a research team) read them all, we used machine learning to scale up information about tone from our human readers. Essentially, we helped the computer learn from the sample of speeches coded by hand about which words indicate that a speech is about immigration (say, "border" or "illegal"), and which speeches are pro-immigration (a score of +1), neutral (a score of 0), or anti-immigration (a score of −1). The results of this analysis are presented in Figure 8.

By classifying all of the speeches about immigration in the *Congressional Record*, we uncovered a number of notable findings. First, when congressmen and senators spoke about immigration in the past (up through around 1940), their tone was consistently negative.[4] Speeches were larded with inflammatory rhetoric about "stamp[ing] out these Chinese dens" and "breaking up the traffic in alien girls." Of immigrants more broadly, many politicians declared it "undesirable to have an unlimited quantity of an alien people who cannot assimilate."[5]

Moreover, Republican and Democratic representatives in that period were equally likely to give anti-immigration speeches. Here's one Democratic senator, speaking in favor of immigration restriction in

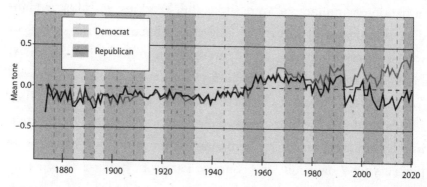

FIGURE 8. Average tone in congressional speeches has become more pro-immigrant over time, but increasingly polarized by party. Source: *Congressional Record*, 1870–present. CREDIT: Illustrations by Patti Isaacs, based on Ran Abramitzky, Leah Boustan, Chris Becker, Dallas Card, Serina Chang, Dan Jurafsky, Julia Mendelsohn, and Rob Voigt, "Computational Analysis of 140 Years of U.S. Political Speeches Reveals More Positive but Increasingly Polarized Framing of Immigration" (working paper, November 2021)

the 1920s: "Shall we permit them to have their way when we have discovered that it is not good for our country for them to continue to come in such large numbers? I ought to speak for America, and so ought you. . . . instead of lending your influence to build up traffic for steamship companies and make rich corrupt immigration agents in bringing people in here who are not fit to become citizens of the United States. And they have been coming, hundreds of them. Thousands and hundreds of thousands of them have come."[6]

Given this widespread negative sentiment, it is not surprising that the typical representative voted to restrict immigration multiple times before their initiatives were finally successful with the Emergency Quota Act of 1921.

Second, the overall tone toward immigration shifted in a clear way from mostly negative to mostly positive within a single generation—in the years between 1945 and 1965. As American soldiers fought fascism alongside immigrants and the children of immigrants, acceptance of immigrants grew. The efforts by President Truman—and later Presidents Kennedy and Johnson—to redefine America as "a nation of immigrants" were successful. Working with Oscar Handlin, a professor of history at Harvard, Truman and his successors worked to rewrite the history of immigration to the United States. As Handlin wrote in the introduction to his classic book *The Uprooted*, "once I thought to write a history of the immigrants in America. Then I discovered that the immigrants *were* American history."[7] In this tale, immigrants were no longer barbarians at the gates, but instead were pioneers who had built the country. Far from being a feared outgroup, immigrants were us.

Third, the new positive tone toward immigration that arose in the 1940s and 1950s helped create the conditions for the reopening of the border in 1965.[8] What's particularly striking is that for nearly thirty years after the border reopened in 1965, the positive sentiment toward immigration did not erode even as immigrant inflows from new sending countries like Mexico, China, and India increased greatly. Instead, right after the passage of the 1965 law, the average tone toward immigration remained positive but our current partisan split on immigration emerged, with the Republican party becoming increasingly disapproving of immigration.

We also analyzed presidential speeches and found that modern presidents (from Truman onward) also tended to be more positive toward immigration than were presidents in the past. Furthermore, modern presidents express more positive sentiment toward immigration than the average representative of their party in the House or Senate. This pattern reflects the fact that presidents tend to keep an eye on the national economy for which immigration can be an engine of growth, whereas representatives are more concerned about sentiment in local areas, where xenophobia and concern about immigration can be rampant. On this metric, the Trump presidency stands out as a notable outlier: the first time in recent memory (and perhaps in American history) that a president exceeded his party in negativity toward immigration.

Today, the partisan divide over immigration is wider than ever, thanks to changes in both major parties. Republican views turned strongly against immigration in the mid-1990s, when unauthorized immigration—particularly into California—became a topic of national concern; Republican sentiment became even more negative after 9/11, when the party tied immigration to terrorism.[9] At the same time, the Democratic party is becoming increasingly pro-immigration. In the 1990s, President Bill Clinton convened an immigration commission that proposed not only heightened border security but also cuts to legal immigration. It is hard to imagine this kind of proposal coming from a Democratic politician today.[10]

Now, for the first time in nearly a century, Republican attitudes toward immigration are as negative as they were during the Age of Mass Migration from Europe. The provocative statements tying immigration to crime and terrorism could very well have been uttered a century ago, if you swap the name of one threat (Islamic terrorists) for another (anarchists or Bolsheviks): "Violent crime seems to go up," said one Republican House member in 2016. "The border is porous. We have people pouring into the country. The Islamic State has made clear they are making use of our porous border and our willingness to harm ourselves by bringing in refugees that will include Islamic State terrorists." Lack of assimilation is another theme that unites the two periods. "So many of them who come here illegally come so ill-prepared for success," lamented another Republican senator. "They come with lack of education; they come with lack of skill; they come with lack of ability or unwillingness to assimilate into the culture. So what happens is they can't find success? Instead of returning back home where maybe they can work within their culture, they settle for our welfare state."[11]

Sentiment toward immigration among the Democrats has also oscillated over the decades, but today it remains higher than ever. Combing through recent speeches from Democratic senators and House members reveals pages of sympathetic stories emphasizing the hardships that refugees faced before arrival and their flourishing in the United States, as well as hard-nosed economic numbers emphasizing immigrants' contribution to economic growth. Never have the two parties been further apart.

From the types of words that representatives use in their speeches, it is clear that Republicans and Democrats view immigrants through different lenses. Republicans are increasingly likely to use words related to crime, illegality, and violence in their speeches about immigration, whereas Democrats use terms related to family and community.

One area where the two parties do agree is in reference to work and the economy: Republicans and Democrats are equally likely to use words like "employee," "pay," "fund" or "tax." So it's not that anti-immigration politicians regularly emphasize that immigrants will "take our jobs." Instead, they sow fear that immigrants threaten the nation's security or simply don't belong.

Elected officials do pay attention to their constituents when choosing what policies to support and what words to use. The positive tone toward immigrants that we measure in recent political speeches mirrors rising positive sentiment in the population as a whole. Contrary to anti-immigrant rhetoric from Republican candidates like Lauren Witzke, Gallup posted the *highest* national support for immigration in the most recent poll. For the past twenty years, Gallup has asked Americans: "On the whole, do you think immigration is a good thing or a bad thing for this country today?" In 2021, a staggering 75 percent of Americans answered that immigration was a "good thing." This was up from the low point of 52 percent in 2002, the year after the 9/11 attacks. Respondents are also asked: "In your view, should immigration be kept at its present level, increased or decreased?" In the mid-1990s, a full 65 percent of respondents said that immigration should be decreased; in 2021, that number fell to just 31 percent—the lowest share ever to say that immigration should be decreased.[12]

WHAT YESTERDAY'S IMMIGRANTS TEACH US ABOUT IMMIGRATION POLICY TODAY

Both political speech and public sentiment in the United States are more positive toward immigration than ever before, and our data can help explain why. Our research reveals a striking upward mobility among the children of immigrants, which undermines the view that immigrants from poorer countries will always remain behind. To be sure, for immigrants themselves, the process of moving up from a dockworker or a farmhand in the past or a dishwasher or a gardener today takes time. But if we think of immigration policy on the level of generations, rather than years, we can—and should—take the long view. Our immigration policies should be based on a strong foundation of fact, not on anecdotes and fear.

What does this mean about concrete policy proposals currently on the table? One thing is clear: our immigration system does not need to preselect immigrants based on their wealth or level of education. Rather, if we are willing to plan with the future in mind, we can continue to accept immigrants from poor countries at similar levels to today, even immigrants who arrive without many years of schooling, with the confidence that the American economy will allow their children to rise. It has happened before, and we are seeing it happen again now.

One could worry that what's past is not prologue, to paraphrase Shakespeare. It could be that the newest immigrants—for example, Central Americans fleeing unrest or searching for work—may not fare as well as immigrants in the past. But we have traced out immigrant success across more than one hundred years, and we see very few countries from which the fact of upward mobility does not hold. We find overwhelming evidence that the children of immigrants move up the ladder, regardless of which country immigrants come from—including Mexico and other parts of Latin America.

Of course, one might say that there is no *harm* in selecting for educated immigrants up front. Immigrants with a college degree do well right off the bat. They enjoy high earnings, contribute to scientific innovation, and pay more than their fair share of public funds. But one implication of our research is that we don't need to organize our immigration system around initial skills. There is a strong demand for services that less-educated immigrants provide today in construction, the restaurant industry, child- and eldercare, and agriculture.

Importantly, our research shows that policies designed to deter less-educated immigrants from entering the United States are misguided. Both a century ago and today, the children of poor immigrants rise. Even immigrants earning close to the minimum wage had children who reached at least the midpoint of the income distribution. So even if some immigrant parents live below the poverty line and receive some government assistance, one generation later their children more than pay for their parents' debts.

Furthermore, it would be a mistake to base our nation's immigration policy on the belief that immigrants will remain foreigners, preserving their old ways of life and keeping themselves at arm's length from the dominant culture. There is overwhelming evidence that assimilation is fast and measurable—that over time immigrant populations come to resemble US-born residents, and that new generations form distinct identities as Americans.

A question remains about what to do about the estimated 11 million undocumented immigrants living in the United States. The last major legislation to address the lives of undocumented immigrants—the Immigration Reform and Control Act (IRCA)—passed in 1986 under President Reagan. This bill was pitched as a "grand bargain" between left and right: Democrats wanted a pathway to citizenship for the 2.7 million undocumented immigrants living in the United States at the time, while Republicans pushed for new sanctions on hiring undocumented immigrant workers. As President

George H. W. Bush later said in describing a related piece of legislation, the goal was to "open the 'front door'" to legal immigration while "clos[ing] the 'back door' on illegal immigration."[13] But there was little enforcement of the new rules that forbade hiring undocumented immigrants. With plentiful work opportunities still available, undocumented entry continued, souring the right on the idea of future immigration deals.[14]

Efforts at comprehensive immigration reform have run aground several times in the past decade. Despite the fact that most Americans support immigrants who entered the United States as children without papers, Congress has repeatedly failed to pass the DREAM Act to create a route to permanent residency for this special group. With legislative action foreclosed, the Obama administration used an executive order to create the Deferred Action program (DACA), offering temporary work permits for undocumented immigrants who arrived as children.

Any hope of finding a bipartisan solution to the dilemma of undocumented immigration was set back during the Trump administration. The Trump White House chipped away at our immigration system bit by bit. One of the administration's first acts, which activists on the left branded the "Muslim Ban," was to suspend immigration from countries said to harbor terrorists. Trump also tightened the process for claiming asylum, requiring some asylum seekers to wait on the Mexican side of the border while holding many—including children—in detention centers on the US side. During the COVID crisis, the Trump administration used public safety concerns to justify additional restrictions on popular, legal forms of immigrant entry—including restrictions on international students and skilled workers on H1-B visas.

Despite the many sharp changes to administrative rules, Trump's more serious efforts to remake the immigration system through new legislation—including a proposal to slash entry visas and allocate the remaining slots to immigrants with higher degrees or a high-paid job offer—went nowhere.[15] President Biden was able to reverse many of the smaller steps in just his first month in office, mainly through the use of executive orders.[16] Family separations at the border ended. Construction halted on the wall. The "public charge" rule banning immigrants who might take public assistance was rescinded.[17]

Immigration policy seems stuck in a holding pattern: Democratic presidents pass new rules to protect one group; Republican presidents pass different rules to clamp down on another. The harder questions—whether to expand the slots for legal entry, how to address the eleven million undocumented immigrants already living in the country—cannot be accomplished through executive action alone. Any action to create a real pathway to citizenship for the existing undocumented population needs to go through a legislative process—but the prospects for such bipartisan reform seem dim.[18]

The evidence-based story that we tell in this book suggests a way forward. At least half of the country can trace their ancestry to the first or second peak of the Immigration U: more than seventy million Americans are descendants of the Age of Mass Migration from Europe, while nearly eighty million are immigrants themselves or children of recent immigrants. These generations of immigrants have more to unite them than to divide them. By expanding Kennedy's concept of "a nation of immigrants" to include recent arrivals alongside immigrants who disembarked at Ellis Island a century ago, we as Americans can lay the groundwork for a second "grand bargain."

It may seem wildly optimistic to imagine that today's splintered politics can create anything that looks like consensus. But we are heartened by the fact that when we released earlier studies about the children of immigrants, our message reached a wider spectrum of Americans than would ever seem possible. Desus and The Kid Mero on Showtime, sure—but also progressives, whose message was "See, immigrant groups contribute to the country"; conservatives, who crowed that "America works! Anyone can make it here"; and libertarians, who praised the search for opportunity and the resulting mobility. Even after four years of "Make America Great Again"-style anti-immigrant messaging, we still believe that the one symbol that can unite this great nation is the promise of the Statue of Liberty.

We believe that politicians who take this message seriously will succeed: that immigrants contribute to our economy through science, innovation, and vital services; that the children of immigrants from nearly every poor country move up to the middle in the next generation; that immigrants are just as keen to become Americans now as in the past; and that America is a country that embraces this diversity and lets in new ideas. Indeed, it is hard to imagine any gathering that is more patriotic than a naturalization ceremony welcoming new Americans from around the globe. A positive and optimistic message about immigration is broadly popular and might even be a political winner if politicians embrace it proudly, rather than cringing from it out of fear of backlash. We can reclaim the legacy and continued prospect for prosperity that is the promise of America's Streets of Gold.

IMMIGRATION POLICY IN AMERICA: A BRIEF TIMELINE

1790: NATURALIZATION ACT   ● 1790
- "Free white persons" residing in US for two years and all children of US citizens deemed eligible for citizenship

● **1800**

1882: CHINESE EXCLUSION ACT   ● 1882
- Prohibited immigration of all Chinese laborers

1891: IMMIGRATION ACT   ● 1891
- Centralized immigration enforcement authority to the federal government from the states

● **1900**

1917: LITERACY REQUIREMENT   ● 1917
- Added a literacy requirement for entry
- Expanded the "Asiatic barred zone," excluding all Asians and Pacific Islanders (until 1952)

1921 & 1924: COUNTRY OF ORIGIN QUOTAS   ● 1921 & 1924
- Introduced quotas favoring immigrants from Northwest Europe
- Cut slots for legal entry to 150,000 annually, down from nearly a million entrants a year

1942: BRACERO PROGRAM   ● 1942
- Allowed entry of temporary Mexican workers, who were mostly employed in agriculture

1948: DISPLACED PERSONS ACT   ● 1948
- Provided some entry slots for displaced persons in Europe at the end of WWII.

1952: IMMIGRATION AND NATIONALITY ACT   ● 1952
- Minor revision of national origins quota system from 1924
- Repealed the exclusion of Asian immigrants but quotas for entry remained low
- Followed by the Refugee Relief Act in 1953, providing slots to refugees from Communist countries

1965: IMMIGRATION AND NATIONALITY ACT   ● 1965
- Replaced quota system based on national origin with hemisphere caps
- Expanded number of slots for legal entry
- Prioritized family reunification and skilled labor
- No person could be "discriminated against in the issuance of an immigration visa because of . . . race, sex, nationality, place of birth or place of residence"

1975: INDOCHINA MIGRATION AND REFUGEE ASSISTANCE ACT   ● 1975
- Allowed ~130,000 refugees from Vietnam, Laos, and Cambodia

1980: REFUGEE ACT   ● 1980
- Created a new permanent procedure for refugee admissions

1986 ● **1986: IMMIGRATION REFORM AND CONTROL ACT**
- Provided pathway to citizenship for undocumented residents who arrived in US before 1983 (2.7 million)
- Sanctions on employers who hire undocumented workers
- The number of crimes included for deportation kept expanding through 1980s and 1990s

1990 ● **1990: IMMIGRATION ACT OF 1990**
- Increased quota cap for legal immigration by 50%

1996 ● **1996: ILLEGAL IMMIGRATION REFORM AND RESPONSIBILITY ACT**
- Reduced government benefit eligibility for immigrants
- Mandated tracking of entry-exit to prevent visa overstays (US-VISIT)
- Established programs for local law enforcement to cooperate with immigration enforcement
- Instituted "expedited removal" for noncitizens at border without proper documents

2000 ●

2006 ● **2006: SECURE FENCE ACT5**
- Authorized 700 miles of fence on border

2009 ● **2009: SECURE COMMUNITIES**
- Coordinated technology and information between FBI, Immigration and Customs Enforcement (ICE), and local police

2012 ● **2012: DEFERRED ACTION FOR CHILDHOOD ARRIVALS (DACA)**
- Granted a two-year renewable period of legal status for some undocumented individuals who entered the US before the age of 16

2017–2020 ● **2017–2020: TRUMP CHANGES REFUGEE AND ASYLUM PROGRAMS**
- Imposed multiple travel bans on arrivals from a list of Muslim-majority countries
- Limited the number refugee admissions as low as ~15,000 in 2020 (down from 85,000 in 2016)
- New process for asylum applicants, contributing to massive backlog of applicantss

2017–2020 ● **2017–2020: TRUMP'S WAR ON THE SOUTHERN BORDER**
- Announced that Administration will prosecute parents who cross the border with their children, ultimately separating families
- Declared a state of emergency at the southern border in a failed attempt to secure funding for a border wall

2020 ● **2020: COVID PANDEMIC RESTRICTIONS**
- Many travel restrictions for people entering and leaving the country

Acknowledgments

T HE WORK UNDERLYING THIS BOOK IS BASED ON RESEARCH projects with multiple coauthors, including a number of our former graduate students. Our coauthors include Katherine Eriksson and Santiago Pérez (both on the faculty at the University of California, Davis), as well as Philip Ager (University of Mannheim), Chris Becker (Stanford), Dallas Card (University of Michigan), Peter Catron (University of Washington), Serina Chang (Stanford), Elior Cohen (Kansas City Fed), Dylan Connor (Arizona State), Elisa Jácome (Northwestern), Casper Worm Hansen (University of Copenhagen), Stephanie Hao (Princeton), Dan Jurafsky (Stanford), and Rob Voigt (Northwestern).

We appreciate the help of numerous graduate and undergraduate research assistants at Stanford, Princeton, and UCLA, particularly Helen Kissel and Myera Rashid. We also thank Jaime Arellano-Bover, Alvaro Calderon, Kelsey Carido, Jenna Kowalski, Bailey Palmer, Pam Poteh, Lorenzo Rosas, Antigone Xenopoulos, David Yang, and Tom Zohar. We appreciate each and every person who took the time to respond to our immigration survey, and we are especially grateful to Mariano (Tino) Cuéllar, Lucy Koh, Eunsook Koh, and Harlan Platt for sharing their inspiring family immigration stories.

This book owes its existence to our agent, Margo Fleming, who first saw its value as a "string of pearls." We thank Marina Krakovsky, who read every single word with the precision of a fine jeweler, and our editor, John Mahaney, who made our words shine.

Our graduate advisors encouraged us to ask big questions about the world, while also paying attention to the smallest details. We will forever be the students of our teachers: Joe Ferrie, Claudia Goldin, Larry Katz, Bob Margo, and Joel Mokyr.

A generous community of economic historians and other scholars read our book and provided insightful comments. We thank Ariel Bino, Michael Clemens, Elizabeth Cohen, Claudia Goldin, Naomi Lamoreaux, Melvin Lopata, Bob Margo, Ana Raquel Minian, Joel Mokyr, Juan Moreno-Cruz, Melanie Morten, Santiago Pérez, Paul Rhode, Debra Satz, and Gavin Wright. We appreciate funding from the National Science Foundation and the Russell Sage Foundation for some of the studies we discuss in these pages. Leah acknowledges the support of the Industrial Relations Section at Princeton University, and the encouragement of the WC cheering section.

From Leah: I expected to write this book while on sabbatical abroad, experiencing life as a (temporary) immigrant far from my place of birth. Instead, I finished the manuscript within the four walls of my family home in Princeton, New Jersey, as COVID shut down international travel in March 2020. I thank my husband, Ra'anan Boustan, for his deep love of family and his commitment to equality in all things, and our three children, Gil, Haskel, and Mira, who share with their parents a passion for books and stories. May our streets of gold let you grow up to be whoever you want to be.

From Ran: Even though I chose to become an immigrant and live far away from home, my family selflessly encouraged and supported me despite the separation. I thank my wife, Noya, for her endless support, strength, and dedication. You are my best friend and soulmate, and there is nobody else I would rather walk with through the adventure of life. And our boys, Roee, Ido, and Tom, who are growing up to be wonderful human beings. Nothing makes me prouder.

Leah and Ran are both immigrants and the descendants of immigrants. To our many ancestors, especially to Annie, Chaim, Pearl, Jack, Ida, Louis, Minnie, Leopold, Gus, Jerry, Matthew, Roslyn, Harlan, and Margie, and to Moshe, Rachel, Baruch, Breindel, and the Lopata family—without your bravery, we would not be here.

Notes

CHAPTER 1: "I CAME WITH FIFTY CENTS AND THAT'S IT!"

1. "Hasan Minhaj & Bodega Boys: Street Interviews w/ Children of Immigrants," *Desus & Mero* on Showtime, video, 4:44, November 14, 2019, https://youtu.be/H05btFii4K0.

2. "Desus and Mero Talk Hit Show, How They Met + Dealing w/ New Fame," *The Angie Martinez Show*, video, 13:11, February 24, 2017, https://youtu.be/DkLmufIk8SY.

3. Jazmine Hughes, "How 'Desus & Mero' Conquered Late Night," *New York Times*, June 18, 2018, www.nytimes.com/2018/06/18/magazine/how-desus-mero-conquered-late-night.html.

4. All *Desus & Mero* quotes from "Hasan Minhaj & Bodega Boys."

5. Philissa Cramer, "Jon Ossoff Had a Totem of His American Jewish Heritage in His Pocket When He Joined the Senate," *Jewish News of Northern California*, January 21, 2021, www.jweekly.com/2021/01/21/jon-ossoff-had-a-totem-of-his-american-jewish-heritage-in-his-pocket-when-he-joined-the-senate/.

6. We coded stated reason for immigration from 1,190 immigrants who spoke with the Ellis Island Foundation. Of these respondents, 1,106 (93 percent) provided a reason for immigration. We describe this dataset in more detail in Chapter 4. Transcripts and audio files of the interviews can be found at

the Statue of Liberty–Ellis Island Foundation Oral History Library, https:// heritage.statueofliberty.org/oral-history-library.

7. Ran Abramitzky, Leah Platt Boustan, and Katherine Eriksson, "Europe's Tired, Poor, Huddled Masses: Self-Selection and Economic Outcomes in the Age of Mass Migration," *American Economic Review* 102, no. 5 (2012): 1832–1856.

8. David McKenzie, Steven Stillman, and John Gibson, "How Important Is Selection? Experimental vs. Non-experimental Measures of the Income Gains from Migration," *Journal of the European Economic Association* 8, no. 4 (2010): 913–945; Gordon H. Hanson, "Illegal Migration from Mexico to the United States," *Journal of Economic Literature* 44, no. 4 (December 2006): 869–924.

9. "Largest U.S. Immigrant Groups over Time, 1960-Present," Migration Policy Institute, accessed September 14, 2021, www.migrationpolicy.org /programs/data-hub/charts/largest-immigrant-groups-over-time.

10. Ethan M. Forman, "Georgia Senator Jon Ossoff's Jewish Family Began Its American Dream in Peabody," *Jewish Journal*, March 11, 2021, https:// jewishjournal.org/2021/03/11/georgia-senator-jon-ossoffs-jewish-family -began-its-american-dream-in-peabody/.

11. Barry R. Chiswick, "The Effect of Americanization on the Earnings of Foreign-Born Men," *Journal of Political Economy* 86, no. 5 (October 1978): 897–921; Timothy J. Hatton, "The Immigrant Assimilation Puzzle in Late Nineteenth-Century America," *Journal of Economic History* 57, no. 1 (March 1997): 34–62.

12. Alfredo Corchado, *Homelands: Four Friends, Two Countries, and the Fate of the Great Mexican-American Migration* (New York: Bloomsbury, 2018).

13. Alejandro Portes and Rubén G. Rumbaut, *Legacies: The Story of the Immigrant Second Generation* (Berkeley: University of California Press, 2001).

14. Raj Chetty, Nathaniel Hendren, Maggie R. Jones, and Sonya R. Porter, "Race and Economic Opportunity in the United States: An Intergenerational Perspective," *Quarterly Journal of Economics* 135, no. 2 (May 2020): 711–783. See also Debopam Bhattacharya and Bhashkar Mazumder, "A Nonparametric Analysis of Black-White Differences in Intergenerational Income Mobility in the United States," *Quantitative Economics* 2, no. 3 (November 2011): 335–379.

15. William H. Frey, "What the 2020 Census Will Reveal About America: Stagnating Growth, an Aging Population, and Youthful Diversity," Brookings Institution, January 11, 2021, www.brookings.edu/research/what-the-2020 -census-will-reveal-about-america-stagnating-growth-an-aging-population -and-youthful-diversity/.

16. Farhad Manjoo, "The World Might Be Running Low on Americans," *New York Times*, May 20, 2021, www.nytimes.com/2021/05/20/opinion/the -world-might-be-running-low-on-americans.html. See also Matthew Yglesias, *One Billion Americans: The Case for Thinking Bigger* (New York: Penguin Random House, 2020).

17. Alberto Alesina, Armando Miano, and Stefanie Stantcheva, "Immigration and Redistribution," NBER Working Paper 24733, National Bureau of Economic Research, June 2018.

18. Schelly, "Ellis Island: Was Your Name Changed?" *MyHeritage Blog*, November 6, 2017, https://blog.myheritage.com/2017/11/ellis-island-was -your-name-changed/.

CHAPTER 2: FACT-CHECKING THE PAST

1. For more details, see quoteresearch, "In God We Trust; Others Must Provide Data," Quote Investigator, accessed September 14, 2021, https:// quoteinvestigator.com/2017/12/29/god-data/.

2. The program for the economic history conference that we attended at the Huntington Gardens is here: http://economichistory.ucla.edu/wp-content /uploads/sites/69/2017/07/All-UC-May-2008-Program.pdf.

3. Chibuike Oguh, "Blackstone to Acquire Ancestry.com for $4.7 Billion," Reuters, August 24, 2020, www.reuters.com/article/us-ancestry-m-a -blackstonegroup/blackstone-to-acquire-ancestry-com-for-4-7-billion -idUSKBN25K0R4.

4. See, for example, Stephan Thernstrom, *Poverty and Progress: Social Mobility in a Nineteenth Century City* (Cambridge, MA: Harvard University Press, 1964).

5. Brendan Graham lyrics to "Isle of Hope, Isle of Tears," Irish Folk Songs, www.irish-folk-songs.com/isle-of-hope-isle-of-tears-lyrics-and-guitar -chords.html.

6. Sam Roberts, "A New Verse in the Ballad of Ellis Island's First Immigrant," *New York Times*, March 30, 2016, www.nytimes.com/2016/03/31 /nyregion/a-new-verse-in-the-ballad-of-ellis-islands-first-immigrant.html.

7. Sheila Langan, "Genealogist Finds Annie Moore's Living Relatives," *Irish Central*, January 1, 2020, www.irishcentral.com/roots/genealogy /genealogist-finds-annie-moores-living-relatives.

8. Megan Smolenyak, "$1,000 Reward for Ellis Island's Little Orphan Annie," *Megan's Roots World* (blog), July 17, 2006, http://megansrootsworld .blogspot.com/2006/07/1000-reward-for-ellis-islands-little.html.

9. Enslaved persons were transported to the United States until 1808, and this population could be considered involuntary immigrants. However,

enslaved persons were not listed by name in the census before the Civil War. The first enumeration to include the formerly enslaved was conducted in 1870, and by this time, most of the population who had been born abroad had since died.

10. Claudia D. Goldin and Lawrence F. Katz, *The Race Between Education and Technology* (Cambridge, MA: Harvard University Press, 2009).

11. For more details on linking algorithms, see Ran Abramitzky, Leah Platt Boustan, Katherine Eriksson, James J. Feigenbaum, and Santiago Pérez, "Automated Linking of Historical Data," *Journal of Economic Literature* 59, no. 3 (September 2021): 865–918.

12. The seventy-two-year rule for the release of census records was passed in 1978, perhaps to match the length of an average life span. Russell Heimlich, "The '72-Year Rule' Governs Release of Census Records," Pew Research Center, April 9, 2012, www.pewresearch.org/fact-tank/2012/04/09/the-72-year-rule-governs-release-of-census-records/.

13. If the Ran Abramitzkys of the world were identical to the John Smiths in all their characteristics, this would not be a problem for our analysis. But people with rarer names tend to have slightly higher socioeconomic status than individuals with more common names. We therefore use statistical techniques of reweighting to correct for this small bias.

14. If name changers like the Platnichkys were more primed for success, we might understate immigrant progress in the past; the opposite would be true if name changers were a less successful group. We checked for this concern by comparing the names of immigrants in our sample to immigrants in the full population. We would be worried if immigrants in our sample had distinctly foreign names, as this could be a sign that our sample disproportionately includes immigrants who keep their old name, yet we do not find economically meaningful differences on this dimension. Ran Abramitzky, Leah Platt Boustan, and Katherine Eriksson, "A Nation of Immigrants: Assimilation and Economic Outcomes in the Age of Mass Migration," *Journal of Political Economy* 122, no. 3 (June 2014): 498.

15. As it turns out, the 1940 census was digitized by two independent companies. We found that the names listed on these versions of the 1940 census files disagreed by at least one character—with a Miles becoming a Mike, for example—around once every ten times.

16. Kelsey Piper, "Study: Many of the 'Oldest' People in the World May Not Be as Old as We Think," *Vox*, August 8, 2019, www.vox.com/2019/8/8/20758813/secrets-ultra-elderly-supercentenarians-fraud-error.

17. Some linking methods are better at avoiding false matches, while others do a better job at finding many true matches. For example, more conservative

approaches require that a match only be declared when there is no other person with the same name and birthplace within five years around the reported age, whereas more expansive approaches will link anyone who has the same (unique) attributes, even if there is another prospective match who is one year older or younger. See Abramitzky et al., "Automated Linking of Historical Data," 865–918.

18. Adam Goodman, *The Deportation Machine: America's Long History of Expelling Immigrants* (Princeton: Princeton University Press, 2020), 3–4.

CHAPTER 3: A BRIEF HISTORY OF IMMIGRATION TO AMERICA

1. Alberto Alesina, Armando Miano, and Stefanie Stantcheva, "Immigration and Redistribution," NBER Working Paper 24733, National Bureau of Economic Research, June 2018.

2. Among the earliest migrants to North America arriving before 1700 were indentured servants, having entered into agreements to work for some period of time for a company or "master" in exchange for their passage to the New World. The number of European immigrants arriving under such labor contracts declined throughout the eighteenth century, eventually replaced by "free" immigrants. David Eltis, ed., *Coerced and Free Migration: Global Perspectives* (Palo Alto: Stanford University Press, 2002); Christopher Tomlins, "Reconsidering Indentured Servitude: European Migration and the Early American Labor Force, 1600–1775," *Labor History* 42, no. 1 (2001): 5–43; David W. Galenson, "The Rise and Fall of Indentured Servitude in the Americas: An Economic Analysis," *Journal of Economic History* 44, no. 1 (March 1984): 1–26.

3. Raymond L. Cohn, "Mortality on Immigrant Voyages to New York, 1836–1853," *Journal of Economic History* 44, no. 2 (June 1984): 289–300; Raymond L. Cohn, "The Determinants of Individual Immigrant Mortality on Sailing Ships, 1836–1853," *Explorations in Economic History* 24, no. 4 (October 1987): 371–391.

4. Vilhelm Moberg, *The Emigrants* (St. Paul: Minnesota Historical Society Press, 1995), 284, 292.

5. George Wilson Pierson, *Tocqueville in America* (Baltimore: Johns Hopkins University Press, 1996), 43.

6. For more details, see Ran Abramitzky and Leah Boustan, "Immigration in American Economic History," *Journal of Economic Literature* 55, no. 4 (December 2017): 1311–1345.

7. In 1900, only one hundred thousand of the five million immigrants in the United States were born in either China or Japan (2 percent of the

total). However, these immigrant groups have a fascinating history. For example, between 1864 and 1869, thousands of Chinese migrants helped construct America's first transcontinental railroad; see the Chinese Railroad Workers in North America Project at Stanford University (http://web.stanford.edu /group/chineserailroad/cgi-bin/website/). Chinese immigrants worked in many industries throughout the western states, from retail to mining (see Hannah Postel, "Ghettoized in Gold Mountain? Chinese Segregation in 19th Century California" [unpublished manuscript, 2021].

8. Beth Lew-Williams, *The Chinese Must Go: Violence, Exclusion, and the Making of the Alien in America* (Cambridge, MA: Harvard University Press, 2018).

9. Congress banned indentured servants and other immigrants arriving on work contracts in 1885, which had been an important means of financing immigration from Asia. Walton Look Lai and Tan Chee-Beng, eds., *The Chinese in Latin America and the Caribbean* (Leiden, Netherlands: Brill, 2010); Lomarsh Roopnarine, "Indian Migration During Indentured Servitude in British Guiana and Trinidad, 1850–1920," *Labor History* 52, no. 2 (2011): 173–191.

10. Josiah Strong, *Our Country: Its Possible Future and Its Present Crisis* (Baltimore: Baker & Taylor for Home Missionary Society, 1891).

11. Jenna Johnson and Abigail Hauslohner, "'I Think Islam Hates Us': A Timeline of Trump's Comments About Islam and Muslims," *Washington Post*, May 20, 2017, www.washingtonpost.com/news/post-politics/wp/2017 /05/20/i-think-islam-hates-us-a-timeline-of-trumps-comments-about-islam -and-muslims/.

12. The consequences of this unequal treatment came into tragic relief with the rise of Hitler in 1933. No more than 250,000 Jewish refugees were allowed to enter the United States from 1933 to 1944, a number of entrants that equals only 4 percent of the Jewish deaths in the Holocaust. After the war ended, Presidents Truman and Eisenhower both negotiated with Congress to accept additional refugees, first displaced persons from World War II and then refugees from Communist countries and from other conflicts around Europe, but again the numbers were small.

13. On these conscious efforts to reframe the history of immigration to the United States, see Jia Lynn Yang, *One Mighty and Irresistible Tide: The Epic Struggle over American Immigration, 1924–1965* (New York: W.W. Norton, 2020), 182–194.

14. Paul Overberg and John McCormick, "Census Data Show America's White Population Shrank for the First Time," *Wall Street Journal*, August 12, 2021, www.wsj.com/articles/census-race-population-redistricting -changes-11628714807.

15. A. Naomi Paik, *Bans, Walls, Raids, Sanctuary: Understanding U.S. Immigration for the Twenty-First Century* (Berkeley: University of California Press, 2020), 28.

16. Douglas S. Massey and Karen A. Pren, "Unintended Consequences of US Immigration Policy: Explaining the Post–1965 Surge from Latin America," *Population and Development Review* 38, no. 1 (July 2012): 1–29 (see Figure 1).

17. Timothy J. Hatton and Jeffrey G. Williamson, *The Age of Mass Migration: Causes and Economic Impact* (Oxford, UK: Oxford University Press, 1998).

18. Hidetaka Hirota, *Expelling the Poor: Atlantic Seaboard States and the Nineteenth-Century Origins of American Immigration Policy* (Oxford, UK: Oxford University Press, 2016).

19. Adam Goodman, *The Deportation Machine: America's Long History of Expelling Immigrants* (Princeton: Princeton University Press, 2020), 29. We calculate that around one in 1,000 immigrants were deported in 1910 because 500 immigrants were deported per year, relative to average entry of 584,000. From 1910–1920, deportations rose to around 3,000 per year. Since 1965, the United States has deported around 50 million immigrants, and we estimate that around twice that number have entered the country from 1965–2020 (both legally and illegally).

20. Sasha Ingber and Rachel Martin, "Immigration Chief: 'Give Me Your Tired, Your Poor Who Can Stand On Their Own 2 Feet,'" NPR, August 13, 2019, www.npr.org/2019/08/13/750726795/immigration-chief -give-me-your-tired-your-poor-who-can-stand-on-their-own-2-feet.

21. Jennifer Mendelsohn, "Their Own Two Feet," *Jennifer Mendelsohn* (blog), August 30, 2019, https://clevertitletk.medium.com/their-own-two-feet -8ddd1dbb1602.

22. Elizabeth F. Cohen, *Illegal: How America's Lawless Immigration Regime Threatens Us All* (London: Hachette UK, 2020); Mae M. Ngai, "The Strange Career of the Illegal Alien: Immigration Restriction and Deportation Policy in the United States, 1921–1965," *Law and History Review* 21, no. 1 (Spring 2003): 69–107.

23. Erika Lee, *At America's Gates: Chinese Immigration During the Exclusion Era, 1882–1943* (Chapel Hill: University of North Carolina Press, 2003).

24. Paik, *Bans, Walls, Raids, Sanctuary*, 50.

25. Cohen, *Illegal*, 97.

26. Julia G. Young, *Mexican Exodus: Emigrants, Exiles, and Refugees of the Cristero War* (Oxford: Oxford University Press, 2015).

27. Jongkwan Lee, Giovanni Peri, and Vasil Yasenov, "The Employment Effects of Mexican Repatriations: Evidence from the 1930's," NBER Working

Paper 23885, National Bureau of Economic Research, September 2017; Goodman, *The Deportation Machine*, 37–72.

28. Goodman, 3–4. These deportations can occur with or without formal legal proceedings, either as a response to being in the country without papers or to committing one of an expanding list of crimes (even for legal permanent residents). In the years after 9/11, immigration authorities were increasingly coordinating with local police departments to enforce immigration laws.

29. In recent years, there have been around four hundred thousand undocumented entrants per year, compared to one million legal immigrant entries, or around 28 percent of the total inflow each year. See Jeffery S. Passel and D'Vera Cohn, "U.S. Unauthorized Immigrant Total Dips to Lowest Level in a Decade," Pew Research Center, November 27, 2018, www.pewresearch .org/hispanic/2018/11/27/u-s-unauthorized-immigrant-total-dips-to-lowest -level-in-a-decade/.

30. Cynthia Feliciano, "Educational Selectivity in U.S. Immigration: How Do Immigrants Compare to Those Left Behind?," *Demography* 42, no. 1 (February 2005): 131–152; David McKenzie and Hillel Rapoport, "Network Effects and the Dynamics of Migration and Inequality: Theory and Evidence from Mexico," *Journal of Development Economics* 84, no. 1 (September 2007): 1–24; Jeffrey Grogger and Gordon H. Hanson, "Income Maximization and the Selection and Sorting of International Migrants," *Journal of Development Economics* 95, no. 1 (2011): 42–57; Michael Andrew Clemens and Mariapia Mendola, "Migration from Developing Countries: Selection, Income Elasticity, and Simpson's Paradox," IZA Discussion Paper 13612, IZA Institute of Labor Economics, 2020.

31. Jens Manuel Krogstad and Jynnah Radford, "Education Levels of U.S. Immigrants Are on the Rise," Pew Research Center, September 14, 2018, www.pewresearch.org/fact-tank/2018/09/14/education-levels-of-u-s -immigrants-are-on-the-rise/; Rukmini S., "Only 8.15% of Indians Are Graduates, Census Data Show," *The Hindu*, April 1, 2016, https://www.thehindu .com/news/national/only-815-of-indians-are-graduates-census-data-show /article7496655.ece.

32. Leslie Casimir, "Data Show Nigerians the Most Educated in the U.S.," *Houston Chronicle*, May 20, 2008, www.chron.com/news/article/Data -show-Nigerians-the-most-educated-in-the-U-S-1600808.php. The percentages quoted in the text come from the authors' own calculations from the 2015–2019 American Community Survey and from the 2010 data from https://ourworldindata.org/tertiary-education. Note that Nigeria does not collect information on the percentage of the population that holds a tertiary

degree, and so we report the share of youth who enroll in postsecondary education within five years of graduating from high school.

33. Ran Abramitzky, Leah Platt Boustan, and Katherine Eriksson, "Europe's Tired, Poor, Huddled Masses: Self-Selection and Economic Outcomes in the Age of Mass Migration," *American Economic Review* 102, no. 5 (August 2012): 1832–1856.

34. In our research on Norway, we were able to compare brothers within the same family with access to different levels of wealth due to quirks of the inheritance system. Families in Northern and Western Norway practiced primogeniture, a set of inheritance practices that passed family property to the oldest brother. In those regions, the oldest brothers of families with land were far less likely to move to the United States than their younger brothers raised in the same household. In general, brothers who stood to inherit family land—and thus expected to be wealthier if they remained at home—were less likely to move to the United States than brothers who were not in line for inheritance. See Ran Abramitzky, Leah Platt Boustan, and Katherine Eriksson, "Have the Poor Always Been Less Likely to Migrate? Evidence from Inheritance Practices During the Age of Mass Migration," *Journal of Development Economics* 102 (May 2013): 2–14.

35. Dylan Shane Connor, "The Cream of the Crop? Geography, Networks, and Irish Migrant Selection in the Age of Mass Migration," *Journal of Economic History* 79, no. 1 (2019): 139–175; Yannay Spitzer and Ariell Zimran, "Migrant Self-Selection: Anthropometric Evidence from the Mass Migration of Italians to the United States, 1907–1925," *Journal of Development Economics* 134 (2018): 226–247.

36. Statue of Liberty–Ellis Island Foundation Oral History Library, accessed September 14, 2021, https://heritage.statueofliberty.org/oral-history -library.

CHAPTER 4: CLIMBING THE LADDER

1. Hamilton Holt, *The Life Stories of Undistinguished Americans as Told by Themselves* (Oxfordshire, UK: Routledge, 1999 [orig. pub. 1906]).

2. The triumphant immigrant journey from poverty to prosperity features in most high school textbooks today. The *New York Times* published an exposé documenting how high school textbooks in different states present controversial historical events—like suburbanization—through a partisan lens, favoring the progressive view in blue states and the conservative understanding in red states. Yet, we found very little that differed in the treatment of the Age of Mass Migration in textbooks used in red and blue

states. The textbooks we surveyed all referred to the hardships of moving from Europe, the discrimination that immigrants initially faced in American cities, and the eventual success of immigrant generations. Dana Goldstein, "American History Textbooks Can Differ Across the Country, in Ways That Are Shaded by Partisan Politics," *New York Times*, January 12, 2020, www.nytimes.com/interactive/2020/01/12/us/texas-vs-california-history -textbooks.html.

3. Holt, *The Life Stories of Undistinguished Americans*.

4. We are pretty confident that the Rocco we found, Rocco Caruso, is the Rocco we are looking for because other details of his life match up to Holt's story. There are other possible matches for Rocco in the census records but various details do not match. One possible match, Rocco Caresco, arrived too late (1911) to be profiled in Holt's book. This Rocco likely died in New York State in 1916. Another possible match, Rocco Creser, lived in Bridgeport, Connecticut, and eventually worked his way up to owning a lunch counter. However, he reports on his naturalization records that he arrived in the United States with a different last name (Rocco Dieni) and so he is likely not the right person. Furthermore, even though we had access to complete records from that era, we could not locate a single Corresca living in the United States at that time, and from what we can surmise Corresca is not even an Italian surname. We thank Joe Price, director of the BYU Record Linking Lab, for confirming our Rocco is the right match.

5. Kalman Bilchick's story can be found at the Statue of Liberty–Ellis Island Foundation Oral History Library, https://heritage.statueofliberty.org /oral-history-library.

6. Ran Abramitzky, Leah Platt Boustan, and Katherine Eriksson, "A Nation of Immigrants: Assimilation and Economic Outcomes in the Age of Mass Migration." *Journal of Political Economy* 122, no. 3 (June 2014): 467–506. We extend the results in this paper to look at different outcomes and data-linking approaches. You can find these results at https://ranabr.people .stanford.edu/matching-codes.

7. Of course, it is possible that immigrants earned less than US-born workers in the same occupation. Scattered historical surveys suggest that immigrants received lower wages than the existing workforce in the same job title or occupation. Thus, it is possible that historically immigrants from poorer countries have fared even worse than we suspect. Timothy J. Hatton, "The Immigrant Assimilation Puzzle in Late Nineteenth-Century America," *Journal of Economic History* 57, no. 1 (March 1997): 34–62.

8. Other scholars have found similar evidence of slow mobility in payroll records. For example, at the Ford Motor Company, immigrants usually ended their careers in the same occupational positions where they began. Peter Ca-

tron, "Made in America? Immigrant Occupational Mobility in the First Half of the Twentieth Century," *American Journal of Sociology* 122, no. 2 (September 2016): 325–378.

9. David Escamilla-Guerrero, Edward Kosack, and Zachary Ward, "Life After Crossing the Border: Assimilation During the First Mexican Mass Migration," *Explorations in Economic History* 82 (October 2021).

10. Louis Daiberl's story can be found at the Statue of Liberty–Ellis Island Foundation Oral History Library, https://heritage.statueofliberty.org/oral-history-library.

11. Barack Obama, "Remarks by President Obama and Prime Minister Renzi of the Republic of Italy in Arrival Ceremony," Office of the Press Secretary, White House, October 18, 2016, https://obamawhitehouse.archives.gov/the-press-office/2016/10/18/remarks-president-obama-and-prime-minister-renzi-republic-italy-arrival.

12. Eli Watkins and Abby Phillip, "Trump Decries Immigrants from 'Shithole Countries' Coming to the US," CNN, January 12, 2018, https://www.cnn.com/2018/01/11/politics/immigrants-shithole-countries-trump/index.html.

13. Sarah Janecek, "The Bachelor Farmer and the Marriage Vote," *Minneapolis Star Tribune*, October 29, 2012, www.startribune.com/sarah-janecek-in2012-the-bachelor-farmer-and-the-marriage-vote/176332521/.

14. Eric Liu, *A Chinaman's Chance: One Family's Journey and the Chinese American Dream* (New York: PublicAffairs, 2016), 90–91.

15. Darren Lubotsky, "Chutes or Ladders? A Longitudinal Analysis of Immigrant Earnings," *Journal of Political Economy* 115, no. 5 (2007): 820–867; Harriet Orcutt Duleep and Daniel J. Dowhan, "Insights from Longitudinal Data on the Earnings Growth of U.S. Foreign-Born Men," *Demography* 39, no. 3 (August 2002): 485–506. The data for these modern studies comes from earnings records from the Social Security Administration, which keeps track of workers over their career.

16. Ellen Alexander Conley, *The Chosen Shore: Stories of Immigrants* (Berkeley: University of California Press, 2004), 139.

17. The first paper on recent immigrant arrivals raised alarms, suggesting that immigrants who arrived in the 1990s earned less and were not experiencing rapid earnings gains compared to immigrants who arrived before. See George J. Borjas, "The Slowdown in the Economic Assimilation of Immigrants: Aging and Cohort Effects Revisited Again," *Journal of Human Capital* 9, no. 4 (Winter 2015): 483–517. However, recent work that follows immigrants over time (rather than looking at all immigrants in the United States at one point in time) finds recent arrivals are catching up at the same rate as immigrants before. Giovanni Peri and Zachariah Rutledge,

"Revisiting Economic Assimilation of Mexican and Central Americans Immigrants in the United States," IZA Discussion Paper 12976, IZA Institute of Labor Economics, February 2020; Deborah Rho and Seth Sanders, "Immigrant Earnings Assimilation in the United States: A Panel Analysis," *Journal of Labor Economics* 39, no. 1 (January 2021): 37–78; Andrés Villarreal and Christopher R. Tamborini, "Immigrants' Economic Assimilation: Evidence from Longitudinal Earnings Records," *American Sociological Review* 83, no. 4 (August 2018): 686–715; Randall Akee, Jimmy Chin, and Daniel Crown, "Immigrant Earnings Assimilation in the Age of Modern Mass Migration" (unpublished manuscript, 2021). According to Rho and Sanders, to the extent that immigrant catch-up is slower today, the slowdown is due to the fact that a rising share of immigrants are highly educated, and educated immigrants already earn more than the US born and thus have less ground to make up. Some economists argue that immigrants would be converging even faster now than in the past if not for competition with the growing number of immigrant workers in the labor market that erases some of these gains. Christoph Albert, Albrecht Glitz, and Joan Llull, "Labor Market Competition and the Assimilation of Immigrants," IZA Discussion Paper 14641, IZA Institute of Labor Economics, August 2021.

18. Joseph P. Ferrie, "History Lessons: The End of American Exceptionalism? Mobility in the United States Since 1850," *Journal of Economic Perspectives* 19, no. 3 (September 2005): 199–215.

19. William J. Collins and Ariell Zimran, "Working Their Way Up? US Immigrants' Changing Labor Market Assimilation in the Age of Mass Migration," NBER Working Paper 26414, National Bureau of Economic Research, October 2019.

20. Barry R. Chiswick, "The Effect of Americanization on the Earnings of Foreign-Born Men," *Journal of Political Economy* 86, no. 5 (October 1978): 897–921.

21. George J. Borjas, "Assimilation, Changes in Cohort Quality, and the Earnings of Immigrants," *Journal of Labor Economics* 3, no. 4 (October 1985): 463–489.

22. For contemporary estimates of return migration, see Christian Dustmann and Joseph-Simon Görlach, "The Economics of Temporary Migrations," *Journal of Economic Literature* 54, no. 1 (March 2016): 98–136, and Jonathan J. Azose and Adrian E. Raftery, "Estimation of Emigration, Return Migration, and Transit Migration Between All Pairs of Countries," *Proceedings of the National Academy of Sciences* 116, no. 1 (January 2019): 116–122. For historical estimates, see John D. Gould, "European Inter-continental Emigration. The Road Home: Return Migration from the USA," *Journal of European Economic History* 9, no. 1 (Spring 1980): 41,

and Oriana Bandiera, Imran Rasul, and Martina Viarengo, "The Making of Modern America: Migratory Flows in the Age of Mass Migration," *Journal of Development Economics* 102 (May 2013): 23–47.

23. Mark Wyman, *Round-Trip to America: The Immigrants Return to Europe, 1880–1930* (Ithaca, NY: Cornell University Press, 1993), 80.

24. Wyman, 40.

25. Wyman, 129.

26. In modern data, there is some evidence that immigrants are more likely to return to their home country after a spell of unemployment, both in the United States and the Netherlands. Randall Akee and Maggie R. Jones, "Immigrants' Earnings Growth and Return Migration from the U.S.: Examining Their Determinants Using Linked Survey and Administrative Data," NBER Working Paper 25639, National Bureau of Economic Research, March 2019; Govert E. Bijwaard, Christian Schluter, and Jackline Wahba, "The Impact of Labor Market Dynamics on the Return Migration of Immigrants," *Review of Economics and Statistics* 96, no. 3 (July 2014): 483–494.

27. Our study was possible because in 1910 the Norwegian government added extra questions to their population census. One new question asked whether individuals had ever spent time in the United States; of those who had spent time in the United States, the census also asked when they left Norway, when they came back, and what occupation they held while abroad. Around 25 percent of Norwegian migrants ended up returning to Norway.

28. Wyman, *Round-Trip to America*, 139.

29. Mounir Karadja and Erik Prawitz, "Exit, Voice, and Political Change: Evidence from Swedish Mass Migration to the United States," *Journal of Political Economy* 127, no. 4 (August 2019): 1864–1925.

CHAPTER 5: BACKGROUND IS NOT DESTINY

1. Lora Kelley, "I Am the Portrait of Downward Mobility," *New York Times*, April 17, 2020, www.nytimes.com/interactive/2020/04/17/opinion/inequality-economy-1980.html.

2. The exceptional mobility that we find for the children of immigrants is not unique to the United States, but scholars have found that it is more common in New World countries like Canada and Australia than it is today in Europe. For France, Germany, and the UK, see Yann Algan, Christian Dustmann, Albrecht Glitz, and Alan Manning, "The Economic Situation of First and Second-Generation Immigrants in France, Germany and the United Kingdom," *Economic Journal* 120, no. 542 (February 2010): F4–F30. For Australia, see Nathan Deutscher, "What Drives Second Generation Success? The

Roles of Education, Culture, and Context," *Economic Inquiry* 58, no. 4 (October 2020): 1707–1730. For Canada, see Abdurrahman Aydemir, Wen-Hao Chen, and Miles Corak, "Intergenerational Earnings Mobility Among the Children of Canadian Immigrants," *Review of Economics and Statistics* 91, no. 2 (May 2009): 377–397. For the Netherlands, see Anne Gielen and Dinand Webbink, "Migration Selection and Assimilation: Evidence from the Great Migration from Surinam to the Netherlands," working paper, 2019. For Sweden, see Valentin Bolotnyy and Cristina Bratu, "The Intergenerational Mobility of Immigrants and the Native-Born: Evidence from Sweden," working paper, Harvard University, 2018.

3. National Academies of Sciences, Engineering, and Medicine, *The Economic and Fiscal Consequences of Immigration* (Washington, DC: National Academies Press, 2017).

4. Sociologists have documented similar patterns in terms of occupational mobility today. See Stephanie Potochnick and Matthew Hall, "U.S. Occupational Mobility of Children of Immigrants Based on Parents' Origin-Country Occupation," *Demography* 58, no.1 (February 2021): 219–245.

5. The modern data was shared by the Opportunity Insights research team. We report the details on differences between the historical and modern data in an academic paper. See Ran Abramitzky, Leah Platt Boustan, Elisa Jácome, and Santiago Pérez, "Intergenerational Mobility of Immigrants in the United States over Two Centuries," *American Economic Review* 111, no. 2 (February 2021): 580–608.

6. Nancy Rytina, "IRCA Legalization Effects: Lawful Permanent Residence and Naturalization Through 2001." Paper presented at The Effects of Immigrant Legalization Programs on the United States: Scientific Evidence on Immigrant Adaptation and Impacts on U.S. Economy and Society, The Cloister, Mary Woodward Lasker Center, NIH Main Campus, October 25, 2002, www.dhs.gov/xlibrary/assets/statistics/publications/irca0114int.pdf. Rytina reports that "the applicants [for legalization through IRCA] represented most legalization eligible aliens."

7. "Average, Median, Top 1%, and all United States Household Income Percentiles in 2020," Don't Quit Your Day Job, https://dqydj.com/average-median-top-household-income-percentiles/.

8. The rates of social mobility that we document here are not as high as in Canada, Australia, or Europe. Gary Solon, "Cross-Country Differences in Intergenerational Earnings Mobility," *Journal of Economic Perspectives* 16, no. 3 (September 2002): 59–66.

9. Debopam Bhattacharya and Bhashkar Mazumder, "A Nonparametric Analysis of Black-White Differences in Intergenerational Income Mobility in the United States," *Quantitative Economics* 2, no. 3 (November 2011):

335–379; William J. Collins and Marianne H. Wanamaker, "African American Intergenerational Economic Mobility Since 1880," NBER Working Paper 23395, National Bureau of Economic Research, May 2017.

10. See William J. Collins and Ariell Zimran, "The Economic Assimilation of Irish Famine Migrants to the United States," *Explorations in Economic History* 74 (2019): 1–22. The children of Mexican immigrants (not pictured on the graph) were one exception to the strong upward mobility of the past. Other scholars have found that the children of Mexican immigrants living in the United States by 1910 *fell behind* the children of US-born fathers who were raised at the same point in the income distribution. See Edward Kosack and Zachary Ward, "El Sueño Americano? The Generational Progress of Mexican Americans Prior to World War II," *Journal of Economic History* 80, no. 4 (December 2020): 961–995.

11. Tyler Anbinder, *Nativism and Slavery: The Northern Know Nothings and the Politics of the 1850s* (Oxford, UK: Oxford University Press, 1992); Marcella Alsan, Katherine Eriksson, and Gregory Niemesh, "Understanding the Success of the Know-Nothing Party," NBER Working Paper 28078, National Bureau of Economic Research, November 2020; Maeve Higgins, "Joe Biden, the Irishman," *New York Times*, January 28, 2021, www.nytimes.com/2021/01/28/opinion/joe-biden-irish-ireland.html.

12. Cormac Ó'Gráda, *The Great Irish Famine*, New Studies in Economic and Social History (Cambridge, UK: Cambridge University Press, 1995).

13. Philip Kasinitz, Mary C. Waters, John H. Mollenkopf, and Jennifer Holdaway, *Inheriting the City: The Children of Immigrants Come of Age* (New York: Russell Sage Foundation, 2009).

14. Raj Chetty and Nathaniel Hendren, "The Impacts of Neighborhoods on Intergenerational Mobility I: Childhood Exposure Effects," *Quarterly Journal of Economics* 133, no. 3 (August 2018): 1107–1162.

15. Hui Ren Tan, "A Different Land of Opportunity: The Geography of Intergenerational Mobility in the Early 20th-Century US," working paper, 2019; Dylan Shane Connor and Michael Storper, "The Changing Geography of Social Mobility in the United States," *Proceedings of the National Academy of Sciences* 117, no. 48 (December 2020): 30309–30317.

16. J. D. Vance, *Hillbilly Elegy: A Memoir of a Family and Culture in Crisis* (New York: Harper, 2016).

17. Indeed, economists have found that during the Great Recession immigrants were more likely than the US born to leave areas that were particularly hard hit to move elsewhere in search of new work. See Brian C. Cadena and Brian K. Kovak, "Immigrants Equilibrate Local Labor Markets: Evidence from the Great Recession," *American Economic Journal: Applied Economics* 8, no. 1 (January 2016): 257–290.

18. Peter Ganong and Daniel Shoag, "Why Has Regional Income Convergence in the US Declined?," *Journal of Urban Economics* 102 (November 2017): 76–90.

19. Christoph Albert and Joan Monras, "Immigration and Spatial Equilibrium: The Role of Expenditures in the Country of Origin," CEPR Discussion Paper 12842, Center for Economic Policy and Research, 2018.

20. Kirk Semple, "When the Kitchen Is Also a Bedroom: Overcrowding Worsens in New York," *New York Times*, February 29, 2016, www.nytimes .com/2016/03/01/nyregion/overcrowding-worsens-in-new-york-as-working -families-double-up.html.

21. Rebecca Lessem and Carl Sanders, "Immigrant Wage Growth in the United States: The Role of Occupational Upgrading," *International Economic Review* 61, no. 2 (January 2020): 941–972.

22. Rohan Alexander and Zachary Ward, "Age at Arrival and Assimilation During the Age of Mass Migration," *Journal of Economic History* 78, no. 3 (September 2018): 904–937.

23. Economist Nathaniel Hilger finds a similar pattern for the children of Asian immigrants in this period: they, too, earned more than the children of US-born parents despite having fewer years of schooling. Nathaniel Hilger, "Upward Mobility and Discrimination: The Case of Asian Americans," NBER Working Paper 22748, National Bureau of Economic Research, October 2016.

24. James J. Feigenbaum and Hui Ren Tan, "The Return to Education in the Mid-Twentieth Century: Evidence from Twins," *Journal of Economic History* 80, no. 4 (September 2020): 1101–1142.

25. "Hmong Oral History Project: Interview with Cher Vang," created February 3, 1992, Minnesota Historical Society, http://collections.mnhs.org /cms/display.php?irn=10445712.

26. Ellen Alexander Conley, *The Chosen Shore: Stories of Immigrants* (Berkeley: University of California Press, 2004), 164.

27. Not surprisingly, the children of immigrants from higher-income countries tend to earn more themselves. On this phenomenon, see Zachary Ward, "The Not-So-Hot Melting Pot: The Persistence of Outcomes for Descendants of the Age of Mass Migration," *American Economic Journal: Applied Economics* 12, no. 4 (October 2020): 73–102.

28. Trinidad and Tobago has a mixed race population: 35 percent is of Indian heritage, 34 percent is of African heritage, and 23 percent reports mixed heritage. See "Trinidad and Tobago," *The World Factbook*, Central Intelligence Agency, https://www.cia.gov/the-world-factbook/countries/trinidad -and-tobago/.

29. In general, family disadvantage has a stronger effect on the educational outcomes of boys than of girls. More broadly, there are larger Black-white

gaps in upward mobility for sons than for daughters. David Figlio, Krzysztof Karbownik, Jeffrey Roth, and Melanie Wasserman, "Family Disadvantage and the Gender Gap in Behavioral and Educational Outcomes," *American Economic Journal: Applied Economics* 11, no. 3 (July 2019): 338–381; Raj Chetty, Nathaniel Hendren, Maggie R. Jones, and Sonya R. Porter, "Race and Economic Opportunity in the United States: An Intergenerational Perspective," *Quarterly Journal of Economics* 135, no. 2 (May 2020): 711–783.

30. Kasinitz, Holdaway, Waters, and Mollenkopf, *Inheriting the City*, 130, 166.

31. Kasinitz, Holdaway, Waters, and Mollenkopf, 188.

32. Kasinitz, Holdaway, Waters, and Mollenkopf, 319.

33. Devah Pager, "The Mark of a Criminal Record," *American Journal of Sociology* 108, no. 5 (March 2003): 937–975.

34. George J. Borjas, "Ethnic Capital and Intergenerational Mobility," *Quarterly Journal of Economics* 107, no. 1 (February 1992): 123–150.

35. Noah Smith, "US Needs More Skilled Immigrants from Two Countries," *Bloomberg*, November 5, 2019, www.bloomberg.com/opinion/articles /2019-11-05/u-s-needs-more-skilled-immigrants-from-india-and-china.

36. The idea of the 1.5 generation was coined in Rubén Rumbaut, "The Agony of Exile: A Study of the Migration and Adaptation of Indochinese Refugee Adults and Children," in *Refugee Children: Theory, Research, and Services*, ed. Frederick L. Ahearn Jr. and Jean L. Athey (Baltimore: Johns Hopkins University Press, 1991), 53–91. He argued that children adjust much more rapidly and flexibly than adults to a new society, leading to an "adaptation lag" between the old and the young. This parent-child conflict can be especially acute for refugees but applies in some way to all immigrants. Scholars can't agree exactly where to draw the line on who is in the 1.5 generation, so researchers content themselves with a fuzzier definition of immigrants who arrive young enough to adapt quickly but old enough to have some experience with the home country, agreeing that "there is not a single-best, all-purpose representation" of this group. Quote is from Dowell Myers, Xin Gao, and Amon Emeka, "The Gradient of Immigrant Age-at-Arrival Effects on Socioeconomic Outcomes in the U.S.," *International Migration Review* 43, no. 1 (March 2009): 205–229.

37. Audrey Beck, Miles Corak, and Marta Tienda, "Age at Immigration and the Adult Attainments of Child Migrants to the United States," *Annals of the American Academy of Political and Social Science* 643, no. 1 (September 2012): 134–159.

38. Alejandro Portes, and Rubén G. Rumbaut, *Legacies: The Story of the Immigrant Second Generation* (Berkeley: University of California Press, 2001).

39. Ying Pan, "The Impact of Legal Status on Immigrants' Earnings and Human Capital: Evidence from the IRCA 1986," *Journal of Labor Research*

33, no. 2 (June 2012): 119–142; see also Sherrie A. Kossoudji and Deborah A. Cobb-Clark, "Coming Out of the Shadows: Learning About Legal Status and Wages from the Legalized Population," *Journal of Labor Economics* 20, no. 3 (July 2002): 598–628, and Joan Monras, Javier Vasquez-Grenno, and Ferran Elias, "Understanding the Effects of Granting Work Permits to Undocumented Immigrants" (unpublished manuscript, 2020).

40. Roberto G. Gonzales, preface to *Lives in Limbo: Undocumented and Coming of Age in America* (Berkeley: University of California Press, 2016).

41. Jose Antonio Vargas, "My Life as an Undocumented Immigrant," *New York Times*, June 22, 2011, https://www.nytimes.com/2011/06/26/magazine /my-life-as-an-undocumented-immigrant.html..

42. Gonzales, *Lives in Limbo*, 124.

43. Gonzales, 177.

44. Zachary Liscow and William Gui Woolston, "Does Legal Status Matter for Educational Choices? Evidence from Immigrant Teenagers," *American Law and Economics Review* 20, no. 2 (September 2018): 318–381.

45. Elira Kuka, Na'ama Shenhav, and Kevin Shih, "Do Human Capital Decisions Respond to the Returns to Education? Evidence from DACA," *American Economic Journal: Economic Policy* 12, no. 1 (February 2020): 293–324; Catalina Amuedo-Dorantes and Francisca Antman, "Schooling and Labor Market Effects of Temporary Authorization: Evidence from DACA," *Journal of Population Economics* 30, no. 1 (January 2017): 339–373.

46. D'Vera Cohn and Jeffrey S. Passel, "A Portrait of Unauthorized Immigrants in the United States," Pew Research Center, April 14, 2009, www.pewresearch.org/hispanic/2009/04/14/a-portrait-of-unauthorized -immigrants-in-the-united-states/.

CHAPTER 6: BECOMING AMERICAN

1. The quotations are from the stage directions at the beginning of Israel Zangwill, *The Melting-Pot* (Baltimore: Lord Baltimore, 1921; Project Gutenberg, 2007), www.gutenberg.org/files/23893/23893-h/23893-h.htm.

2. Zangwill.

3. "Israel Zangwill and the Melting Pot," Theodore Roosevelt Center, June 24, 2020, www.theodorerooseveltcenter.org/Blog/Item/Melting%20Pot.

4. Joseph Bucklin Bishop, ed., *Theodore Roosevelt and His Time Shown in His Own Letters*, vol. 2 of 2 (New York: Charles Scribner's Sons, 1920).

5. "Gordon, Milton Myron 1918–," Encyclopedia.com, September 22, 2021, www.encyclopedia.com/arts/educational-magazines/gordon-milton -myron-1918.

6. Milton Myron Gordon, *Assimilation in American Life: The Role of Race, Religion, and National Origins* (New York: Oxford University Press, 1964).

7. Alejandro Portes and Min Zhou, "The New Second Generation: Segmented Assimilation and Its Variants," *Annals of the American Academy of Political and Social Science* 530, no. 1 (November 1993): 7496; Alejandro Portes, Patricia Fernández-Kelly, and William Haller, "Segmented Assimilation on the Ground: The New Second Generation in Early Adulthood," *Ethnic and Racial Studies* 28, no. 6 (2005): 1000–1040; Mary C. Waters, Van C. Tran, Philip Kasinitz, and John H. Mollenkopf, "Segmented Assimilation Revisited: Types of Acculturation and Socioeconomic Mobility in Young Adulthood," *Ethnic and Racial Studies* 33, no. 7 (July 2010): 1168–1193.

8. We use the term "assimilation" interchangeably with "incorporation" or "integration." See Laila Lalami, "What Does It Take to 'Assimilate' in America?," *New York Times*, August 1, 2017, www.nytimes.com/2017/08/01/magazine/what-does-it-take-to-assimilate-in-america.html.

9. Richard Alba and Victor Nee, "Rethinking Assimilation Theory for a New Era of Immigration," *International Migration Review* 31, no. 4 (December 1997): 826–874; Richard Alba and Victor Nee, *Remaking the American Mainstream: Assimilation and Contemporary Immigration* (Cambridge, MA: Harvard University Press, 2003). See also Russell A. Kazal, "Revisiting Assimilation: The Rise, Fall, and Reappraisal of a Concept in American Ethnic History," *American Historical Review* 100, no. 2 (April 1995): 437–471; Mary C. Waters and Tomás R. Jiménez, "Assessing Immigrant Assimilation: New Empirical and Theoretical Challenges," *Annual Review of Sociology* 31, no. 1 (August 2005): 105–125.

10. Tomás Jiménez, *The Other Side of Assimilation: How Immigrants Are Changing American Life* (Oakland: University of California Press, 2017).

11. Eric Liu, *A Chinaman's Chance: One Family's Journey and the Chinese American Dream* (New York: PublicAffairs, 2014), 86–87.

12. David Miller, *Strangers in Our Midst: The Political Philosophy of Immigration* (Cambridge, MA: Harvard University Press, 2016), 9.

13. Alex Nowrasteh and Andrew Forrester, "Immigrants Recognize American Greatness: Immigrants and Their Descendants Are Patriotic and Trust America's Governing Institutions," Cato Institute Immigration Research and Policy Brief 10 (February 2019).

14. Rush Limbaugh, "Hyphenated Americans and Immigration," *The Rush Limbaugh Show*, March 31, 2014, www.rushlimbaugh.com/daily/2014/03/31/hyphenated_americans_and_immigration/.

15. Sociologists have documented rapid assimilation for the second generation in the contemporary period, using both qualitative and quantitative

methods. Julie Park and Dowell Myers, "Intergenerational Mobility in the Post-1965 Immigration Era: Estimates by an Immigrant Generation Cohort Method," *Demography* 47 (May 2010): 369–392; Philip Kasinitz, John H. Mollenkopf, Mary C. Waters, and Jennifer Holdaway, *Inheriting the City: The Children of Immigrants Come of Age* (New York: Russell Sage Foundation, 2009). For additional work on the comparison of assimilation rates between the past and the present, see Jacob L. Vigdor, *From Immigrants to Americans: The Rise and Fall of Fitting In* (New York: Rowman & Littlefield, 2010).

16. "Immigration," Gallup, https://news.gallup.com/poll/1660/immigration .aspx.

17. Tomás Jiménez, *The Other Side of Assimilation*, 191.

18. Christian Dustmann and Francesca Fabbri, "Language Proficiency and Labour Market Performance of Immigrants in the UK," *Economic Journal* 113, no. 489 (July 2003): 695–717; Hoyt Bleakley and Aimee Chin, "Language Skills and Earnings: Evidence from Childhood Immigrants," *Review of Economics and Statistics* 86, no. 2 (May 2004): 481–496; Jacob Nielsen Arendt, Iben Bolvig, Mette Foged, Linea Hasager, and Giovanni Peri, "Integrating Refugees: Language Training or Work-First Incentives?" NBER Working Paper 26834, National Bureau of Economic Research, March 2020.

19. Alfredo Corchado, *Homelands: Four Friends, Two Countries, and the Fate of the Great Mexican-American Migration* (London: Bloomsbury, 2018), 279.

20. Czeslaw Milosz, *Native Realm: A Search for Self-Definition* (New York: Farrar, Straus and Giroux, 2002 [orig. pub. 1968]), 22, 91, 138.

21. Ran Abramitzky, Leah Platt Boustan, and Katherine Eriksson, "Cultural Assimilation During the Age of Mass Migration," NBER Working Paper 22381, National Bureau of Economic Research, July 2016.

22. Our own calculations from the 2019 American Community Survey.

23. Ran Abramitzky, Leah Boustan, Peter Catron, Dylan Connor, and Rob Voigt, "Refugees without Assistance: English-Language Attainment and Economic Outcomes in the Early Twentieth Century," *SocArXiv*, December 14, 2021, https://doi.org/10.31235/osf.io/429jp.

24. Victor Kuperman, Hans Stadthagen-Gonzalez, and Marc Brysbaert, "Age-of-Acquisition Ratings for 30,000 English Words," *Behavior Research Methods* 44, no. 4 (December 2012): 978–990.

25. Nick Miroff, "Trump Cuts Refugee Cap to Lowest Level Ever, Depicts Them on Campaign Trail as a Threat and Burden," *Washington Post*, October 1, 2020, www.washingtonpost.com/immigration/trump-cuts-refugee -cap/2020/10/01/a5113b62-03ed-11eb-8879-7663b816bfa5_story.html; Charles Davis, "A New Low: In Biden's First Year, the US Is on Track to Resettle Even Fewer Refugees Than Under Trump," *Business Insider*, August 12, 2021, https://news.yahoo.com/low-bidens-first-us-track-192826743.html.

26. Michelle Hackman, "Afghan Refugees in the U.S.: How They're Vetted, Where They're Going and How to Help," *Wall Street Journal*, September 3, 2021, www.wsj.com/articles/afghan-refugees-in-the-u-s-how-theyre-vetted -where-theyre-going-and-how-to-help-11630677004.

27. Emilie Adams's and Wadih Zogby's stories can be found at the Statue of Liberty–Ellis Island Foundation Oral History Library, https://heritage .statueofliberty.org/oral-history-library.

28. Alice Fishman's story can be found at the Statue of Liberty–Ellis Island Foundation Oral History Library, https://heritage.statueofliberty.org /oral-history-library.

29. Kalena E. Cortes, "Are Refugees Different from Economic Immigrants? Some Empirical Evidence on the Heterogeneity of Immigrant Groups in the United States," *Review of Economics and Statistics* 86, no. 2 (May 2004): 465–480; Jérôme Adda, Christian Dustmann, and Joseph-Simon Görlach, "The Dynamics of Return Migration, Human Capital Accumulation, and Wage Assimilation," IZA Discussion Paper 14333, IZA Institute of Labor Economics, 2021; Sascha O. Becker, Irena Grosfeld, Pauline Grosjean, Nico Voigtländer, and Ekaterina Zhuravskaya, "Forced Migration and Human Capital: Evidence from Post-WWII Population Transfers," *American Economic Review* 110, no. 5 (May 2020): 1430–1463.

30. Cevat Giray Aksoy and Panu Poutvaara, "Refugees' and Irregular Migrants' Self-Selection into Europe: Who Migrates Where?," IZA Discussion Paper 12800, IZA Institute of Labor Economics, 2019.

31. Ellen Alexander Conley, *The Chosen Shore: Stories of Immigrants* (Berkeley: University of California Press, 2004), 46–61.

32. Margaret Besheer, "UN: Many Syrian Refugees Educated, Seeking Better Lives," Voice of America, December 8, 2015, www.voanews.com/a/un -many-syrian-refugees-educated-seeking-better-lives/3093871.html.

33. Aimee Chin and Kalena E. Cortes, "The Refugee/Asylum Seeker," in *Handbook of the Economics of International Migration*, vol. 1A, ed. Barry R. Chiswick and Paul W. Miller (Amsterdam: North-Holland, 2015), 585–658.

34. David M. Cutler, Edward L. Glaeser, and Jacob L. Vigdor, "Is the Melting Pot Still Hot? Explaining the Resurgence of Immigrant Segregation," *Review of Economics and Statistics* 90, no. 3 (February 2008): 478–497.

35. Katherine Eriksson and Zachary Ward, "The Residential Segregation of Immigrants in the United States from 1850 to 1940," *Journal of Economic History* 79, no. 4 (December 2019): 989–1026.

36. Madhulika Shankar Khandelwal, *Becoming American, Being Indian: An Immigrant Community in New York City* (Ithaca, NY: Cornell University Press, 2002), 15.

37. Statue of Liberty–Ellis Island Foundation Oral History Library, https://heritage.statueofliberty.org/oral-history-library.

38. In some cases, immigrant neighborhoods emerge out of necessity, when immigrant families face discrimination trying to buy or rent property in more integrated areas. Puente, a neighborhood east of Los Angeles, has long been settled by Mexican Americans who were excluded from other areas. Leticia Mendoza, whose family moved to Southern California from Mexico in the 1880s, remembers that "we [Mexican Americans] had a barrio, and it was from Central up to Valley Boulevard. We were not allowed to buy a home outside of Central. We were all segregated. We all lived in this barrio, and we all knew each other." In the 1920s and 1930s, students with Mexican and Japanese ancestry were sent to segregated schools. The deeds to some houses explicitly forbade the property from ever being transferred to certain groups—often to Black buyers, but sometimes also to Jews and members of other immigrant groups. Quote from Gilda L. Ochoa, *Becoming Neighbors in a Mexican American Community: Power, Conflict, and Solidarity* (Austin: University of Texas Press, 2004), 5051.

39. Lawrence Bobo and Camille L. Zubrinsky, "Attitudes on Residential Integration: Perceived Status Differences, Mere In-Group Preference, or Racial Prejudice?" *Social Forces* 74, no. 3 (March 1996): 883–909; Camille Zubrinsky Charles, "Neighborhood Racial-Composition Preferences: Evidence from a Multiethnic Metropolis," *Social Problems* 47, no. 3 (August 2000): 379–407; William A. V. Clark, "Ethnic Preferences and Ethnic Perceptions in Multi-Ethnic Settings," *Urban Geography* 23, no. 3 (2002): 237–256.

40. Cutler, Glaeser, and Vigdor, "Is the Melting Pot Still Hot?"

41. Jennifer Lee, *Civility in the City: Blacks, Jews, and Koreans in Urban America* (Cambridge, MA: Harvard University Press, 2002), 36–37.

42. Illsoo Kim, *New Urban Immigrants: The Korean Community in New York* (Princeton: Princeton University Press, 2014), 226.

43. Kim, 232.

44. Christian Dustmann, Albert Glitz, Uta Schönberg, and Herbert Brücker, "Referral-Based Job Search Networks," *Review of Economic Studies* 83, no. 2 (2016): 514–546; Kaivan Munshi, "Networks in the Modern Economy: Mexican Migrants in the U.S. Labor Market," *Quarterly Journal of Economics* 118, no. 2 (May 2003): 549–599.

45. Kasinitz, Mollenkopf, Waters, and Holdaway, *Inheriting the City*, 182.

46. Ran Abramitzky, Leah Platt Boustan, and Dylan Connor, "Leaving the Enclave: Historical Evidence on Immigrant Mobility from the Industrial Removal Office," NBER Working Paper 27372, National Bureau of Economic Research, June 2020. However, we note that the case of refugees in Scandinavia suggests that immigrants benefit from living near *at least a*

few others from their home country. Refugees who arrived in Sweden and Denmark in the mid-1980s from countries like Iran, Sri Lanka, and Lebanon were assigned to cities and towns all over the country to avoid overconcentration in the largest cities of Stockholm and Copenhagen. Refugees who were assigned to live near fellow countrymen fared better than refugees who were assigned to be alone. See Anna Piil Damm, "Ethnic Enclaves and Immigrant Labor Market Outcomes: Quasi-Experimental Evidence," *Journal of Labor Economics* 27, no. 2 (April 2009): 281–314; Per-Anders Edin, Peter Fredriksson, and Olof Åslund, "Ethnic Enclaves and the Economic Success of Immigrants: Evidence from a Natural Experiment," *Quarterly Journal of Economics* 118, no. 1 (February 2003): 329–357.

47. Graham Hodges, "Lower East Side," in *The Encyclopedia of New York City*, 2nd ed., ed. Kenneth T. Jackson (New Haven, CT: Yale University Press, 2010).

48. Claudia D. Goldin and Lawrence F. Katz, *The Race Between Education and Technology* (Cambridge, MA: Harvard University Press, 2009).

49. Zhenchao Qian and Daniel T. Lichter, "Social Boundaries and Marital Assimilation: Interpreting Trends in Racial and Ethnic Intermarriage," *American Sociological Review* 72, no. 1 (February 2007): 68–94.

50. Dan Rodríguez-García, "Intermarriage and Integration Revisited: International Experiences and Cross-Disciplinary Approaches," *Annals of the American Academy of Political and Social Science* 662, no. 1 (November 2015): 8–36. For a recent survey of the literature, see Alícia Adserà and Ana Ferrer, "Immigrants and Demography: Marriage, Divorce, and Fertility," in *Handbook of the Economics of International Migration*, vol. 1A, ed. Barry R. Chiswick and Paul W. Miller (Amsterdam: North-Holland, 2015), 315–374.

51. In a mechanical sense, intermarriage rates might be lower for smaller immigrant groups, or for groups that send more men than women to the United States. Yet, as this paper shows, adjusting for these factors does not change the basic patterns. See Abramitzky, Boustan, and Eriksson, "Cultural Assimilation During the Age of Mass Migration."

52. Joel Perlmann and Mary C. Waters, "Intermarriage Then and Now: Race, Generation, and the Changing Meaning of Marriage," in *Not Just Black and White: Historical and Contemporary Perspectives on Immigration, Race and Ethnicity in the US*, ed. Nancy Foner and George Frederickson (New York: Russell Sage Foundation, 2004), 262–277.

53. Barry R. Chiswick and Christina Houseworth, "Ethnic Intermarriage Among Immigrants: Human Capital and Assortative Mating," *Review of Economics of the Household* 9, no. 2 (June 2011): 149–180.

54. Pratikshya Bohra-Mishra and Douglas S. Massey, "Intermarriage Among New Immigrants in the USA," *Ethnic and Racial Studies* 38, no. 5 (2015): 734–758.

55. Conley, *The Chosen Shore*, 82–83.

56. Kasinitz, Mollenkopf, Waters, and Holdaway, *Inheriting the City*, 232.

57. Ryan Nobles and Donald Judd, "Georgia Republican Senator Willfully Mispronounces Kamala Harris' Name at Trump Rally," CNN, October 17, 2020, https://www.cnn.com/2020/10/16/politics/david-perdue-kamala-harris/index.html.

58. Maya was around the nine-hundredth most common name in 1967 when Maya Harris was born, but rose to the sixty-first most common name in 2019. See "Maya," BabyNames.com, www.babynames.com/name/maya.

59. One study finds that immigrant families who had access to early radio broadcasts in their city were more likely to pick American-sounding names for their kids, including the names of famous baseball players. Gianluca Russo, "Mass Media and Cultural Assimilation: Broadcasting the American Dream on the Radio" (unpublished manuscript, 2020).

60. Robert C. Smith, "Mexicans: Social, Educational, Economic, and Political Problems and Prospects in New York," in *New Immigrants in New York*, ed. Nancy Foner (New York: Columbia University Press, 2001), 295.

61. Reyna Grande, *The Distance Between Us: A Memoir* (New York: Simon and Schuster, 2012), 171–172.

62. Wajahat Ali, "For Muslim-Americans, Baby Aidan or Baby Muhammad?," *New York Times*, October 3, 2015, www.nytimes.com/2015/10/04/opinion/sunday/for-muslim-americans-baby-aidan-or-baby-muhammad.html.

63. Ran Abramitzky, Leah Boustan, and Katherine Eriksson, "Do Immigrants Assimilate More Slowly Today Than in the Past?" *American Economic Review: Insights* 2, no. 1 (March 2020): 125–141.

64. Vasiliki Fouka, "How Do Immigrants Respond to Discrimination? The Case of Germans in the US During World War I," *American Political Science Review* 113, no. 2 (March 2019): 405–422; Martin Hugo Saavedra, "Kenji or Kenneth? Pearl Harbor and Japanese-American Assimilation," *Journal of Economic Behavior and Organization* 185 (2021): 602–624; Diane S. Lauderdale, "Birth Outcomes for Arabic-Named Women in California Before and After September 11," *Demography* 43, no. 1 (February 2006): 185–201.

65. Philip Oreopoulos, "Why Do Skilled Immigrants Struggle in the Labor Market? A Field Experiment with Thirteen Thousand Resumes," *American Economic Journal: Economic Policy* 3, no. 4 (November 2011): 148–171.

66. Ran Abramitzky, Leah Boustan, Katherine Eriksson, and Stephanie Hao, "Discrimination and the Returns to Cultural Assimilation in the Age of Mass Migration," *AEA Papers and Proceedings* 110 (May 2020): 340–346.

67. This policy of forced assimilation backfired: German American students who grew up under the bans in Indiana and Ohio were *less* likely to

assimilate than their counterparts in neighboring states. Instead, German immigrants in Indiana and Ohio were more likely to marry a fellow German spouse and to give their children German names. Vasiliki Fouka, "Backlash: The Unintended Effects of Language Prohibition in U.S. Schools After World War I," *Review of Economic Studies* 87, no. 1 (January 2020): 204–239.

68. Laws requiring English instruction in public school were somewhat successful at encouraging literacy, but had limited effects on fostering American identity. Immigrant children attending English-only schools were more likely to learn to read, particularly if their own parents could not speak English, but they were no more likely to naturalize as US citizens later in life. See Adriana Lleras-Muney and Allison Shertzer, "Did the Americanization Movement Succeed? An Evaluation of the Effect of English-Only and Compulsory Schooling Laws on Immigrants," *American Economic Journal: Economic Policy* 7, no. 3 (August 2015): 258–290.

CHAPTER 7: DOES IMMIGRANT SUCCESS HARM THE US BORN?

1. Philip Bump, "A Reporter Pressed the White House for Data. That's When Things Got Tense," *Washington Post*, August 2, 2017, www.washington post.com/news/politics/wp/2017/08/02/a-reporter-pressed-the-white-house -for-data-thats-when-things-got-tense/.

2. Janet Adamy and Anthony DeBarros, "U.S. Population Growth, an Economic Driver, Grinds to a Halt," *Wall Street Journal*, July 25, 2021, www .wsj.com/articles/u-s-population-growth-slows-birth-rate-decline-economic -risk-11627231536.

3. Jens Manuel Krogstad, Mark Hugo Lopez, and Jeffrey S. Passel, "A Majority of Americans Say Immigrants Mostly Fill Jobs U.S. Citizens Do Not Want," Pew Research Center, June 10, 2020, www.pewresearch.org/fact-tank /2020/06/10/a-majority-of-americans-say-immigrants-mostly-fill-jobs-u-s -citizens-do-not-want/.

4. "Insights Animation: The Economic Benefits of Immigration," Yale School of Management, video, 3:38, May 23, 2017, https://youtu.be /6nCY2Ncvk-g.

5. Patricia Cortes, "The Effect of Low-Skilled Immigration on US Prices: Evidence from CPI Data," *Journal of Political Economy* 116, no. 3 (June 2008): 381–422.

6. Bradley Jones, "Majority of Americans Continue to Say Immigrants Strengthen the U.S.," Pew Research Center, January 31, 2019, www .pewresearch.org/fact-tank/2019/01/31/majority-of-americans-continue-to -say-immigrants-strengthen-the-u-s/.

7. "Donald Trump Presidential Campaign Announcement Full Speech (C-SPAN)," C-SPAN, video, 47:09, June 16, 2017, https://youtu.be /apjNfkysjbM.

8. David Stradling, *Cincinnati: From River City to Highway Metropolis* (Charleston, SC: Arcadia, 2003), 51; Carol Poh Miller and Robert Anthony Wheeler, *Cleveland: A Concise History, 1796–1996*, vol. 1 (Bloomington: Indiana University Press, 1997), 81.

9. Our calculations from historical census data. We use the micro-data from IPUMS from 1900 onward and the published tabulations in 1890 because the micro-data was lost in that year.

10. After July 1, 1927, the allocation of quota slots was shifted again to a "national origins" formula based on estimates of the national origins of the white population of the United States in 1790. This rule further restricted immigration from Southern and Eastern European countries and favored immigration from the United Kingdom and Ireland over Germany and Scandinavia. See Desmond S. King, *Making Americans: Immigration, Race, and the Origins of the Diverse Democracy* (Cambridge, MA: Harvard University Press, 2002).

11. Gary Richardson, "The Origins of Anti-immigrant Sentiments: Evidence from the Heartland in the Age of Mass Migration," *BE Journal of Economic Analysis & Policy* 5, no. 1 (June 2005): 1–48.

12. "Immigration Restriction," Harry Laughlin and Eugenics: A Selection of Historical Objects from Harry H. Laughlin Papers, Truman State University, https://historyofeugenics.truman.edu/altering-lives/immigration -restriction/.

13. Jeremiah Jenks and W. Jett Lauck, *The Immigration Problem: A Study of American Immigration Conditions and Needs* (New York: Funk & Wagnalls, 1922), 195.

14. Edward Alfred Steiner, *The Immigrant Tide: Its Ebb and Flow* (New York: Fleming H. Revell, 1909), 190–191.

15. Peter H. Wang, "Farmers and the Immigration Act of 1924," *Agricultural History* 49, no. 4 (October 1975): 647–652.

16. Edith Abbott, "Immigration Restriction—Economic Results and Prospects," *American Economic Review* 17, no. 1 (March 1927): 127–132.

17. Paul H. Douglas, *Real Wages in the United States, 1890–1926* (Boston: Houghton Mifflin, 1930), 247.

18. David Card, "Immigrant Inflows, Native Outflows, and the Local Labor Market Impacts of Higher Immigration," *Journal of Labor Economics* 19, no. 1 (January 2001): 22–64.

19. You can watch an animated video that illustrates this research strategy: "What Is the Economic Impact of Closing the Border?," Econimate, video, 7:08, March 30, 2020, https://youtu.be/_uOORAsQ6nE.

20. Ran Abramitzky, Philipp Ager, Leah Platt Boustan, Elior Cohen, and Casper W. Hansen, "The Effects of Immigration on the Economy: Lessons from the 1920s Border Closure," *American Economic Journal: Applied Economics*, forthcoming. See also Marco Tabellini, "Gifts of the Immigrants, Woes of the Natives: Lessons from the Age of Mass Migration," *Review of Economic Studies* 87, no. 1 (January 2020): 454–486.

21. In Chicago, immigrants were replaced with "blacks and Mexicans . . . [contributing to] the increasing presence of these two groups within Chicago's factories during the decade [1920–1929]" (Lizabeth Cohen, *Making a New Deal: Industrial Workers in Chicago, 1919–1939* [Cambridge, UK: Cambridge University Press, 1990], 165). Mexican immigrants also pursued opportunities in rural areas. "After World War I, Chicanos or Mexican-Americans gradually replaced Russian Germans in the sugar beet fields as migrant workers" (Frederick C. Luebke, "Ethnic Group Settlement on the Great Plains," *Western Historical Quarterly* 8, no. 4 [October 1977]: 421).

22. William J. Collins, "When the Tide Turned: Immigration and the Delay of the Great Black Migration," *Journal of Economic History* 57, no. 3 (September 1997): 607–632.

23. Byron Lew and Bruce Cater, "Farm Mechanization on an Otherwise 'Featureless' Plain: Tractors on the Northern Great Plains and Immigration Policy of the 1920s," *Cliometrica* 12, no. 2 (May 2018): 181–218.

24. Jonathan R. Clark, Robert S. Huckman, and Bradley R. Staats, "Learning from Customers: Individual and Organizational Effects in Outsourced Radiological Services," *Organization Science* 24, no. 5 (September–October 2013): 1539–1557.

25. Binyamin Appelbaum, "With Fewer Immigrants, More Jobs? Not So, Economists Say," *New York Times*, August 4, 2017, www.nytimes.com/2017/08/03/us/politics/legal-immigration-jobs-economy.html.

26. Dustin McLochlin, "Whom We Shall Welcome: Immigration Reform During the Great Society" (PhD diss., Bowling Green State University, 2014), 107.

27. "New Door for Braceros?," *New York Times*, December 9, 1964, www.nytimes.com/1964/12/09/archives/new-door-for-braceros.html.

28. "California Meets Snag on Braceros; Plan to Replace Mexicans on Farms Is Set Back," *New York Times*, December 31, 1964, www.nytimes.com/1965/01/01/archives/california-meets-snag-on-braceros-plan-to-replace-mexicans-on-farms.html.

29. Julie Benell to Lyndon Johnson, January 22, 1965, LBJ Library, WHCF LA Box 18, LA 5 12/26/64–3/9/65.

30. Philip L. Martin, *Promise Unfulfilled: Unions, Immigration, and the Farm Workers* (Ithaca, NY: Cornell University Press, 2003).

31. Michael A. Clemens, Ethan G. Lewis, and Hannah M. Postel, "Immigration Restrictions as Active Labor Market Policy: Evidence from the Mexican Bracero Exclusion," *American Economic Review* 108, no. 6 (June 2018): 1468–1487.

32. Clemens, Lewis, and Postel, 1468–1487.

33. Donna Vestal, "A Century of Produce: The First-Aisle Department," *The Packer*, July 2, 2019 (orig. pub. 1993), www.thepacker.com/news/industry/century-produce-first-aisle-department.

34. Douglas S. Massey and Karen A. Pren, "Unintended Consequences of US Immigration Policy: Explaining the Post-1965 Surge from Latin America," *Population and Development Review* 38, no. 1 (March 2012): 1–29.

35. Jens Manuel Krogstad, Jeffrey S. Passel, and D'Vera Cohn, "5 Facts About Illegal Immigration in the U.S.," Pew Research Center, June 12, 2019, www.pewresearch.org/fact-tank/2019/06/12/5-facts-about-illegal-immigration-in-the-u-s/.

36. Daniel Politi, "Donald Trump in Phoenix: Mexicans Are 'Taking Our Jobs' and 'Killing Us,'" *Slate*, July 12, 2015, https://slate.com/news-and-politics/2015/07/donald-trump-in-phoenix-mexicans-are-taking-our-jobs-and-killing-us.html.

37. Douglas S. Massey, Jorge Durand, and Karen A. Pren, "Why Border Enforcement Backfired," *American Journal of Sociology* 121, no. 5 (March 2016): 1557–1600.

38. John Gramlich and Luis Noe-Bustamante, "What's Happening at the U.S.-Mexico Border in 5 Charts," Pew Research Center, November 1, 2019, www.pewresearch.org/fact-tank/2019/11/01/whats-happening-at-the-u-s-mexico-border-in-5-charts/.

39. Ted Robbins, "San Diego Fence Provides Lessons in Border Control," NPR, April 6, 2006, www.npr.org/templates/story/story.php?storyId=5323928.

40. Treb Allen, Cauê de Castro Dobbin, and Melanie Morten, "Border Walls," NBER Working Paper 25267, National Bureau of Economic Research, November 2018. One interesting element of this study is how the research team was able to study illegal entry, given that undocumented migrants try to stay hidden and don't show up in official databases unless they are apprehended by border patrol. All Mexican immigrants—whether legal or illegal—are eligible to get an identification card called a *matrícula consular* at the Mexican consulate once they arrive in the United States. The card lists current place of residence in the United States and city or village of origin in Mexico. Data from registrations for consular cards allowed these scholars to count the number of Mexican immigrants arriving in each US city from each Mexican place of origin.

41. Robbins, "San Diego Fence Provides Lessons."

42. For an estimate of the number of undocumented Mexican immigrants in the United States, see Ana Gonzales-Barrera and Jens Manuel Krogstad, "What We Know About Illegal Immigration from Mexico," Pew Research Center, June 28, 2019, www.pewresearch.org/fact-tank/2019/06/28/what-we-know-about-illegal-immigration-from-mexico/.

43. Ana Raquel Minian, *Undocumented Lives: The Untold Story of Mexican Migration* (Cambridge, MA: Harvard University Press, 2018); Massey, Pren, and Durand, "Why Border Enforcement Backfired." See also Douglas S. Massey, Jorge Durand, and Nolan J. Malone, *Beyond Smoke and Mirrors: Mexican Immigration in an Era of Economic Integration* (New York: Russell Sage Foundation, 2002).

44. Manuela Angelucci, "US Border Enforcement and the Net Flow of Mexican Illegal Migration," *Economic Development and Cultural Change* 60, no. 2 (January 2012): 311–357; Rebecca Lessem, "Mexico-US Immigration: Effects of Wages and Border Enforcement," *Review of Economic Studies* 85, no. 4 (October 2018): 2353–2388.

45. Gonzales-Barrera and Krogstad, "What We Know About Illegal Immigration."

46. Story from José Manuel Garcia, *Voices from Mariel: Oral Histories of the 1980 Cuban Boatlift* (Gainesville: University Press of Florida, 2018), 36–42.

47. "Mariel Boatlift," GlobalSecurity.org, www.globalsecurity.org/military/ops/mariel-boatlift.htm.

48. Story from Garcia, *Voices from Mariel*, 120.

49. Nathaniel Sheppard Jr., "Economic Standings Reflect Attitudes on Cuban Refugees; Asks for Expulsion Money Changes Attitudes Economic Blessing," *New York Times*, June 30, 1980, www.nytimes.com/1980/06/30/archives/economic-standings-reflect-attitudes-on-cuban-refugees-asks-for.html.

50. David Card, "The Impact of the Mariel Boatlift on the Miami Labor Market," *ILR Review* 43, no. 2 (January 1990): 245–257. For a less optimistic view on the effect of immigrant arrivals on Black workers, see: George J. Borjas, Jeffrey Grogger, and Gordon H. Hanson, "Immigration and the Economic Status of African-American Men," *Economica* 77, no. 306 (April 2010): 255–282. This paper is based on immigrant arrivals into education-age cells.

51. George J. Borjas, "The Wage Impact of the Marielitos: A Reappraisal." *ILR Review* 70, no. 5 (October 2017): 1077–1110.

52. Giovanni Peri and Vasil Yasenov, "The Labor Market Effects of a Refugee Wave: Synthetic Control Method Meets the Mariel Boatlift," *Journal of Human Resources* 54, no. 2 (2019): 267–309.

53. Michael A. Clemens and Jennifer Hunt, "The Labor Market Effects of Refugee Waves: Reconciling Conflicting Results," *ILR Review* 72, no. 4 (2019): 818–857.

54. Story from Garcia, *Voices from Mariel*, 62–63.

55. Ethan Lewis, "How Did the Miami Labor Market Absorb the Mariel Immigrants?" Working Paper 04-3, Federal Reserve Bank of Philadelphia, January 2004.

56. Jens Manuel Krogstad and Jynnah Radford, "Education Levels of U.S. Immigrants Are on the Rise," Pew Research Center, September 14, 2018, www.pewresearch.org/fact-tank/2018/09/14/education-levels-of-u-s-immigrants-are-on-the-rise/.

57. Shai Bernstein, Rebecca Diamond, Timothy McQuade, and Beatriz Pousada, "The Contribution of High-Skilled Immigrants to Innovation in the United States," Working Paper 3748, Stanford Graduate School of Business, November 2018.

58. Jennifer Hunt, "Which Immigrants Are Most Innovative and Entrepreneurial? Distinctions by Entry Visa," *Journal of Labor Economics* 29, no. 3 (July 2011): 417–457.

59. Jens Hainmueller and Michael J. Hiscox, "Attitudes Toward Highly Skilled and Low-Skilled Immigration: Evidence from a Survey Experiment," *American Political Science Review* 104, no. 1 (March 2010): 61–84.

60. William R. Kerr and William F. Lincoln, "The Supply Side of Innovation: H-1B Visa Reforms and U.S. Ethnic Invention," *Journal of Labor Economics* 28, no. 3 (July 2010): 473–508.

61. George J. Borjas and Kirk B. Doran, "The Collapse of the Soviet Union and the Productivity of American Mathematicians," *Quarterly Journal of Economics* 127, no. 3 (August 2012): 1143–1203.

62. Gina Kolata, "Soviet Scientists Flock to U.S., Acting as Tonic for Colleges," *New York Times*, May 8, 1990, www.nytimes.com/1990/05/08/us/soviet-scientists-flock-to-us-acting-as-tonic-for-colleges.html.

63. Stan Atshuller, "The Rise of Quantitative Hedge Funds," Novus, December 9, 2016, www.novus.com/blog/rise-quant-hedge-funds; Gregory Zuckerman and Bradley Hope, "The Quants Run Wall Street Now," *Wall Street Journal*, May 21, 2017, www.wsj.com/articles/the-quants-run-wall-street-now-1495389108.

64. Petra Moser and Shmuel San, "Immigration, Science, and Invention. Lessons from the Quota Acts," working paper, SSRN, March 2020.

65. D. Nachmansohn, *German-Jewish Pioneers in Science 1900–1933: Highlights in Atomic Physics, Chemistry, and Biochemistry* (New York: Springer-Verlag, 1979).

66. Henry Cabot Lodge, "Lynch Law and Unrestricted Immigration," *North American Review* 152, no. 414 (May 1891): 602–612.

67. "Remarks by President Trump in Briefing on Keeping American Communities Safe: The Takedown of Key MS-13 Criminal Leaders," Trump White House Archives, July 15, 2020, https://trumpwhitehouse.archives .gov/briefings-statements/remarks-president-trump-briefing-keeping-american -communities-safe-takedown-key-ms-13-criminal-leaders/.

68. Michael T. Light, Jingying He, and Jason P. Robey, "Comparing Crime Rates Between Undocumented Immigrants, Legal Immigrants, and Native-Born US Citizens in Texas," *Proceedings of the National Academy of Sciences* 117, no. 51 (December 2020): 32340–32347.

69. Kristin F. Butcher and Anne Morrison Piehl, "Recent Immigrants: Unexpected Implications for Crime and Incarceration," *ILR Review* 51, no. 4 (July 1998): 654–679.

70. Elisa Jácome, "The Effect of Immigration Enforcement on Crime Reporting: Evidence from Dallas," *Journal of Urban Economics* 128 (March 2022).

71. Mathieu Couttenier, Sophie Hatte, Mathias Thoenig, and Stephanos Vlachos, "The Logic of Fear—Populism and Media Coverage of Immigrant Crimes," CEPR Discussion Paper 13496, Center for Economic Policy and Research, January 2019.

72. Michael T. Light and Ty Miller, "Does Undocumented Immigration Increase Violent Crime?," *Criminology* 56, no. 2 (May 2018): 370–401.

73. Rowena Gray and Giovanni Peri, "Importing Crime? The Effect of Immigration on Crime in the United States, 1880–1930," January 5, 2018. Slides available at www.aeaweborg.

74. Brian Bell, Francesco Fasani, and Stephen Machin, "Crime and Im- migration: Evidence from Large Immigrant Waves" *Review of Economics and Statistics* 95, no. 4 (October 2013): 1278–1290; Milo Bianchi, Paolo Buonanno, and Paolo Pinotti, "Do Immigrants Cause Crime?," *Journal of the European Economic Association* 10, no. 6 (December 2012): 1318–1347.

75. Adrian Florido, "Picture an America with #TacoTrucksOnEvery Corner," WNYC, September 2, 2016, www.wnyc.org/story/picture-an -america-with-tacotrucksoneverycorner/.

76. Bryan, "The History of Beer in America," Great Fermentations, June 27, 2016, www.greatfermentations.com/the-history-of-beer-in-america/.

77. Dina M. Di Maio, *Authentic Italian: The Real Story of Italy's Food and Its People* (self-pub., 2018).

78. John Mariani, "How Immigrants from Everywhere Made American Food the Most Diverse in the World," *Forbes*, April 13, 2020, www.forbes

.com/sites/johnmariani/2020/04/13/how-immigrants-from-everywhere
-made-american-food-the-most-diverse-in-the-world/.

79. Francesca Mazzolari and David Neumark, "Immigration and Product Diversity," *Journal of Population Economics* 25, no. 3 (July 2012): 1107–1137.

80. Howard Reich, "How Immigrants Created America's Mix Tape," *Chicago Tribune*, July 12, 2013, www.chicagotribune.com/entertainment /ct-xpm-2013-07-12-ct-ae-0714-immigrant-music-20130713-story.html.

CHAPTER 8: A SECOND GRAND BARGAIN

1. Lauren Witzke (@LaurenWitzkeDE), "Most third-world migrants can not assimilate into civil societies. Prove me wrong," Twitter, October 7, 2020, 11:43 a.m. Account has since been suspended.

2. Henry C. Lodge, "The Restriction of Immigration," *North American Review* 152, no. 410 (January 1891): 27–36.

3. Ran Abramitzky, Chris Becker, Leah Boustan, Dallas Card, Serina Chang, Dan Jurafsky, and Rob Voigt, "Computational Analysis of 140 Years of U.S. Political Speeches Reveals More Positive but Increasingly Polarized Framing of Immigration" (working paper, 2021).

4. In the period before 1940, we find that the average tone was negative, with a value of around −0.2. This number is not small, because many speeches are coded as neutral: for example, an average of −0.2 might arise if, for every ten speeches, there were four negative speeches, two positive speeches, and four neutral speeches.

5. Snippets of speeches from Senator Blease (D-SC), Representative Richardson (D-AL), and Representative Calkins (R-IN) given on May 9, 1930, January 11, 1910, and March 14, 1882.

6. Speech of Senator Heflin (D-AL), April 17, 1924.

7. Oscar Handlin, *The Uprooted: The Epic Story of the Great Migrations That Made the American People* (Philadelphia: University of Pennsylvania Press, 2002 [orig. pub. 1951]).

8. Nowadays, the average speech has a positive tone of 0.1—which comes about, for example, when for every ten speeches, 2.5 speeches are negative (down from 4) and 3.5 speeches are positive (up from 2), while 4 speeches are still neutral.

9. Jeffrey S. Passel and D'Vera Cohn, "Overall Number of US Unauthorized Immigrants Holds Steady Since 2009," Pew Research Center, September 20, 2016, https://www.pewresearch.org/hispanic/2016/09/20/overall -number-of-u-s-unauthorized-immigrants-holds-steady-since-2009/. The undocumented migrant population rose by nearly two million from 1990 to 1995, or around one thousand a day. California had just elected an anti-

immigrant governor, Pete Wilson, and passed a series of ballot initiatives that limited immigrant access to public services. In 1994, President Clinton implemented Operation Gatekeeper to raise funding for border patrol.

10. Robert Pear, "Clinton Embraces a Proposal to Cut Immigration by a Third," *New York Times*, June 8, 1995, www.nytimes.com/1995/06/08/us /clinton-embraces-a-proposal-to-cut-immigration-by-a-third.html.

11. Speech of Representative Gohmert (R-TX), July 14, 2016, and from Representative Fleming (R-LA), July 8, 2013.

12. Mohamed Younis, "Americans Want More, Not Less, Immigration for First Time," Gallup, July 1, 2020, https://news.gallup.com/poll/313106 /americans-not-less-immigration-first-time.aspx. See this site for updated 2021 numbers: https://news.gallup.com/poll/1660/immigration.aspx.

13. Daniel Mann, "George H. W. Bush's Legacy on Immigration," George P. Mann & Associates, December 5, 2018, https://greencard-us.com /george-h-w-bushs-legacy-on-immigration/.

14. Elizabeth F. Cohen, *Illegal: How America's Lawless Immigration Regime Threatens Us All* (London: Hachette UK, 2020).

15. Tal Kopan, "How to Earn 'Points' to Come to the US Under Trump's Immigration Plan," CNN, August 2, 2017, www.cnn.com/2017/08/02 /politics/cotton-perdue-trump-bill-point-system-merit-based/index.html.

16. Sarah Stillman, "The Race to Dismantle Trump's Immigration Policies," *New Yorker*, February 1, 2021, www.newyorker.com/magazine/2021/02/08 /the-race-to-dismantle-trumps-immigration-policies.

17. "The Biden Plan for Securing Our Values as a Nation of Immigrants," Democratic National Committee website for Joe Biden/Kamala Harris, https://joebiden.com/immigration/.

18. Heather Caygle, Sarah Ferris, and Lauran Barrón-López, "'It Would Be Very Difficult': Dems Prepare for Heartburn over Biden Immigration Plan," *Politico*, February 11, 2021, https://www.politico.com/news/2021/02/11/house -democrats-biden-immigration-plan-468720.

Index

RAN ABRAMITZKY is professor of economics and the senior associate dean of the social sciences at Stanford University, a research associate at the National Bureau of Economic Research, a senior fellow at the Stanford Institute for Economic Policy Research, and a former co-editor of *Explorations in Economic History.*

Weaving his family story together with extensive economic and historical data, Abramitzky's prizewinning scholarly book, *The Mystery of the Kibbutz,* examines how communities based on income equality survived in Israel for over a century, and the conditions under which more equal societies can thrive.

LEAH BOUSTAN is professor of economics at Princeton University, where she is the director of the Industrial Relations Section. She is also a codirector of the Development of the American Economy Program at the National Bureau of Economic Research and co-editor at *American Economic Journal: Applied Economics.*

Her prizewinning scholarly book, *Competition in the Promised Land,* examines the effect of the Great Black Migration from the rural South during and after World War II. Boustan has written for the *New York Times,* the *American Prospect,* and *Slate.* With more than thirty thousand Twitter followers, she is among the most followed economists in the world; she regularly tweets about immigration.

PublicAffairs is a publishing house founded in 1997. It is a tribute to the standards, values, and flair of three persons who have served as mentors to countless reporters, writers, editors, and book people of all kinds, including me.

I. F. STONE, proprietor of *I. F. Stone's Weekly*, combined a commitment to the First Amendment with entrepreneurial zeal and reporting skill and became one of the great independent journalists in American history. At the age of eighty, Izzy published *The Trial of Socrates*, which was a national bestseller. He wrote the book after he taught himself ancient Greek.

BENJAMIN C. BRADLEE was for nearly thirty years the charismatic editorial leader of *The Washington Post*. It was Ben who gave the *Post* the range and courage to pursue such historic issues as Watergate. He supported his reporters with a tenacity that made them fearless and it is no accident that so many became authors of influential, best-selling books.

ROBERT L. BERNSTEIN, the chief executive of Random House for more than a quarter century, guided one of the nation's premier publishing houses. Bob was personally responsible for many books of political dissent and argument that challenged tyranny around the globe. He is also the founder and longtime chair of Human Rights Watch, one of the most respected human rights organizations in the world.

•   •   •

For fifty years, the banner of Public Affairs Press was carried by its owner Morris B. Schnapper, who published Gandhi, Nasser, Toynbee, Truman, and about 1,500 other authors. In 1983, Schnapper was described by *The Washington Post* as "a redoubtable gadfly." His legacy will endure in the books to come.

Peter Osnos, *Founder*

9·14·22